MARCO POLO'S
SILK ROAD
THE ART OF THE JOURNEY

MARCO POLO'S
SILK ROAD
THE ART OF THE JOURNEY

AN ITALIAN AT THE
COURT OF KUBLAI KHAN

INTRODUCTION BY JOHN MASEFIELD

WATKINS PUBLISHING
LONDON

Marco Polo's Silk Road: The Art of the Journey

First published in the United Kingdom and USA in 2011 by
Watkins Publishing, Sixth Floor, Castle House, 75–76 Wells Street, London W1T 3QH

Conceived, created and designed by Watkins Publishing

Managing Editor: Christopher Westhorp
Managing Designer: Suzanne Tuhrim
Designer: Daniel Sturges
Picture Research: Julia Ruxton
Map: Garry Walton

British Library Cataloguing-in-Publication Data:
A CIP record for this book is available from the British Library

    Library of Congress Cataloging-in-Publication Data

Polo, Marco, 1254-1323?
  Marco Polo's Silk Road : the art of the journey, an Italian at the court of the Kublai Khan.
    p. cm.
  ISBN 978-1-78028-015-8
  1. Polo, Marco, 1254-1323?--Travel--Silk Road. 2. Silk Road--Description and travel. 3. Asia--Discovery and
exploration. I. Title.
  G370.P9P635 2011
  915.04'2--dc22
                              2011012025

ISBN: 978-1-78028-015-8

10 9 8 7 6 5 4 3 2 1

Typeset in Minion Pro
Colour reproduction by Colourscan
Printed in China by Imago

NOTES:
There are minor differences between some spellings of names and places in the introduction and those used
in the remainder of this book, but these differences will not confuse the reader. This edition is based principally
on the 1903 Yule translation, with notes added throughout that have been drawn largely from Henry Yule (1903)
and William Marsden (1908). For further information about versions of Polo's text, please see the note that
accompanies the Further Reading on page 264.

Prelim captions: Page 1 A commemorative medallion bearing a portrait of Marco Polo, nineteenth century.
Page 2 The central Tian Shan, the large mountain range in modern-day Kazakhstan that is to the northeast
of Kashgar (Cascar, see page 77) and forms the northern boundary of the Taklamakan Desert.

Distributed in the USA and Canada by
Sterling Publishing Co., Inc., 387 Park Avenue South, New York, NY 10016-8810

For information about custom editions, special sales, premium and corporate purchases,
please contact Sterling Special Sales Department at 800-805-5489 or specialsales@sterlingpub.com.

CONTENTS

Introduction by John Masefield   8
Itinerary   15

**MARCO POLO'S
SILK ROAD –**
THE ART OF THE JOURNEY

PROLOGUE   18

CHAPTER

1   How the two brothers Polo
set forth from Constantinople
to traverse the world   20

2   How the two brothers
went on beyond Soldaia   20

3   How the two brothers came to
the city of Bokhara and fell in
with certain envoys there   22

4   How the two brothers took
the envoys' counsel and
went to the court of the
Great Khan   23

5   How the two brothers arrived
at the court of the Great
Khan   23

6   How the Great Khan asked
all about the manners of the
Christians, and particularly
about the pope of Rome   24

7   How the Great Khan sent the
two brothers as his envoys to
the pope   25

8   How the Great Khan gave
them a tablet of gold bearing
his orders   25

9   How the two brothers
came to the city of Acre   27

10   How the two brothers again
departed from Venice, on their
way back to the Great Khan,
and took with them Marco,
the son of Nicolo   28

11   How the two brothers set out
from Acre, and Marco along
with them   29

12   How the two brothers presented
themselves before the new
pope   29

13   How Nicolo and Maffeo,
accompanied by Marco,
travelled to the court of the
Great Khan   30

14   How Nicolo and Maffeo
Polo and Marco presented
themselves before the Great
Khan   31

15   How the emperor sent Marco
on an embassy   31

16   How Marco returned from the
mission whereon he had been
sent   32

17   How Nicolo, Maffeo and Marco
asked leave of the Great Khan to
go their own way   32

18   How the two brothers and
Marco took leave of the Great
Khan and returned to their own
country   34

MAP MARCO POLO'S
TRAVELS TO THE EAST   38

BOOK I

ACCOUNT OF REGIONS
VISITED OR HEARD OF ON
THE JOURNEY FROM THE
LESSER ARMENIA TO
THE COURT OF THE GREAT
KHAN AT CHANDU

CHAPTER

1   Here the book begins; and first
it speaks of Lesser Armenia   42

2   Concerning the province of
Turcomania   42

3   Description of Greater
Armenia   43

4   Of Georgiania and the kings
thereof   44

5   Of the kingdom of Mausul   45

6   Of the great city of Baudas,
and how it was taken   46

7   How the calif of Baudas took
counsel to slay all the Christians
in his lands   49

8   How the Christians were in
great dismay because of what
the calif had said   50

9   How the one-eyed cobbler
was desired to pray for the
Christians   51

10   How the prayer of the one-eyed
cobbler caused the mountain
to move   51

11   Of the noble city of Tauris   52

12   Of the monastery of
St Barsamo on the
borders of Tauris   53

13   Of the great country of Persia;
with some account of the
three kings   53

14   What befell when the three
kings returned to their own
country   54

15   Of the eight kingdoms of Persia,
and how they are named   55

16   Concerning the great city
of Yasdi   56

17   Concerning the kingdom
of Kermán   57

18   Of the city of Camadi and
its ruins; also touching the
Karauna robbers   58

19   Of the descent to the city
of Hormuz   61

20   Of the wearisome and desert
road that has now to be
travelled   64

21   Concerning the city of Cobinan
and the things that are made
there   65

22   Of a certain desert that
continues for eight days'
journey   65

23   Concerning the Old Man
of the Mountain   66

24   How the Old Man
used to train his Assassins   67

25   How the Old Man
came by his end   68

26   Concerning the city of
Sapurgan   69

27 Of the city of Balc   69

28 Of Taican, and the mountains of salt. Also of the province of Casem   70

29 Of the province of Badashan   72

30 Of the province of Pashai   74

31 Of the province of Keshimur   75

32 Of the great river of Badashan   75

33 Of the kingdom of Cascar   77

34 Of the great city of Samarkand   77

35 Of the province of Yarcan   78

36 Of a province called Cotan   80

37 Of the province of Pein   80

38 Of the province of Charchan   81

39 Of the city of Lop and the great desert   81

40 Concerning the great province of Tangut   83

41 Of the province of Camul   85

42 Of the province of Chingintalas   87

43 Of the province of Sukchur   88

44 Of the city of Campichu   89

45 Of the city of Etzina   90

46 Of the city of Caracoron   91

47 Of Genghis, and how he became the First Khan of the Tartars   93

48 How Genghis mustered his people to march against Prester John   94

49 How Prester John marched to meet Genghis   94

50 The battle between Genghis Khan and Prester John   96

51 Of those who did reign after Genghis Khan, and of the customs of the Tartars   96

52 Concerning the customs of the Tartars   98

53 Concerning the God of the Tartars   100

54 Concerning the Tartar customs of war   101

55 Concerning the administering of justice among the Tartars   103

56 Sundry particulars of the plain beyond Caracoron   106

57 Of the kingdom of Erguiul, and province of Sinju   107

58 Of the kingdom of Egrigaia   109

59 Concerning the province of Tanduc, and the descendants of Prester John   109

60 Concerning the khan's palace of Chagan Nor   111

61 Of the city of Chandu, and the khan's palace there   112

BOOK II: PART I

THE GREAT KHAN, HIS COURT AND CAPITAL

CHAPTER

1   Of Kublai Khan, the Great Khan now reigning, and of his great power   119

2   Concerning the revolt of Nayan, who was uncle to the Great Khan Kublai   120

3   How the Great Khan marched against Nayan   121

4   Of the battle that the Great Khan fought with Nayan   122

5   How the Great Khan caused Nayan to be put to death   124

6   How the Great Khan went back to the city of Cambaluc   125

7   How the khan rewarded the valour of his captains   125

8   Concerning the person of the Great Khan   126

9   Concerning the Great Khan's sons   128

10 Concerning the palace of the Great Khan   129

11 Concerning the city of Cambaluc   131

12 How the Great Khan maintains a guard of 12,000 horse, which are called keshican   133

13 The fashion of the Great Khan's table at his high feasts   134

14 Concerning the great feast held by the Great Khan every year on his birthday   135

15 Of the great festival which the khan holds on New Year's Day   136

16 Concerning the 12,000 barons who receive robes of cloth of gold from the emperor on the great festivals, thirteen changes apiece   139

17 How the Great Khan enjoineth his people to supply him with game   139

18 Of the lions and leopards and wolves that the khan keeps for the chase   140

19 Concerning the two brothers who have charge of the khan's hounds   141

20 How the emperor goes on a hunting expedition   141

21 Rehearsal of the way the year of the Great Khan is distributed   144

22 Concerning the city of Cambaluc and its great traffic and population   145

23 Concerning the oppressions of Achmath the bailo, and the plot that was formed against him   148

24 How the Great Khan causeth the bark of trees, made into something like paper, to pass for money over all his country   151

25 Concerning the twelve barons who are set over all the affairs of the Great Khan   153

26 How the khan's posts and runners are sped through many lands and provinces   154

27 How the emperor bestows help on his people, when they are afflicted with dearth or murrain   156

28 How the Great Khan causes trees to be planted by the highways   157

29 Concerning the rice-wine drunk by the people of Cathay   158

30 Concerning the black stones that are dug in Cathay, and are burnt for fuel 159

31 How the Great Khan caused stores of corn to be made, to help his people withal in time of dearth 159

32 Of the charity of the emperor to the poor 161

33 Concerning the astrologers in the city of Cambaluc 162

34 Concerning the religion of the Cathayans; their views as to the soul; and their customs 163

BOOK II: PART II

JOURNEY TO THE WEST AND SOUTHWEST OF CATHAY

CHAPTER

35 Here begins the description of the interior of Cathay; and first of the River Pulisanghin 167

36 Account of the city of Juju 168

37 The kingdom of Taianfu 169

38 Concerning the castle of Caichu, the Golden King and Prester John 171

39 How Prester John treated the Golden King his prisoner 172

40 Concerning the great river Caramoran and the city of Cachanfu 173

41 Concerning the city of Kenjanfu 174

42 Concerning the province of Cuncun, which is right wearisome to travel through 175

43 Concerning the province of Acbalec Manzi 176

44 Concerning the province of Sindafu 176

45 Concerning the province of Tibet 178

46 Further discourse concerning Tibet 182

47 Concerning the province of Caindu 184

48 Concerning the province of Carajan 186

49 Concerning a further part of the province of Carajan 187

50 Concerning the province of Zardandan 190

51 Wherein is related how the king of Mien and Bangala vowed vengeance against the Great Khan 193

52 Of the battle that was fought by the Great Khan's host and his seneschal against the king of Mien 195

53 Of the great descent that leads toward the kingdom of Mien 197

54 Concerning the city of Mien, and the two towers that are therein, one of gold, and the other of silver 197

55 Concerning the province of Bangala 199

56 Discourses on the province of Caugigu 201

57 Concerning the province of Anin 201

58 Concerning the province of Coloman 202

59 Concerning the province of Cuiju 202

BOOK II: PART III

JOURNEY SOUTHWARD THROUGH THE EASTERN PROVINCES OF CATHAY AND MANZI

CHAPTER

60 Concerning the cities of Cacanfu and Changlu 207

61 Concerning the city of Chinangli, and that of Tadinfu, and the rebellion of Liytan 208

62 Concerning the noble city of Sinjumatu 209

63 Concerning the cities of Linju and Piju 212

64 Concerning the city of Siju, and the great river Caramoran 213

65 How the Great Khan conquered the province of Manzi 215

66 Concerning the city of Coiganju 217

67 Of the cities of Paukin and Cayu 217

68 Of the cities of Tiju, Tinju and Yanju 218

69 Concerning the city of Nanghin 219

70 Concerning the very noble city of Saianfu, and how its capture was effected 220

71 Concerning the city of Sinju and the great river Kian 222

72 Concerning the city of Caiju 224

73 Of the city of Chinghianfu 224

74 Of the city of Chinginju and the slaughter of certain Alans there 225

75 Of the noble city of Suju 226

76 Description of the great city of Kinsay, which is the capital of the whole country of Manzi 227

77 Further particulars concerning the great city of Kinsay 233

78 Treating of the yearly revenue that the Great Khan has from Kinsay 235

79 Of the city of Tanpiju and others 236

80 Concerning the kingdom of Fuju 237

81 Concerning the greatness of the city of Fuju 240

82 Of the city and great haven of Zayton 241

EPILOGUE TO THIS EDITION

Conclusion 243

Appendix: Endnotes 244
Further Reading 264
Index 265
Acknowledgments & Picture Credits 270

INTRODUCTION

BY JOHN MASEFIELD

MARCO POLO, the subject of this memoir, was born at Venice in the year 1254. He was the son of Nicolo Polo, a Venetian of noble family, who was one of the partners in a trading house, engaged in business with Constantinople. In the year 1260, this Nicolo Polo, in company with his junior partner, his brother Maffeo, set out across the Euxine[1] on a trading venture to the Crimea. They prospered in their business, but were unable to return to their base, owing to the breaking out of a Tartar war on the road by which they had come. As they could not go back, they went forward, crossing the desert to Bokhara, where they stayed for three years. At the end of the third year (the fifth of their journey) they were advised to visit the Great Khan Kublai, the "Kubla Khan" of Coleridge's poem. A party of the Great Khan's envoys were about to return to Cathay, and the two brothers therefore joined the party, travelling forward, "northward and northeastward", for a whole year, before they reached the *khan*'s court in Cathay. The *khan* received them kindly, and asked them many questions about life in Europe, especially about the emperors, the pope, the Church, and "all that is done at Rome". He then sent them back to Europe on an embassy to the pope, to ask His Holiness to send a hundred missionaries to convert the Cathaians to the Christian faith. He also asked for some of the holy oil from the lamp of the Holy Sepulchre. The return journey of the brothers (from Cathay to Acre) took three years. On their arrival at Acre the travellers discovered that the pope was dead. They therefore decided to return home to Venice to wait until the new pope should be elected. They arrived at Venice in 1269, to find that Nicolo's wife had died during her husband's absence. His son Marco, our traveller, was then fifteen years old. He had probably passed his childhood in the house of one of his uncles at Venice.

Nicolo and Maffeo Polo remained at Venice for a couple of years, waiting for a pope to be elected, but as there seemed to be no prospect of this happening, they determined to return to the Great Khan, to tell him how their mission had failed. They therefore set out again (in 1271) and Marco, now seventeen years old, went with them. At Acre they obtained a letter from a Papal Legate, stating how it came about that the message had not been delivered. They had already obtained some of the holy oil, so that they were free to proceed. They had not gone very far upon their journey when they were recalled to Acre by the above-mentioned Syrian legate, who had just heard that he had been elected pope. The new pope did not send a hundred missionaries, as Kublai had asked, but he appointed instead two preaching friars, who accompanied the Polos as far as Armenia, where rumours of war frightened them into returning. The Polos journeyed on for three years and a half, and arrived at the *khan*'s court (at Shangtu, not far from Pekin) in the middle of 1275. The *khan* received them "honourably and graciously", making much of Marco, "who was then a young gallant". In a little while, when Marco had learned the speech and customs of the "Tartars", the *khan* employed him in public business, sending him as a visiting administrator to several wild and distant provinces. Marco noted carefully the strange customs of these provinces, and delighted the *khan* with his account of them. On one of these journeys Marco probably visited the southern states of India.

After some seventeen years of honourable service with Kublai, the three Venetians became eager to return to Venice. They were rich men, and Kublai was growing old, and they knew that Kublai's death "might deprive them of that public assistance by which alone they could expect to surmount the innumerable difficulties of so long a journey". But Kublai refused to allow them to leave the court, and even "appeared hurt at the application". It chanced, however, that at this time, Arghun, *khan* of Persia, had sent ambassadors to Kublai to obtain the hand of a maiden "from among the relatives of his deceased wife". The maiden, aged seventeen, and very beautiful, was about to accompany the ambassadors to Persia; but the ordinary overland routes to Persia were unsafe, owing to wars among the Tartars. It was necessary for her to travel to Persia by ship. The envoys begged Kublai that the three Venetians might come with them in the ships "as being persons well skilled in the practice of navigation". Kublai granted their request, though not very gladly. He fitted out a splendid squadron of ships, and despatched the three Venetians with the Persians, first granting them the golden tablet, or safe-conduct, which would enable them to obtain supplies on the way. They sailed from a Chinese port about the beginning of 1292.

The voyage to Persia occupied about two years, during which time the expedition lost six hundred men. The *khan* of Persia was dead when they arrived; so the beautiful maiden was handed over to his son, who received her kindly. He gave the Venetians safe-conduct through Persia; indeed he sent them forward with troops of horse, without which, in those troublous days, they could never have crossed the country. As they rode on their way they heard that the great *khan* Kublai, their old master, had died. They arrived safely at Venice some time in the year 1295.

There are some curious tales of their arrival at home. It is said that they were not recognised by their relatives, and this is not strange, for they returned in shabby Tartar clothes, almost unable to speak their native tongue. It was not until they had ripped the seams of the shabby clothes, producing stores of jewels from the lining, that the relatives decided to acknowledge them. (This tale may be read as allegory by those who doubt its truth as history.) Marco Polo did not stay long among his relatives. Venice was at war with Genoa, and the Polo family, being rich, had been called upon to equip a galley, even before the travellers returned from Asia. Marco Polo sailed in command of this galley, in the fleet under Andrea Dandolo, which was defeated by the Genoese off Curzola on the 7th September, 1296. Marco Polo was carried as a prisoner to Genoa, where he remained, in spite of efforts made to ransom him, for about three years, during which time he probably dictated his book in very bad French to one Rustician of Pisa, a fellow-prisoner. He returned to Venice during the year 1299, and probably married shortly afterwards.

Little is known of his life after his return from prison. We know that he was nicknamed "Il Milione" on account of his wonderful stories of Kublai's splendour; but as he was rich and famous the slighting nickname was probably partly a compliment. Colonel Yule, the great editor of Marco Polo, has discovered that he stood surety for a wine-smuggler, that he gave a copy of his book to a French noble, and that he sued a commission agent for the half profits on the sale of some musk. It was at one time thought that he was the Marco Polo who failed (in 1302) to have his water-pipe inspected by the town plumber. This sin has now been laid upon another man of the same name, who "was ignorant of the order on that subject". On the 9th of January, 1324, feeling himself to be growing daily feebler, he made his will, which is still preserved. He named as his trustees his wife Donata and his three daughters, to whom the bulk of his estate was left. He died soon after the execution of this will. He was buried in Venice without the door of the Church of San Lorenzo; but the exact site of the grave is unknown. No known authentic portrait of the man exists; but as in the case of Columbus, there are several fanciful portraits, of which the best dates from the seventeenth century.

Marco Polo's book was not received with faith by his contemporaries. Travellers who see marvellous things, even in our own day (the name of Bruce will occur to everyone),[2] are seldom believed by those who, having stayed at home, have all the consequences of their virtue. When Marco Polo came back from the East, a misty, unknown country, full of splendour and terrors, he could not tell the whole truth. He had to leave his tale half told lest he should lack believers. His book was less popular in the later Middle Ages than the fictions and plagiarisms of Sir John Mandeville. Marco Polo tells of what he saw; the compiler of Mandeville, when he does not steal openly from Pliny, Friar Odoric, and others, tells of what an ignorant person might expect to see, and would, in any case, like to read about, since it is always blessed to be confirmed in an opinion, however ill-grounded it may be. How little Marco Polo was credited may be judged from the fact that the map of Asia was not modified by his discoveries till fifty years after his death.

His book is one of the great books of travel. Even now, after the lapse of six centuries, it remains the chief authority for parts of Central Asia, and of the vast Chinese Empire. Some of his wanderings are hard to follow; some of the places which he visited are hard to identify; but the labour of Colonel Yule has cleared up most of the difficulties, and confirmed most of the strange statements. To the geographer, to the historian, and to the student of Asiatic life, the book of Marco Polo will always be most valuable. To the general reader, the great charm of the book is its romance.

It is accounted a romantic thing to wander among strangers and to eat their bread by the camp-fires of the other half of the world. There is romance in doing thus, though the romance has been over-estimated by those whose sedentary lives have created in them a false taste for action. Marco Polo wandered among strangers; but it is open to anyone (with courage and the power of motion) to do the same. Wandering in itself is merely a form of self-indulgence. If it adds not to the stock of human knowledge, or if it gives not to others the imaginative possession of some part of the world, it is a pernicious habit. The acquisition of knowledge, the accumulation of fact, is noble only in those few who have that alchemy which transmutes such clay to heavenly eternal gold. It may be thought that many travellers have given their readers great imaginative possessions; but the imaginative possession is not measured in miles and parasangs, nor do the people of that country write accounts of birds and beasts. It is only the wonderful traveller who sees a wonder, and only five travellers in the world's history have seen wonders. The others have seen birds and beasts, rivers and wastes, the earth and the (local) fullness thereof. The five travellers are Herodotus, Caspar, Melchior, Balthazar, and Marco Polo himself. The wonder of Marco Polo is this: that he created Asia for the European mind.

When Marco Polo went to the East, the whole of Central Asia, so full of splendour and magnificence, so noisy with nations and kings, was like a dream in men's minds. Europeans touched only the fringe of the East. At Acre, at Byzantium, at the busy cities on the Euxine, the merchants of Europe bartered with the stranger for silks, and jewels and precious balms, brought over the desert at great cost, in caravans from the unknown. The popular conception of the East was taken from the Bible, from the tales of old Crusaders, and from the books of the merchants. All that men knew of the East was that it was mysterious, and that our Lord was born there. Marco Polo, almost the first European to see the East, saw her in all her wonder, more fully than any man has seen her since. His picture of the East is the picture which we all make in our minds when we repeat to ourselves those two strange words, "the East", and give ourselves up to the image which that symbol evokes. It may be that the Western mind will turn to Marco Polo for a conception of Asia long after "Cathay" has become an American colony.

It is difficult to read Marco Polo as one reads historical facts. One reads him as one reads romance; as one would read, for instance, the "Eve of St Mark", or the "Well at the World's End". The East of which he writes is the East of romance, not the East of the Anglo-Indian, with his Simla, his missions to Tibet, and Reuter telegrams. In the East of romance there grows "the tree of the sun, or dry tree" (by which Marco Polo passed), a sort of landmark or milestone, at the end of the great desert. The apples of the sun and moon grow upon that tree. Darius and Alexander fought in its shade. Those are the significant facts about the tree according to Marco Polo. We moderns, who care little for any tree so soon as we can murmur its Latin name, have lost wonder in losing faith.

The Middle Age, even as our own age is, was full of talk of the Earthly Paradise. It may be that we have progressed, in learning to talk of it as a social possibility instead of as a geographical fact. We like to think that the old Venetians went eastward, on their famous journey, half believing that they would arrive there, just as Columbus (two centuries later) half expected to sight land "where the golden blossoms burn upon the trees forever". They did not find the Earthly Paradise; but they saw the splendours of Kublai, one of the mightiest of earthly kings. One feels the presence of Kublai all through the narrative, as the red wine, dropped into the water-cup, suffuses all, or as the string supports the jewels on a trinket. The imagination is only healthy when it broods upon the kingly and the saintly. In Kublai, the reader will find enough images of splendour to make glorious the temple of his mind. When we think of Marco Polo, it is of Kublai that we think; and, apart from the romantic wonder which surrounds him, he is a noble person, worth our contemplation. He is like a king in a romance. It was the task of a kingly nature to have created him as he appears in the book here. It makes us proud and reverent of the poetic gift, many cities, so many gardens, so many fishpools, would be but a name, an image covered by the sands, had he not welcomed two dusty travellers, who came to him one morning from out of the unknown, after long wandering over the world. Perhaps when he bade them farewell the thought occurred to him (as it occurred to that other king in the poem) that he might come to be remembered "but by this one thing",[3] when all his glories were fallen from him, and he lay silent, the gold mask upon his face, in the drowsy tomb, where the lamp, long kept alight, at last guttered, and died, and fell to dust.

JOHN MASEFIELD (December 1907)

ITINERARY

The elder Polos, when they left Constantinople in the year 1260, had not planned to go far beyond the northern borders of the Euxine. They first landed at Soldaia, in the Crimea, then an important trading city. From Soldaia they journeyed in a northerly and east–northeasterly direction to Sara, or Sarra, a vast city on the Volga, where King Cambuscan lived, and to Bolgara, or Bolghar, where they stayed for a year. Going south a short distance to Ucaca, another city on the Volga, they journeyed direct to the southeast, across the northern head of the Caspian, on the sixty days march to Bokhara, where they stayed for three years. From Bokhara they went with the Great Khan's people northward to Otrar, and thence in a northeasterly direction to the court of the *khan* near Pekin. On their return journey, they arrived at the sea-coast at Layas, in Armenia. From Layas they went to Acre, and from Acre to Negropont in Roumania, and from Negropont to Venice, where they stayed for about two years.

On the second journey to the East, with the young Marco Polo, they sailed direct from Venice to Acre towards the end of the year 1271. They made a short journey southward to Jerusalem, for the holy oil, and then returned to Acre for letters from the Papal Legate. Leaving Acre, they got as far as Layas, in Armenia, before they were recalled by the newly elected pope. On setting out again, they returned to Layas, at that time a great city, where spices and cloth of gold were sold, and from which merchants journeying to the East generally started. From Layas they pushed northward into Turcomania, past Casaria and Sivas, to Arzingan, where the people wove "good buckrams". Passing Mount Ararat, where Noah's Ark was supposed to rest, they heard stories of the Baku oil-fields. From here they went to the southeastward, following the course of the Tigris to Bandas. From Bandas they seem to have made an unnecessary journey to the Persian Gulf. The book leads one to suppose they travelled by way of Tauriz, Yezd, and Kerman, to the port of Ormuz, as though they intended to take ship there. They could, however, have progressed more swiftly had they followed the Tigris to Busrah, there taken ship upon the Gulf, and sailed by way of Keis or Kisi to Ormuz. After visiting Ormuz, they returned to Kerman by another road, and then pushed on, over the horrible salt desert of Kerman, through Khorassan to Balakshan. It is possible that their journey was broken at Balakshan, owing to the illness of Marco, who speaks of having at some time stayed nearly a year here to recover his health. On leaving Balakshan they proceeded through the high Pamirs to Kashgar, thence southeastward by way of Khotan, not yet buried under the sands, to the Gobi desert. The Gobi desert, like all deserts, had a bad name as being "the abode of many evil spirits, which amuse travellers to their destruction". The Polos crossed the Gobi in the usual thirty days, halting each night by the brackish ponds which make the passage possible. After crossing the desert, they soon entered China. At Kan Chau, one of the first Chinese cities which they visited, they may have stayed for nearly a year, on account of "the state of their concerns", but this stay probably took place later, when they were in Kublai's service. They then crossed the province of Shen-si, into that of Shan-si, finally arriving at Kai-ping-fu, where Kublai had built his summer pleasure garden.

On the return journey, the Polos set sail from the port of Zaitum, in the province of Fo-Kien. They hugged the Chinese coast (in order to avoid the Pratas and Pracel Reefs) and crossed the Gulf of Tong King to Champa in the southeast of Cambodia. Leaving Champa, they may have made some stay at Borneo, but more probably they sailed direct to the island of Bintang, at the mouth of the Straits of Malacca, and to Sumatra, where the fleet was delayed for five months by the blowing of the contrary monsoon. The ships seem to have waited for the monsoon to change in a harbour on the northeast coast, in the kingdom of Sumatra. On getting a fair wind, they passed by the Nicobar and Andaman Islands, and then shaped a course for Ceylon. They put across to the coast of Coromandel, and may perhaps have coasted as far to the northward upon the Madras coast as Masulipatam. On the Bombay side, they would seem to have hugged the coast as far as they could, as far perhaps as Surat, in the Gulf of Cambay; but it is just possible that the descriptions of these places were taken from the tales of pilots, and that his fleet put boldly out to avoid the coast pirates. Marco Polo tells us much about Aden, and about towns on the Arabian coasts; but the fleet probably never touched at them. All that is certainly known is that they arrived at Ormuz, in the Persian Gulf, and passed inland to Khorassan. On leaving Khorassan they journeyed overland, through Persia and Greater Armenia, until they came to Trebizonda on the Euxine Sea. Here they took ship, and sailed home to Venice, first touching at Constantinople and at Negropont. "And this was in the year 1295 of Christ's Incarnation."

J.M.

PROLOGUE

GREAT EMPERORS, KINGS, dukes, marquises, earls, knights, and all other people who desire to know the diversity of the races of mankind, as well as the diversity of kingdoms, provinces and regions of all parts of the East, read this book. You will find in it the most marvellous things and the characteristics of the peoples of Armenia, Persia [and] the land of the Tartars ... as they are described in the present work by Marco Polo, a wise and learned citizen of Venice, who states distinctly what things he saw and what things he heard from others whose accounts he trusted. For this book will be a truthful one. From the creation of Adam to the present day, no man, of whatever generation or nation he may have been, ever saw or inquired into so many and such great things as has Marco Polo. For that reason he thought that the things he had seen and heard should be compiled in writing for the benefit of other people. I may tell you that in acquiring this knowledge he spent twenty-six years in those various parts of the world. Thereafter, as an inmate of the prison at Genoa, he caused

Rustichello of Pisa,[1] who was in the said prison, to put the whole thing in writing, and this happened in the year of our Lord 1298.[2]

How the TWO BROTHERS POLO set forth from CONSTANTINOPLE to TRAVERSE THE WORLD

IT CAME TO pass in the year of Christ 1260,[3] when Baldwin was reigning at Constantinople,[4] that Nicolo Polo, the father of Marco, and Maffeo Polo, the brother of Nicolo, were at the said city of Constantinople, where they had gone from Venice with a rich and varied cargo of merchandise. After mature deliberation it was decided that they should continue into the Black Sea, so they acquired many fine and costly jewels and crossed the sea to Soldaia.[5]

How the TWO BROTHERS went on BEYOND SOLDAIA

HAVING STAYED A while at Soldaia they thought it well to extend their journey further. So they travelled until they reached the court of a Tartar chief named Barka Khan, whose residences were at Sarai and Bolgara.[6] Barka treated the two brothers with great honour, so they laid the jewels before him and presented them for his acceptance. The liberality of this conduct struck him with admiration; and being unwilling that they should surpass him in generosity, he not only directed double the value of the jewels to be paid to them, but made them in addition several rich presents.

After they had spent a year at the court the brothers desired to revisit their native country, but were impeded by the sudden outbreak of war between Barka and Alaü, lord of the eastern Tartars. Alaü was victorious, in consequence of which the brothers could not attempt to return by the way they came. It was recommended to

them to proceed in an easterly direction so as to skirt the limits of Barka's territories. Accordingly they made their way to a town named Oukaka,[7] then they crossed the Tigris[8] and travelled for seventeen days across a desert,[9] where they found only Tartars with their herds.

CHAPTER 3

How the TWO BROTHERS *came to the*
CITY OF BOKHARA *and* FELL IN
with CERTAIN ENVOYS *there*

… THEY ARRIVED at length at a well-built city called Bokhara, belonging to the dominions of Persia. Here, unable to proceed farther, they remained three years. It happened while these brothers were in Bokhara, that a person of consequence … made his appearance there. He was proceeding as ambassador from Alaü to the Great Khan,

supreme chief of all the Tartars, named Kublai, whose residence was at the extremity of the continent, in a direction between northeast and east.[10] ... he was gratified at meeting and conversing with these brothers, who had now become proficient in the Tartar language; and after associating with them for several days ... he proposed to them that they should accompany him to the presence of the Great Khan, who ... had not hitherto been visited by any person from their country ....

CHAPTER 4

How the TWO BROTHERS
TOOK THE ENVOYS' COUNSEL and went
to the COURT of the GREAT KHAN

CONVINCED AS THEY were that their endeavours to return homeward would expose them to the most imminent risks, they agreed to this proposal, and ... set out on their journey in the suite of the ambassador, attended by several Christian servants whom they had brought with them from Venice. An entire year was consumed before they were enabled to reach the imperial residence, in consequence of the extraordinary delays occasioned by the snows and the swelling of the rivers, which obliged them to halt until [they] ... had subsided. Many things worthy of admiration were observed by them in the progress of their journey, but which are here omitted, as they will be described by Marco Polo, in the sequel of the book.

CHAPTER 5

How the TWO BROTHERS ARRIVED
at the COURT of the GREAT KHAN

BEING INTRODUCED TO the presence of Kublai the travellers were received by him with the condescension and affability that belonged to his character, and as they were the first Latins who had made their appearance in that country, they were entertained and honoured .... [He] made earnest inquiries on the subject of the western parts of the world, of the emperor of the Romans,[11] and of other Christian kings and princes. He wished to be informed of their relative consequence, the extent of their possessions, the manner in which justice was administered in their several kingdoms and principalities, and how they conducted themselves in warfare.

CHAPTER 6

How the GREAT KHAN *asked all about*
the MANNERS *of the* CHRISTIANS, *and*
PARTICULARLY *about the* POPE *of* ROME

ABOVE ALL HE questioned them about the pope, the affairs of the Church, and the religious worship and doctrine of the Christians. They gave appropriate answers upon all of these points, and they expressed themselves always in becoming terms; insomuch that the Great Khan, holding them in high estimation, frequently commanded their attendance.

CHAPTER 7

How the GREAT KHAN *sent*
the TWO BROTHERS *as his*
ENVOYS *to the* POPE

WHEN HE HAD obtained all the information that the two brothers communicated with so much good sense, he expressed himself well satisfied, and having formed in his mind the design of employing them as his ambassadors to the pope ... he proposed ... that they should accompany one of his officers, named Khogatal, on a mission to the Holy See in Rome. His object was to make a request to His Holiness that he would send 100 men of learning, thoroughly acquainted with the principles of the Christian religion, as well as with the seven arts,[12] and qualified to prove to the learned of his dominions by just and fair argument, that the faith professed by Christians is superior to, and founded upon more evident truth than, any other; that the gods of the Tartars and the idols [they] worshipped were only evil spirits, and that they and the people of the East in general were under an error in reverencing them as divinities.[13] He moreover signified his pleasure that upon their return they should bring with them, from Jerusalem, some of the holy oil from the lamp which is kept burning over the sepulchre of our Lord Jesus Christ, whom he professed to hold in veneration and to consider as the true God.[14]

CHAPTER 8

How the GREAT KHAN *gave them a*
TABLET *of* GOLD *bearing* HIS ORDERS

HAVING HEARD THESE commands addressed to them by the *khan* they humbly prostrated themselves before him, declaring their willingness ... to perform, to the utmost of their ability, whatever might be the royal will. Upon which he caused letters, in the

Tartarian language, to be written in his name to the pope of Rome, and these he delivered into their hands. He likewise gave orders that they should be furnished with a golden tablet displaying the imperial cipher, according to the usage established by his majesty; in virtue of which the person bearing it, together with his whole suite, are safely conveyed and escorted from station to station by the governors of all places within the imperial dominions, and are entitled, during the time of their residing in any city, castle, town, or village, to a supply of provisions and everything necessary for their accommodation.

Being thus … commissioned they took their leave of the Great Khan, and set out … but had not proceeded more than twenty days when … Khogatal, their companion, fell ill in the city named Alaü. In this dilemma it was determined, upon consulting all who were present, and with the approval of the man himself, that they should leave him behind. In the prosecution of their journey they derived essential benefit from … the royal tablet, which procured them attention in every place through which they passed. Their expenses were defrayed, and escorts were furnished. But notwithstanding these advantages, so great were the natural difficulties they had to encounter, from the extreme cold, the snow, the ice, and the flooding of the rivers, that their progress was unavoidably tedious, and three

years elapsed before they were enabled to reach a seaport in Lesser Armenia,[15] named Laiassus.[16]

CHAPTER 9

How the TWO BROTHERS *came to the* CITY *of* ACRE

THEY DEPARTED FROM Laiassus and arrived at Acre[17] in the month of April, 1269, and there learned, with extreme concern, that Pope Clement IV was recently dead. A legate whom he had appointed was at this time resident in Acre, one Theobald Visconti of Piacenza, and to him they gave an account of what they had in command from the Great Khan of Tartary. He advised them by all means to await the election of another pope, and when that should take place, to proceed with the object of their embassy. Approving of this counsel, they determined upon employing the interval in a visit to their families in Venice. They accordingly embarked at Acre in a ship bound to Negropont, and from thence went on to Venice, where Nicolo Polo found that his wife, whom he had left with child at his departure, was dead, after having been delivered of a son,

who received the name of Marco, and was now of the age of fifteen years.[18] This is the Marco by whom the present work is composed, and who will give therein a relation of all those matters of which he has been an eyewitness.

CHAPTER 10

How the TWO BROTHERS *again* DEPARTED *from* VENICE, *on their* WAY BACK *to the* GREAT KHAN, *and took with them* MARCO, *the* SON *of* NICOLO

IN THE MEANTIME the election of a pope was retarded by so many obstacles that they remained two years in Venice[19] ... ; when at length, becoming apprehensive that the Great Khan might be displeased at their delay, or might suppose it was not their intention to revisit, they judged it expedient to return to Acre; and on this occasion they took with them young Marco Polo. Under

the sanction of the legate they made a visit to Jerusalem, and there provided themselves with some of the oil belonging to the lamp of the Holy Sepulchre. As soon as they were furnished with letters from the legate bearing testimony to the fidelity with which they had endeavoured to execute the *khan*'s commission, and explaining that the pope had not yet been chosen, they proceeded to Laiassus.

CHAPTER 11

How the TWO BROTHERS set out FROM ACRE,
and MARCO along WITH THEM

SCARCELY HOWEVER HAD they taken their departure when the legate received messengers from Italy ... announcing his own elevation to the papal chair; and he thereupon assumed the name of Gregory X. Considering that he was now in a situation that enabled him fully to satisfy the wishes of the Tartar sovereign, he hastened to transmit letters to the king of Armenia, communicating to him the event of his election, and requesting, in case the ambassadors who were on their way to the court of the Great Khan should not have already quitted his dominions, that he would give directions for their immediate return. These letters found them still in Armenia, and with great alacrity they obeyed the summons to repair once more to Acre; for which purpose the king furnished them with an armed galley; sending at the same time an ambassador from himself, to offer his congratulations to the sovereign pontiff.

CHAPTER 12

How the TWO BROTHERS presented
themselves before the NEW POPE

UPON THEIR ARRIVAL, His Holiness received them in a distinguished manner, and immediately dispatched them with letters papal, accompanied by two friars of the Order of Preachers,[20] who happened to be on the spot; men of letters and of science, as well as profound theologians. One of them was named Fra Nicolo da Vicenza, and the other, Fra Guielmo da Tripoli. To them he gave licence and authority to ordain priests, to consecrate bishops, and to grant absolution as fully as he could do in his own person. He also entrusted them with valuable presents, and among these, several handsome vases of crystal, to be delivered to the Great Khan in his name, along with his benediction. Having taken leave, they again steered their course to the port of Laiassus,[21] where they landed, and from thence proceeded into the country of Armenia.

Here they received intelligence that the *soldan* of Babylonia, named Bundokdari, had invaded the Armenian territory with a numerous army, and had overrun and laid waste the country to a great extent.[22] Terrified at these accounts, and apprehensive for their lives, the two friars determined not to proceed further, and delivering over to the Venetians the letters and presents entrusted to them by the pope, they placed themselves under the protection of the master of the Knights Templar, and with him returned directly to the coast.

CHAPTER 13

How NICOLO *and* MAFFEO,
ACCOMPANIED *by* MARCO, TRAVELLED
to the COURT *of the* GREAT KHAN

NICOLO, MAFFEO AND Marco, however, undismayed by perils or difficulties … passed the borders of Armenia and prosecuted their journey. After crossing deserts … and passing many dangerous defiles they advanced so far … that at length they gained information of the Great Khan, who then had his residence in a large and magnificent city named Clemenfu.[23] Their whole journey to this place occupied no less than three years and a half …. The Great Khan having notice of their approach … and being aware how much they must have suffered from fatigue … gave orders to prepare in every place through which they were to pass whatever might be requisite to their comfort. By these means, and through the blessing of God, they were conveyed in safety to the royal court.

CHAPTER 14

How NICOLO and MAFFEO POLO and MARCO PRESENTED THEMSELVES before the GREAT KHAN

UPON THEIR ARRIVAL they were ... graciously received by the Great Khan, in a full assembly of his principal officers. When they drew nigh to his person, they paid their respects by prostrating themselves on the floor. He immediately commanded them to rise, and to relate to him the circumstances of their travels, with all that had taken place in their negotiation with His Holiness. ... The letters and the presents from Pope Gregory were then laid before him, and, upon hearing the former read, he bestowed much commendation on the fidelity, the zeal and the diligence of his ambassadors; and receiving with due reverence the oil from the Holy Sepulchre, he gave directions that it should be preserved with religious care. Upon his observing Marco Polo, and inquiring who he was, Nicolo made answer, "This is your servant, and my son"; upon which the Great Khan replied, "He is welcome, and it pleases me much", and he caused him to be enrolled amongst his attendants of honour. And ... as long as the said brothers and Marco remained in the court of the Great Khan, they were honoured even above his own courtiers.

CHAPTER 15

How the EMPEROR sent MARCO on an EMBASSY

MARCO WAS HELD in high estimation and respect by all belonging to the court. He ... adopted the manners of the Tartars, and acquired a proficiency in four languages .... Finding him thus accomplished, his master put his talents for business to the proof and sent him on an important concern of state to a city named Karazan,[24] situated ... six months' journey from the imperial residence; on which occasion he conducted himself with so much wisdom and prudence in the ... affairs entrusted to him, that his services became highly acceptable.

CHAPTER 16

How MARCO RETURNED *from*
the MISSION *whereon* HE HAD BEEN SENT

ON HIS PART, perceiving that the Great Khan took a pleasure in hearing accounts of whatever was new to him respecting the customs and manners of people, and the peculiar circumstances of distant countries, he endeavoured, wherever he went, to obtain correct information on these subjects, and made notes of all he saw and heard, in order to gratify the curiosity of his master.

In short, during seventeen years that he continued in his service, he rendered himself so useful, that he was employed on confidential missions to every part of the empire and its dependencies .... Under such circumstances it was that Marco Polo had the opportunity of acquiring a knowledge, either by his own observation, or what he collected from others, of so many things, until his time unknown, respecting the eastern parts of the world, and which he diligently and regularly committed to writing, as in the sequel will appear.

And by this means he obtained so much honour, that he provoked the jealousy of the other officers of the court.

CHAPTER 17

How NICOLO, MAFFEO *and* MARCO ASKED LEAVE
of the GREAT KHAN *to go their* OWN WAY

OUR VENETIANS HAVING now resided many years at the

imperial court, and in that time having realized considerable wealth, felt a strong desire to revisit their native country .... It became the more decidedly their object when they reflected on the advanced age of the Great Khan, whose death ... might deprive them of that public assistance by which alone they could expect to surmount the innumerable difficulties of so long a journey, and reach their homes in safety; which ... in his lifetime, and through his favour, they might reasonably hope to accomplish. Nicolo Polo accordingly took an opportunity one day, when he observed him to be more than usually cheerful, of ... soliciting on behalf of himself and his family to be indulged with his majesty's gracious permission for their departure. But far from showing himself disposed to comply with the request, he appeared hurt at the application, and asked what motive they could have for wishing to expose themselves to all the inconveniences and hazards of a journey in which they might probably lose their lives. If gain, he said, was their object, he was ready to give them the double of whatever they possessed, and to gratify them with honours to the extent of their desires; but that, from the regard he bore to them, he must positively refuse their petition.

It happened, about this period, that a queen named Bolgana, the wife of Arghun,[25] died, and as her last request ... conjured her husband that no one might succeed to her place on his throne and in his affections who was not a descendant of her own family, now settled under the dominion of the Great Khan, in the country of Cathay.[26] Desirous of complying with this solemn entreaty, Arghun deputed three of his nobles ... as his ambassadors to the Great Khan with a request that he might receive a bride from among the relatives of his deceased queen. The application was taken in good part, and ... choice was made of a damsel aged seventeen whose name was Kogatin, and of whom the ambassadors highly approved. When everything was arranged for their departure ... they received from the Great Khan a gracious dismissal and set out on their return by the way they came.

Having travelled for eight months, their further progress was obstructed ... by fresh wars that had broken out amongst the Tartar princes. Much against their inclinations, therefore, they [returned] to the court of the Great Khan, to whom they stated the interruption they had met with. About the time of their reappearance, Marco Polo happened to arrive from a voyage he had made, with a few vessels under his orders, to some parts of the East Indies,[27] and reported ... the circumstances of his own navigation, which, he said, was performed in those seas with the utmost safety. This latter observation having reached the ears of the three ambassadors, who were extremely anxious to return to their own country ... they sought a conference with our Venetians, whom they found equally desirous of revisiting their home; and it was settled between them that the former, accompanied by their young queen, should ... represent to [the Great Khan] with what convenience and security they might effect their return by sea; whilst the voyage would be attended with less expense than the journey by land, and be performed in a shorter time .... Should his majesty incline to give his consent to their adopting that mode of conveyance, they were then to urge him to suffer the three Europeans, as being persons well skilled in the practice of navigation, to accompany them until they should reach the territory of King Arghun. The *khan* upon receiving this application showed by his countenance that it was exceedingly displeasing to him, averse as he was to parting with the Venetians. Feeling nevertheless that he could not with propriety do otherwise than consent, he yielded to their entreaty.

CHAPTER 18

HOW *the* TWO BROTHERS *and* MARCO TOOK LEAVE
of the GREAT KHAN *and* RETURNED
to THEIR OWN COUNTRY

HAD IT NOT been that he found himself constrained by the importance and urgency of this peculiar case, they would never otherwise have obtained permission to withdraw themselves from his service. He sent for them, however, and addressed them with much kindness and condescension, assuring them of his regard, and requiring from them a promise that when they should have resided some time in Europe and with their own family, they would return to him once more. With this object in view he caused them to be furnished with the golden tablet (or royal *chop*), which contained his order for their having free and safe conduct through every part of his dominions, with the needful supplies for themselves and their attendants. He likewise gave them authority to act in the capacity of his ambassadors to the pope, the kings of France, England[28] and Spain, and the other Christian princes.

At the same time preparations were made for the equipment of fourteen ships .... On them were embarked the ambassadors, having the queen under their protection, together with Nicolo, Maffeo and Marco Polo.[29] ... After about three months, they arrived at ... Java .... Taking their departure from thence, they employed eighteen months in the Indian seas before they were enabled to reach the place of their destination in the territory of King Arghun[30] and ... between the day of their sailing and that of their arrival ... of the three ambassadors, only one ... survived the voyage; whilst of all the ladies and female attendants one only died.

Upon landing they were informed that King Arghun had died some time before,[31] and that the government ... was then administered, on behalf of his son, who was still a youth, by a person of the name of Ki-akato.[32] From him they desired to receive instructions as to the manner in which they were to dispose of the princess, whom ... they had conducted thither. His answer was that they ought to present the lady to Kasan, the son of Arghun, who was then ... on the borders of Persia, where an army of 60,000 men was assembled for the purpose of guarding certain passes against the irruption of the enemy.

This they proceeded to carry into execution [then] they returned to the residence of Ki-akato .... Here ... they reposed ... for ... nine months.[33] When they took their leave he furnished them with four golden tablets .... Their inscription began with invoking the blessing of the Almighty upon the Great Khan .... It then proceeded to direct that the three ambassadors, as his representatives, should be treated throughout his dominions with due honour, that their expenses should be defrayed, and that they should be provided with the necessary escorts. All this was fully complied with, and from many places they were protected by bodies of 200 horse; nor could this have been dispensed with as the government of Ki-akato was unpopular, and the people were disposed to commit insults and proceed to outrages, which they would not have dared to attempt under the rule of their proper sovereign.

In the course of their journey our travellers received intelligence of the Great Khan (Kublai) having departed this life;[34] which entirely put an end to all prospect of their revisiting those regions. Pursuing, therefore, their intended route, they at length reached the city of Trebizond, from whence they proceeded to Constantinople, then to Negropont, and finally to Venice, at which place, in the enjoyment of health and abundant riches, they safely arrived in the year 1295. On this occasion they offered up their thanks to God, who had now been pleased to relieve them from such great fatigues, after having preserved them from innumerable perils.

The foregoing narrative may be considered as a preliminary chapter, the object of which is to make the reader acquainted with the opportunities Marco Polo had of acquiring a knowledge of the things he describes, during a residence of so many years in the eastern parts of the world. Now we shall begin the Book of the Description of the Divers Things that Marco met with in his Travels.

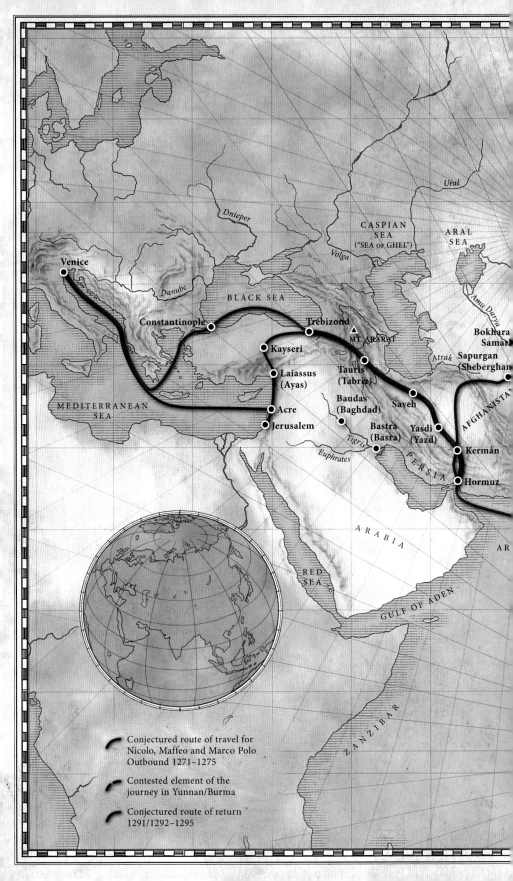

Venice

Dnieper

Danube

CASPIAN
SEA
("SEA of GHEL")

ARAL
SEA

Ural

BLACK SEA

Volga

Amu Darya

Constantinople

Trebizond

MT. ARARAT

Bokhara
Samar
Sapurgan
(Sheberghan)

Kayseri

Tauris
(Tabriz)

Atrak

Laiassus
(Ayas)

Baudas
(Baghdad)

Saveh

AFGHANISTAN

Acre

Yasdi
(Yazd)

Jerusalem

Bastra
(Basra)

Kermán

MEDITERRANEAN
SEA

Tigris

Euphrates

PERSIA

Hormuz

ARABIA

AR

RED
SEA

GULF OF ADEN

Z A N Z I B A R

Conjectured route of travel for
Nicolo, Maffeo and Marco Polo
Outbound 1271–1275

Contested element of the
journey in Yunnan/Burma

Conjectured route of return
1291/1292–1295

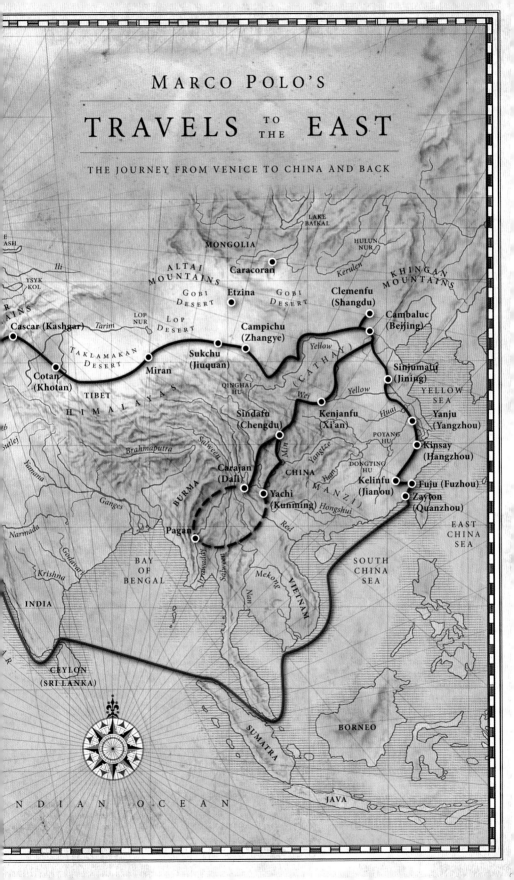

ACCOUNT OF REGIONS VISITED

OR HEARD OF ON THE

JOURNEY

FROM THE

LESSER ARMENIA

TO THE COURT OF THE

GREAT KHAN

AT CHANDU

CHAPTER 1

HERE *the* BOOK BEGINS;
and FIRST *it* SPEAKS *of* LESSER ARMENIA

THERE ARE TWO Armenias, the Greater and the Lesser. The Lesser Armenia is governed by a certain king, who maintains a just rule in his dominions, but is himself subject to the Tartar.[1] The country contains numerous towns and villages, and there is an abundance of all necessaries of life, as well as those things which contribute to its comfort. Game, both beasts and birds, is in plenty. It must be said, however, that it is by no means a healthy region.[2] In former times the gentry were valiant soldiers, but nowadays they are great drinkers and worthless. They have a city upon the sea, which is called Layas, at which there is a great trade. For you must know that all the spicery, and the cloths of silk and gold, and the other valuable wares that come from the interior, are brought to that city. Its port is frequented by merchants from Venice, Genoa, and many other places, who trade in all the rich commodities. Those persons who would travel to the interior (of the East) ... usually proceed in the first instance to this port of Layas.[3]

CONCERNING *the* PROVINCE *of* TURCOMANIA

IN TURCOMANIA[4] THERE are three classes of people. The Turcomans, who follow the law of Muhammad, are a rude people and dull of intellect. They dwell among the mountains and downs, seeking good pasture for their cattle. Excellent horses, known as Turquans,[5] are reared in their country, and fine mules, which are very valuable. The other two classes are the Armenians and the Greeks, who live in the towns, occupying themselves with trade and handicrafts. They weave the finest and handsomest carpets in the world, and also rich silks of crimson and other colours. Their chief cities are Conia, Savast … and Casaria.[6] All these people are subject to the Great Khan, the emperor of the Tartars, as their suzerain.

C H A P T E R   3

DESCRIPTION *of* GREATER ARMENIA

THIS IS A great country. It begins at a city called Arzinga,[7] at which they weave the best buckram in the world.[8] It possesses also the best baths from natural springs that are anywhere to be found. The people of the country are Armenians, under the dominion of the Tartars. There are many towns and villages in the country, but the noblest of their cities is Arzinga, which is the see of an archbishop, and then Arziron and Arzizi.

The country is extensive, and in the summer it is frequented by part of the army of the eastern Tartars, because it furnishes them with excellent pasture for their cattle. But in winter they quit this country and go to a warmer region, where they find other good pastures….

And you must know that it is in Armenia that the Ark of Noah exists on the top of a great mountain,[9] on the summit of which snow is so constant that no one can ascend for the snow never melts and is constantly added to by new falls. Below, however, the snow does melt and runs down, producing such abundant vegetation that in summer cattle are sent to pasture from a long way round about, and it never fails them.

The country is bounded on the south by a kingdom called Mosul, the people of which are Jacobite and Nestorian Christians, of whom I shall have more to tell you presently. On the north it is bounded by the Land of the Georgians, of whom also I shall speak. On the confines toward Georgiania there is a fountain from which oil springs in great abundance, insomuch that a hundred shiploads might be taken from it at one time. This oil is not good to use with food, but 'tis good to burn, and is also used to anoint men and camels that have the mange. People come from vast distances to fetch it, for in all the countries round about they have no other oil.[10]

CHAPTER 4

Of GEORGIANIA *and the* KINGS THEREOF

IN GEORGIANIA THE king is usually styled David Melic.[11] One part of his country is subject to the Tartar and the other part remains in his possession; it is situated between two seas, the Greater (Euxine) on the northern (western) side and the Abuku (Caspian) on the other (eastern) side. The people are handsome, expert archers and valiant soldiers. They are Christians of the Greek Rite, and they have a fashion of wearing their hair cropped short, like clergy.[12]

This is the province that Alexander could not pass into when he wished to penetrate northward, because of a narrow and perilous pass, which has the sea on one side and mountainous woodland impassable to horsemen on the other. The pass extends for four miles, and a handful of men might hold it against all the world. Alexander constructed a wall to prevent the people beyond from coming to attack him, and this obtained the name of the Iron Gate.[13]

This is where it is said that Alexander shut up the Tartars between two mountains – not that they were really Tartars in those days, but were instead a people called Comanians and many besides.

In this province all the forests are of box-wood.[14] There are numerous towns and villages, and silk is produced in abundance. They also weave cloths of gold .... The country produces the best goshawks in the world, which are called *avigi*. It has no lack of anything, and the people live by trade and handicrafts. 'Tis a very mountainous region, and full of narrow defiles and fortresses such that the Tartars have never been able to subdue it entirely.

There is ... a certain convent of nuns called St Leonard's, about which I have to tell you a very wonderful circumstance. Near the church in question there is a great lake at the foot of a mountain, and in this lake no fish can be found, great or small, throughout the year until Lent. On the first day of Lent there is an abundance of the finest fish in the world, and it continues until Easter. After that they are found no more until Lent comes round again; and so 'tis every year. 'Tis really a great miracle![15]

That sea whereof I spoke as coming so near the mountains is called the Sea of Ghel or Ghelan, and extends about 700 miles.[16] It is twelve days' journey distant from any other sea, and into it flows the great River Euphrates and many others, whilst it is surrounded by mountains. Of late the merchants of Genoa have begun to navigate this sea, carrying ships across and launching them thereon. It is from the country on this sea that the silk called *ghelle* is brought.[17] (The said sea produces quantities of fish, especially sturgeon, at the river-mouths salmon, and other big kinds of fish.[18])

CHAPTER 5

Of the KINGDOM of MAUSUL

ON THE FRONTIER of Armenia toward the southeast is the kingdom of Mausul. It is a very great kingdom,[19] and inhabited by several different kinds of people.

First there is a kind of people called Arabians, who worship Muhammad.[20] Then there are Nestorian and Jacobite Christians who have a patriarch who creates archbishops, abbots and prelates whom he sends to every quarter – to India, to Baudas or to Cathay – just as the pope of Rome does in the Latin countries. For you must know that there is a great number of Christians in those countries, but they are all Jacobites and Nestorians; Christians indeed, but not in the fashion enjoined by the pope ....[21]

All the cloths of gold and silk that we call *mosolin*s are made in this country and those merchants called Mosolins, who carry for sale such quantities of spicery and pearls and cloths of silk and gold, are also from this kingdom.[22]

In the mountains there is a race of people called Kurds. Some of them are Christians and some are Muslims; but they are all unprincipled and delight in robbing from the merchants.

CHAPTER 6

Of the GREAT CITY *of* BAUDAS,
and HOW *it was* TAKEN

BAUDAS IS A great city, which used to be the seat of the *calif* of all Muslims in the world, just as Rome is the seat of the pope of all the Christians.[23] A great river flows through the city, and by this river you can descend to the Sea of India.[24] Many merchants use the river to transport their goods, travelling eighteen days from Baudas to a city called Kisi,[25] where they enter the Sea of India. As you go from Baudas to Kisi there is a great city called Bastra, surrounded by woods, in which grow the best dates in the world.[26]

In Baudas they weave many kinds of silkstuffs and gold brocades,[27] and many another beautiful tissue richly wrought with figures of beasts and birds. Islamic law is studied here, as are magic, physics, astronomy, geomancy and physiognomy. It is the noblest and greatest city in all those regions.

Now it came to pass on a day in the year of Christ 1255, that

the lord of the Tartars of the Levant, whose name was Alaü, brother to the Great Khan now reigning, gathered a mighty host and took Baudas by storm.[28] It was a great enterprise, for in Baudas there were more than 100,000 horse, besides footsoldiers. And when Alaü had taken the place he found a tower of the *calif*'s that was full of gold and silver and other treasure – the greatest accumulation of treasure in one spot that ever was known. When he beheld that great heap Alaü was astonished, and, summoning the *calif*, he said: "*Calif*, tell me now why thou hast gathered such a huge treasure? What didst thou mean to do therewith? Knewest thou not that I was … coming against thee with so great an host to cast thee forth of thine heritage? Wherefore didst thou not take of thy gear and employ it in paying knights and soldiers to defend thee and thy city?"

The *calif* said never a word. So Alaü continued, "Now then, *calif*, since I see what a love thou hast borne thy treasure, I will give it thee

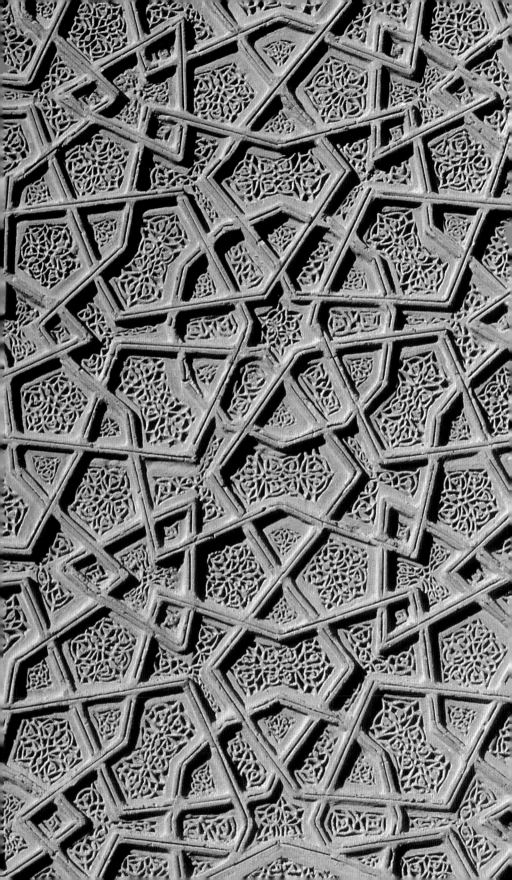

to eat!" So he shut the *calif* up in the tower and bade that neither meat nor drink should be given him, saying, "Now, *calif*, eat of thy treasure as much as thou wilt, since thou art so fond of it; for never shalt thou have aught else to eat!"

The *calif* lingered in the tower four days, and then died like a dog. Truly his treasure would have been of more service to him had he bestowed it upon men who would have defended his kingdom and his people, rather than let himself be taken and … put to death. Howbeit, since that time, there has been never another *calif*, either at Baudas or anywhere else.[29]

Now I will tell you of a great miracle that befell at Baudas, wrought by God on behalf of the Christians.

HOW *the* CALIF *of* BAUDAS TOOK COUNSEL *to* SLAY ALL *the* CHRISTIANS *in* HIS LANDS

IT WAS IN the year of Christ[30] … that there was a *calif* at Baudas who bore a great hatred to Christians, and was taken up day and night with the thought of how he might either bring those that were in his kingdom over to his own faith, or might procure them all to be slain. And he used daily to take counsel about this with the devotees and learned men of his faith, for they all bore the Christians like malice.

Now it happened that the *calif*, with those learned men of his, got hold of a passage in the Gospel where it states that if a Christian had faith as a grain of mustard seed, and should bid a mountain be removed, it would be removed.[31] They were delighted, for it seemed to them the very thing whereby either to force all the Christians to change their faith, or to bring destruction upon them all. The *calif* therefore called together all the Christians in his territories, who were extremely numerous. And when they had come before him, he showed them the Gospel and made them read the text which I have mentioned. And when they had read it he asked them if that was the truth? The Christians answered that it assuredly was so. "Well," said the *calif,* "since you say that it is the truth, I will give you a choice. Among such a number of you there must needs surely be this small amount of faith; so you must either move that mountain there" – and he pointed to a mountain in the neighbourhood – "or you shall die an ill death; unless you choose to eschew death by all becoming Muslims and adopting our Holy Law. To this end I give you a respite of ten days; if the thing be not done by that time, ye shall die or become Muslims." And when he had said this he dismissed them, to consider what was to be done in this strait wherein they were.

CHAPTER 8

HOW *the* CHRISTIANS *were in* GREAT DISMAY
because of WHAT *the* CALIF HAD SAID

ON HEARING WHAT the *calif* had said the Christians were in great dismay, but they lifted all their hopes to God that He would help them in this their strait. All the wisest of the Christians took counsel together, but they had no resource except to turn to Him from whom all good things do come, beseeching Him to protect them from the cruel *calif.*

So they were all gathered together in prayer, men and women, for eight days and eight nights. And whilst they were thus engaged it was revealed to a bishop in a vision that he should find a certain cobbler,[32] who had but one eye, and that through his prayer God in His goodness would grant the request because of the cobbler's holy life.

This cobbler led a life of great uprightness and chastity, he fasted and kept from all sin, went daily to church to hear mass, and gave daily a portion of his gains to God. And how he came to have but one eye was this. It happened one day that a woman came to him to have a pair of shoes made, and she showed him her foot that he might take her measure. Now she had a very beautiful foot and leg; and the cobbler in taking her measure was conscious of sinful thoughts. And he had often heard it said that "if thine eye offend thee, pluck it out and cast it from thee", rather than sin. So, as soon as the woman had departed, he took the awl that he used in stitching, and drove it into his eye and destroyed it.

So you can judge what a holy, just, righteous man he was.

CHAPTER 9

HOW *the* ONE-EYED COBBLER *was* *desired to* PRAY *for the* CHRISTIANS

NOW WHEN THIS vision had visited the bishop several times, he related the whole matter to the Christians, and they agreed to summon the cobbler. On hearing their request the cobbler made many excuses, declaring that he was not at all so good a man as they represented. But they persisted in their request with so much sweetness, that at last he said he would ... do what they desired.

CHAPTER 10

HOW *the* PRAYER *of the* ONE-EYED COBBLER CAUSED *the* MOUNTAIN *to* MOVE

AND WHEN THE appointed day was come, all the Christians got up early, men and women, small and great, more than 100,000 persons, and went to church, and heard holy mass. And after mass had been sung, they all went forth in a great procession to the plain in front of the mountain, carrying the precious cross before them, loudly singing and greatly weeping as they went. And when they arrived at the spot, there they found the *calif* with his host armed to slay them if they would not change their faith; for the Muslims believed not in the least that God would grant such a favour to the Christians. These latter stood indeed in great fear and doubt, but nevertheless they rested their hope on their God Jesus Christ.

So the cobbler threw himself before the cross, and stretched out his hands toward heaven and made this prayer: "Blessed Lord God Almighty, I pray unto Thy people, insomuch that they perish not, nor Thy faith be cast down, nor abused nor flouted. Not that I am in the least worthy to prefer such request unto Thee; but for Thy great power and mercy I beseech Thee to hear this prayer from me Thy servant full of sin."

And when he had ended his prayer to God, and whilst the *calif* and all the Muslims and other people there were looking on, the mountain rose out of its place and moved to the spot which the *calif* had pointed out! And when the *calif* and all his guards beheld this they were so amazed by the wonderful miracle that God had wrought for the Christians that many of the Muslims became Christians. And even the *calif* secretly became a Christian. When he died they found a little cross hung round his neck and therefore the Muslims would not entomb him with the other *califs*, but put him in a place apart. The Christians exulted greatly at this miracle, and returned to their homes full of joy, giving thanks to their Creator for that which He had done.[33]

CHAPTER 11

Of the NOBLE CITY

of TAURIS

TAURIS IS A great and noble city, situated in a great province called Yrac, in which are many other towns and villages. But as Tauris is the most noble I will tell you about it.[34]

The men of Tauris get their living by trade and handicrafts, for they weave many kinds of beautiful and valuable stuffs of silk and gold. The city has such a good position that merchandise is brought thither from India, Baudas, Cremesor,[35] and many other regions; and that attracts many Latin merchants, especially Genoese, to buy goods and transact other business there; it is also a great market for precious stones.

The Taurisians are themselves poor creatures and are a great medley of different peoples. There are Armenians, Nestorians, Jacobites, Georgians, Persians and Muslims, who are the majority of the city's natives. The city is surrounded with charming gardens, full of many varieties of fruits....

... From Tauris to Persia is a journey of twelve days.

CHAPTER 12

Of the MONASTERY *of* ST BARSAMO
on the BORDERS *of* TAURIS

ON THE BORDERS of Tauris there is a monastery called after Barsamo, a most devout saint.[36] There is an abbot, with many monks, who wear a habit like that of the Carmelites, and these to avoid idleness are continually knitting woollen girdles. These they place upon the altar of St Barsamo during the service, and when they go about the province soliciting alms (like the Brethren of the Holy Spirit) they present them to their friends and to people of distinction, for they are excellent things to remove rheumatic pains....

CHAPTER 13

Of the GREAT COUNTRY *of* PERSIA;
with SOME ACCOUNT *of the* THREE KINGS

PERSIA IS A great country, which in ancient times was illustrious and powerful; but the Tartars have destroyed it.

In Persia is the city of Saba, from which the three *magi* set out when they went to worship Jesus Christ .... One of these was called Gaspar, the second Melchior and the third Balthasar. Messer Marco

Polo asked many questions of the people of that city as to those three *magi*, but no one could tell him anything, except that the three were buried there. However, at a place three days' journey distant he found a village called Cala Ataperistan,[37] which means "the castle of the fire-worshippers". And the name is rightly applied, for the people there do worship fire, and I will tell you why.

They relate that in ancient times three kings of that country went away to worship a prophet that was born, and they carried with them three manner of offerings – frankincense, gold and myrrh – in order to ascertain whether that prophet were God, an earthly king, or a physician.[38] For, said they, if he take the incense he is God; if he take the gold, then he is an earthly king; if he take the myrrh he is a physician. So it came to pass when they had come to the place where the child was born, the youngest of the three kings went in first, and found the child apparently just of his own age; so he went forth again marvelling greatly. The middle one entered next, and like the first he found the child seemingly of his own age; so he also went forth again and marvelled greatly. Lastly, the eldest went in, and as it had befallen the other two, so it befell him. And he went forth very pensive. And when the three had rejoined one another, each told what he had seen; and then they all marvelled the more. So they agreed to go in all three together, and on doing so they beheld the child with the appearance of its true age, which was some thirteen days. Then they adored, and presented their frankincense and gold and myrrh. And the child took all three offerings, and then gave them a small closed box; whereupon the kings departed.

CHAPTER 14

WHAT BEFELL *when the* THREE KINGS RETURNED
to THEIR OWN COUNTRY

AND WHEN THE three kings had ridden many days they said they would see what the child had given them. So they opened the little box, and inside it they found a stone.

On seeing this they began to wonder what the importance of it might be. The significance was this: when they had presented their offerings, the child had accepted all three; and when they saw that, they had said within themselves that He was the True God, and the True King, and the True Physician. And what the gift of the stone implied was that this Faith which had begun in them should abide firm as a rock. For He well knew what was in their thoughts. But they had no understanding at all of this meaning of the gift of the stone, so they cast it into a well. Then straightaway a fire from heaven struck the well.

And when the three kings beheld this marvel they were amazed, and they repented bitterly that they had cast away the stone; for they understood that it had a great and holy meaning. So they took some of that fire and carried it into their own country, where they placed it in a rich and beautiful church. And there the people keep it continually burning, and worship it as a god, and all the sacrifices they offer are kindled with that fire. And if ever the fire becomes extinct they go to other cities round about where the same faith is held, and obtain of that fire from them, and carry it to the church. And this is the reason why the people of this country worship fire. They will often go ten days' journey to get of that fire.[39]

Such then was the story told by the people of that castle to Messer Marco Polo; they declared to him for a truth that such was their history, and that one of the three kings was of the city called Saba, and the second of Ava, and the third of that very castle where they still worship fire, with the people of all the country round about.

CHAPTER 15

Of the EIGHT KINGDOMS *of* PERSIA, *and* HOW THEY ARE NAMED

NOW YOU MUST know that Persia is a very great country and contains eight kingdoms.[40] I will tell you the names of them all. The first kingdom is met with upon entering Persia, and it is called

Casvin; the second is further to the south, and is called Kurdistan; the third is Lor; the fourth Suolstan; the fifth Istanit; the sixth Serazy; the seventh Soncara; the eighth Tunocain, which is at the further extremity of Persia.[41] All these kingdoms lie in a southerly direction except one – Tunocain, which lies toward the east, and borders on the (country of the) Arbre Sol.[42]

In Persia there is a great supply of fine horses; and people take them to India to sell, where they bring high prices, with a single one generally able to fetch 200 *livres tournois*; some will be more, some less, according to the quality.[43] Here also are the finest asses in the world, worth fully thirty marks of silver each, for they are very large, fast, strong and not easily fatigued. Dealers carry their horses to Kisi and Curmosa,[44] two cities on the shores of the Sea of India, and there they meet with merchants who take the horses on to India.

In this country there are many murderous people, so that no day passes without some homicide among them. Were it not for the government, which is that of the Tartars of the Levant, they would do great mischief to merchants; and, indeed, even with the government they often succeed in doing such mischief. Unless merchants be well armed they run the risk of being murdered, or at least robbed of everything; and it sometimes happens that a whole party perishes in this way when not on their guard. The people are all Muslims.

In the cities there are traders and artisans weaving cloths of gold, and silkstuffs of sundry kinds. Plenty of cotton is produced in the country; and an abundance of wheat, barley, millet, and wine, with fruits of all kinds....[45]

CHAPTER 16

CONCERNING *the* GREAT CITY *of* YASDI

YASDI ALSO IS properly in Persia; it is a good and noble city, and has a great amount of trade.[46] They weave there quantities of a certain silk tissue known as *yasdi*, which merchants carry into many quarters to dispose of. The people are Muslims.

When you leave this city to travel further, you ride for seven days over great plains, finding a place of refuge in only three places. There are many fine woods (producing dates) upon the way, such as one can easily ride through; and in them there is great sport to be had in hunting and hawking, there being partridges and quails and an abundance of other game, so that the merchants who pass that way have plenty of diversion. There are also wild asses, handsome creatures. At the end of those seven marches over the plain you come to a fine kingdom called Kermán.

CHAPTER 17

CONCERNING *the* KINGDOM *of* KERMÁN

KERMÁN IS A kingdom which is also properly in Persia, and formerly it had a hereditary prince. Since the Tartars conquered the country, the Tartar sends to administer whatever governor he pleases. In this kingdom are produced the stones called turquoises in great abundance; they are found in the mountains, where they are extracted from the rocks. There are also plenty of veins of steel and *ondanique*.[47] The people are very skilful in making accoutrements of war; their saddles, bridles, spurs, swords, bows, quivers, and arms of every kind, are very well made indeed according to the fashion of those parts. The ladies of the country and their daughters also produce exquisite needlework in the embroidery of silkstuffs in different colours, with figures of beasts and birds, trees and flowers, and a variety of other patterns. They work hangings for the use of noblemen so deftly that they are marvels to see, as well as cushions, pillows, quilts, and all sorts of things.[48]

In the mountains of Kermán are found the best falcons in the world.[49] They are inferior in size to the Peregrine, red on the breast, under the neck, and between the thighs; their flight so swift that no bird can escape them.

On quitting the city you ride on for seven days, always finding ... villages and handsome houses .... When you have ridden for seven days you come to a mountain, and when you have got to the top of the pass you find a great descent that takes two days. All along you find an abundance of fruits; and in former days there were plenty of inhabited places on the road, but now there is none; and you meet with only a few people looking after their cattle at pasture. From the city of Kermán to this descent, the cold in winter is so great that you can scarcely abide it, even with a great quantity of clothing.

CHAPTER 18

Of the CITY *of* CAMADI *and its* RUINS; *also* TOUCHING *the* KARAUNA ROBBERS

AFTER YOU HAVE ridden downhill those two days, you find yourself in a vast plain, and at the beginning there is a city called Camadi,[50] which formerly was a great and noble place, but now is of little consequence, for the Tartars ... have several times ravaged it. The plain whereof I speak is a very hot region; and the province that we now enter is called Reobarles.

The fruits of the country are dates, pistachios and apples of paradise,[51] with others of the like not found in our cold climate.... And on this plain there is a kind of bird called francolin, but different from the francolin of other countries, for their colour is a mixture of black and white, and the feet and beak are vermilion. The beasts also are peculiar; and first I will tell you of their oxen. These are very large, and all over white as snow; the hair is very short and smooth, which is owing to the heat of the country. The horns are short and thick, not sharp in the point; and between the shoulders they have a round hump some two palms high. There are no handsomer creatures in the world. And when they have to be loaded, they kneel like the camel; once the load is adjusted, they rise. Their load is a heavy one, for they are very strong animals. Then there are sheep here as big as asses; and their tails are so large and fat, that one tail shall weigh some 30lbs. They are fine fat beasts, and afford excellent mutton.[52]

In this plain there are a number of villages and towns which

have lofty walls of mud, made as a defence against the bandits, who are very numerous, and are called Karaunas.[53] And you must know that when these Karaunas wish to make a plundering incursion, they have certain devilish enchantments whereby they bring darkness over the face of day, insomuch that you can scarcely discern your comrade riding beside you; and this darkness they will extend over a space of seven days' journey. They know the country thoroughly, and ride abreast, keeping near one another, sometimes to the number of 10,000, at other times more or fewer. In this way they extend across the whole plain that they are going to harry, and catch every living thing that is found outside of the towns and villages; man, woman, or beast, nothing can escape them! The old men whom they take in this way they butcher; the young men and the women they sell for slaves in other countries; thus the whole land is ruined, and has become well-nigh a desert.

The king of these scoundrels is called Nogodar. This Nogodar had gone to the court of Chagatai, who was the brother of the Great Khan,[54] with some 10,000 horsemen of his, and abode with him; for Chagatai was his uncle. And whilst there Nogodar devised a most audacious enterprise. He left his uncle, who was then in Greater Armenia, and fled with a great body of horsemen – cruel, unscrupulous fellows – first through Badashan, and then through another province called Pashai-Dir, and then through another called Ariora-Keshemur. There he lost a great number of his people and of his horses, for the roads were narrow and perilous. And when he had conquered all those provinces, he entered India at the extremity of a province called Dalivar. He established himself in that city and government, which he seized from the king, Asedin Soldan by name, a man of great power and wealth.[55] And there abideth Nogodar with his army, afraid of nobody and waging war with all the Tartars in his neighbourhood.[56]

Now that I have told you of those scoundrels and their history, I must add the fact that Messer Marco himself was all but caught in such a darkness as that I have told you of; but, as it pleased God, he got off and threw himself into a village that was hard by, called Conosalmi. He lost his whole company except seven persons who escaped along with him. The rest were caught, and some of them sold, some put to death.

CHAPTER 19

Of the DESCENT *to the* CITY *of* HORMUZ

THE PLAIN OF which we have spoken extends in a southerly direction for five days' journey, and then you come to another descent some 20 miles in length, where the road is very bad and full of peril, for there are many robbers and bad characters about. When you have got to the foot of this descent you find another beautiful plain called the Plain of Formosa.[57] This extends for two days' journey; and you find in it fine streams of water with plenty of date-palms and other fruit-trees. There are also many beautiful birds, francolins, popinjays, and other kinds such as we have none of in our country. When you have ridden these two days you come to the Ocean Sea, and on the shore you find a city with a harbour which is called Hormuz.[58] Merchants come thither from India, with ships loaded with spices and precious stones, pearls, cloths of silk and gold, elephants' teeth, and many other wares, which they sell to the merchants of Hormuz, and which these in turn carry all over the world to dispose of again. In fact, 'tis a city of immense trade. There are plenty of towns and villages under it, but it is the capital. The king is called Ruomedam Ahomet.[59] It is a very sickly place, and the heat is tremendous. If any foreign merchant dies there, the king takes all his property.

In this country they make a wine of dates mixed with spices, which is very good. When anyone not used to it first drinks this wine, it causes repeated and violent purging, but afterwards he is all the better for it, and gets fat upon it. The people never eat meat and wheaten bread except when they are ill, and if they take such food when they are in health it makes them ill. Their food when in health consists of dates and salt-fish (tunny) and onions, and this kind of diet they maintain in order to preserve their health.[60]

Their ships are wretched affairs, and many of them get lost; for they have no iron fastenings and are only stitched together with twine made from the husk of the Indian nut.... It keeps well and is not corroded by seawater, but it will not withstand a storm. The ships are not pitched, but are rubbed with fish-oil. They have one mast, one sail and one rudder, and have no deck, but only a cover spread over the cargo when loaded.... They have no iron to make nails, and for this reason they use only wooden trenails in their shipbuilding, and then stitch the planks with twine as I have told you.[61] Hence 'tis a perilous business to voyage in one of those ships, and many of them are lost, for in that Sea of India the storms are often terrible.

The people are black, and are Muslims. The residents avoid living in the cities, for the heat in summer is so great that it would kill them. Hence they go out (to sleep) at their gardens in the country, where there are streams and plenty of water. For all that they would not escape but for one thing that I will mention. The fact is, you see, that in summer a wind often blows across the sands which encompass the plain, so intolerably hot that it would kill everybody, were it not that when they perceive that wind coming they plunge into water up to the neck, and so abide until the wind has ceased.[62] ...

The people sow their wheat and barley and other corn in the month of November, and reap it in the month of March. The dates are not gathered until May, but otherwise there is no grass nor any other green thing, for the excessive heat dries up everything.

When anyone dies they make a great business of the mourning. Women mourn their husbands for four years, and during that time they mourn at least once a day, gathering together their kinsfolk and friends and neighbours for the purpose, making a great weeping and wailing. (And they have women who are mourners by trade, and do it for hire.) Now, we will quit this country.... For the present let us return by another road to the aforesaid city of Kermán, for we cannot get at those countries that I wish to tell you about except through that city. I should tell you first, however, that King Ruomedam Ahomet of Hormuz, which we are leaving, is a liegeman of the king of Kermán.

On the road by which we return from Hormuz to Kermán you meet with some very fine plains, and you also find many natural hot baths; you find plenty of partridges on the road; and there are towns where victual is cheap and abundant, with quantities of dates and other fruits. The wheaten bread, however, is so bitter … that no one can eat it who is not used to it. The baths that I mentioned have excellent virtues; they cure the itch and several other diseases.[63]

Now, then, I am going to tell you about the countries toward the north…. Let us begin.

CHAPTER 20

Of the WEARISOME *and* DESERT ROAD
that has NOW *to be* TRAVELLED

ON DEPARTING FROM the city of Kermán you find the road for seven days most wearisome; and I will tell you how this is.[64] The first three days you meet with no water, or next to none. And what little you do meet with is bitter green stuff, such that no one can drink it; and in fact if you drink a drop of it, it will set you purging ten times at least by the way. It is the same with the salt from those streams; no one dares to make use of it, because of the excessive purging which it occasions. Hence it is necessary to carry water to last these three days; as for the cattle, they must drink the bad water I have mentioned, but it scours them to such a degree that sometimes they die of it. In all those three days you meet with no human habitation; it is all desert, and the extremity of drought. Even of wild beasts there are none, for there is nothing for them to eat.[65]

After those three days of desert you arrive at a stream of fresh water running underground, but along which there are openings here and there at which you can get sight of the stream. It has an abundant supply, and travellers, worn with the hardships of the desert, here rest and refresh themselves and their beasts.[66]

You then enter another desert which extends for four days; it is very much like the former except that you do see some wild asses. And at the termination of these four days of desert the kingdom of Kermán comes to an end and you find another city, called Cobinan.

CHAPTER 21

CONCERNING *the* CITY *of* COBINAN
and the THINGS *that are* MADE THERE

COBINAN IS A large town.[67] The people are Muslim. There is much iron and steel and *ondanique*, and they make steel mirrors of great size and beauty. They also prepare both *tutia* (a thing very good for the eyes)[68] and *spodium*; and I will tell you the process.

They have a vein of a certain earth which has the required quality, and this they put into a great flaming furnace, whilst over the furnace there is an iron grating. The smoke and moisture, expelled from the earth of which I speak, adhere to the iron grating, and thus form *tutia*, whilst the slag that is left after burning is the *spodium*.

CHAPTER 22

Of a CERTAIN DESERT *that* CONTINUES
for EIGHT DAYS' JOURNEY

WHEN YOU DEPART from Cobinan you find yourself again in a desert of surpassing aridity, which lasts for some eight days. Neither fruits nor trees are to be seen, and what water there is is bitter and bad, so that you have to carry both food and water. ... At the end of those eight days you arrive at a province called Tonocain. It ... forms the extremity of Persia toward the north.[69] It also contains an immense plain on which is found the Arbre Sol, which we Christians call the Arbre Sec .... It is a tall and thick tree, having the bark on one side green and the other white; and it produces a husk like that of a chestnut, but without anything in it. The wood is yellow like box, and strong, and there are no other trees near it nor within 100 miles of it, except on one side, where you find trees within about 10 miles' distance. And there, the people of the country tell you, was fought the battle between Alexander and King Darius.[70]

The towns and villages have a great abundance of everything good, for the climate is extremely temperate, being neither very hot nor very cold. The natives are all Muslims, and are a very fine-looking people, especially the women, who are surpassingly beautiful.

CHAPTER 23

CONCERNING *the* OLD MAN *of the* MOUNTAIN

MULEHET IS A country in which the Old Man of the Mountain dwelt in former days; and the name means "Place of the Aram". I will tell you his whole history as related by Messer Marco Polo, who heard it from several natives of that region.

The Old Man was called in their language Aloadin. He had caused a valley between two mountains to be enclosed, and had turned it into a garden, the largest and most beautiful ever seen .... In it were erected pavilions and palaces the most elegant that can be imagined, covered with gilding and exquisite painting. And there were channels flowing with wine and milk and honey and water; and numbers of ladies ... who could play on all manner of instruments, and sung most sweetly, and danced in a manner that it was charming to behold. For the Old Man desired to make his people believe that this was actually paradise. So he had fashioned it after the description that Muhammad gave of paradise, to wit, that it should be a beautiful garden running with conduits of wine and milk and honey and water, and full of lovely women for the delectation of all its inmates. And sure enough the Muslims of those parts believed that it *was* paradise!

Now no man was allowed to enter the garden save those whom he intended to be his *ashishin*. There was a fortress at the entrance to the garden, strong enough to resist all the world, and there was no other way to get in. He kept at his court a number of the youths of the country, from twelve to twenty years of age, such as had a taste for soldiering, and to these he used to tell tales about paradise, just as Muhammad had been wont to do, and they believed in him just as the Muslims believe in Muhammad. Then he would introduce them into his garden, some four, or six, or ten at a time, having first made them drink a certain potion which cast them into a deep sleep, and then causing them to be lifted and carried in. So when they awoke, they found themselves in the garden.[71]

CHAPTER 24

HOW *the* OLD MAN *used to* TRAIN *his* ASSASSINS

WHEN THEREFORE THEY awoke, and found themselves in a place so charming, they deemed that it truly was paradise. And the ladies and damsels dallied with them to their hearts' content, so that they had what young men would; and with their own good will they never would have quitted the place.

Now this prince whom we call the Old One kept his court in grand and noble style, and made those simple hill-folks about him believe firmly that he was a great prophet. And when he wanted one

of his *ashishin* to send on any mission, he would cause that potion whereof I spoke to be given to one of the youths in the garden, and then had him carried into his palace. So when the young man awoke, he found himself in the castle, and no longer in that paradise; whereat he was not well pleased. He was then conducted to the Old Man's presence, and bowed before him with great veneration as believing himself to be in the presence of a true prophet. The prince would then ask whence he came, and he would reply that he came from paradise and that it was exactly as Muhammad had described it. This of course gave the others who stood by, and who had not been admitted, the greatest desire to enter therein.

So when the Old Man would have any prince slain, he would say to such a youth: "Go and slay so-and-so; and when you return my angels shall bear you into paradise. And should you die, I will still send my angels to carry you back into paradise." So he caused them to believe; and thus there was no order of his that they would not affront any peril to execute, for the desire they had to get back into that paradise. And in this manner the Old One got his people to murder anyone whom he desired to get rid of. Thus, too, the great dread that he inspired all princes withal made them become his tributaries in order that he might abide at amity with them.

I should also tell you that the Old Man had certain others under him, who copied his proceedings and acted exactly in the same manner. One of these was sent into the territory of Damascus, and the other into Kurdistan.[72]

CHAPTER 25

HOW *the* OLD MAN *came by his* END

NOW IT CAME to pass, in the year of Christ's Incarnation 1252 that Alaü, lord of the Tartars of the Levant, heard tell of these great crimes of the Old Man, and resolved to make an end of him. So he took and sent one of his barons with a great army to that castle, and they besieged it for three years, but they could not take it, so strong was it. And indeed if they had had food within it never would have been taken. But after being besieged those three years they ran short of victual, and were taken. The Old Man was put to death with all his men (and the castle with its garden of paradise was levelled with the ground). And since that time he has had no successor; and there was an end to all his villainies.[73]

Now let us go back to our journey.

CHAPTER 26

CONCERNING the CITY of SAPURGAN

ON LEAVING THE castle, you ride over fine plains and beautiful valleys, and pretty hillsides producing excellent grass pasture, an abundance of fruits, and all other products. Armies are glad to take up their quarters here on account of the plenty that exists. This kind of country extends for six days' journey, with a goodly number of towns and villages, in which the people are Muslims. Sometimes also you meet with a tract of desert extending for 50 or 60 miles, or somewhat less, and in these deserts you find no water, but have to carry it along with you. The beasts do without drink until you have got across the desert tract and come to watering places.

So after travelling for six days you come to a city called Sapurgan. It has plenty of everything, but especially of the very best melons in the world. They preserve them by paring them into strips and drying them in the sun. When dry they are sweeter than honey.... There is also abundant game here, both of birds and beasts.

CHAPTER 27

Of the CITY of BALC

BALC IS A noble city, though it was much greater in former days.[74] ... There were formerly many fine palaces and buildings of marble, and the ruins of them still remain. The people of the city tell that it was here that Alexander took the daughter of Darius as his wife. Here, you should be told, is the end of the empire of the Tartar lord of the Levant. And this city is also the limit of Persia in the direction between east and northeast. Now, let us quit this city, and I will tell you of another country called Dogana.[75]

When you have quitted the city of which I have been speaking, you ride some twelve days between northeast and east, without finding any human habitation, for the people have all taken refuge in fastnesses among the mountains, on account of the bandits and armies that harassed them. There is plenty of water on the road, and abundance of game; there are lions too. You can get no provisions on the road, and must carry with you all that you require for these twelve days.

CHAPTER 28

Of TAICAN, and the MOUNTAINS of SALT.
ALSO of the PROVINCE of CASEM

AFTER THOSE TWELVE days' journey you come to a fortified place called Taican, where there is a great corn market.[76] It is a fine place, and the mountains that you see toward the south are all composed of salt. People from all the countries round, to some thirty days' journey, come to fetch this salt, which is the best in the world, and is so hard that it can be broken only with iron picks. 'Tis in such abundance that it would supply the whole world to the end of time. (Other mountains there grow almonds and pistachios, which are exceedingly cheap.)

When you leave this town and ride three days further between northeast and east, you meet with many fine tracts full of vines and other fruits, and with a goodly number of habitations, and everything to be had very cheap. The people are Muslims ... whose great delight is in the wine shop; for they have good wine (albeit it be boiled), and are great topers; in truth, they are constantly getting drunk.

They wear nothing on the head but a cord some ten palms' long twisted round it. They are excellent huntsmen, and take a great deal of game; in fact they wear nothing but the skins of the beasts they have taken in the chase, for they make of them both coats and shoes. Indeed, all of them are acquainted with the art of dressing skins for these purposes.[77]

When you have ridden those three days, you find a town called Casem,[78] which is subject to a count. His other towns and villages are on the hills, but through this town there flows a river of some size. There are many porcupines hereabouts, and very large ones too. When hunted with dogs, several of them will get together and huddle close, shooting their quills at the dogs, which get many a serious wound thereby.[79]

This town of Casem is at the head of a province also called Casem. The people have a peculiar language. The peasants who keep cattle abide in the mountains, and have their dwellings in caves, which form fine and spacious houses for them, and are made with ease, as the hills are composed of earth.

After leaving the town of Casem, you ride for three days without finding a single habitation, or anything to eat or drink, so that you have to carry with you everything that you require. At the end of those three days you reach a province called Badashan, about which we shall now tell you.[80]

CHAPTER 29

Of the PROVINCE *of* BADASHAN

BADASHAN IS A province inhabited by people who are Muslims and have a peculiar language. It forms a very great kingdom, and the royalty is hereditary. All those of the royal blood are descended from King Alexander and the daughter of King Darius, who was lord of the vast empire of Persia. And all these kings call themselves in the

Saracen tongue Zulcarniain, which is as much as to say *Alexander*;
and this out of regard for Alexander the Great.[81]

It is in this province that those valuable gems the balas rubies are
found. They are got in certain rocks ... and in the search for them
the people dig great caves underground, just as is done by miners
for silver. There is but one special mountain that produces them,
and it is called Syghinan.[82] The stones are dug on the king's account,
and no one else dares dig in that mountain on pain of forfeiture of
life as well as goods; nor may anyone carry the stones out of the
kingdom. But the king amasses them all, and sends them to other
kings when he has tribute to render, or when he desires to offer a
friendly present; and such only as he pleases he causes to be sold.
Thus he acts in order to keep the balas at a high value; for if he were
to allow everybody to dig, they would extract so many that the world
would be glutted with them, and they would cease to bear any value.
Hence it is that he allows so few to be taken out, and is so strict in
the matter.

There is also in the same country another mountain, in which
azure is found; 'tis the finest in the world, and is got in a vein like
silver.[83] There are also other mountains which contain a great amount
of silver ore, so that the country is a very rich one; but it is also
(it must be said) a very cold one. It produces numbers of excellent
horses, remarkable for their speed. They are not shod at all, although
constantly used in mountainous country, and on very bad roads....[84]

The mountains of this country also supply saker falcons of
excellent flight, and plenty of lanners likewise. Beasts and birds for
the chase there are in great abundance. Good wheat is grown, and
also barley without husk. They have no olive oil, but make oil from
sesame, and also from walnuts.[85]

In the mountains there are vast numbers of sheep 400, 500 or
600 in a flock, and all of them wild ....

Those mountains are so lofty that 'tis a hard day's work, from
morning until evening, to get to the top of them. On getting up,
you find an extensive plain with an abundance of grass and trees,
and copious springs of pure water running down through rocks
and ravines. In those brooks are found trout and many other fish of

dainty kinds; and the air in those regions is so pure, and residence there so healthful, that when the men who dwell below in the towns, and in the valleys and plains, find themselves attacked by any kind of fever or other ailment, they lose no time in going to the hills; and after abiding there two or three days, they quite recover their health through the excellence of that air. And Messer Marco said he had proved this by experience: for when in those parts he had been ill for about a year, but as soon as he was advised to visit that mountain, he did so and got well at once.[86]

In this kingdom there are many strait and perilous passes, so difficult to force that the people have no fear of invasion. Their towns and villages also are on lofty hills, and in very strong positions.[87] They are excellent archers, and much given to the chase indeed, most of them are dependent for clothing on the skins of beasts, for stuffs are very dear among them. The great ladies, however, are arrayed in stuffs, and I will tell you the style of their dress! They all wear drawers made of cotton cloth, and into the making of these some will put 60, 80, or even 100 ells of stuff.[88] This they do to make themselves look large in the hips, for the men of those parts think that to be a great beauty in a woman.

CHAPTER 30

Of the PROVINCE *of* PASHAI

YOU MUST KNOW that ten days' journey to the south of Badashan there is a province called Pashai, the people of which have a peculiar language, and are idolaters of a dark complexion. They are great adepts in sorcery and the diabolic arts. The men wear earrings and brooches of gold and silver set with stones and pearls. The people are crafty. They live upon flesh and rice, and their country is very hot.[89]

Now let us proceed and speak of another country which is seven days' journey from this one toward the southeast, and the name of which is Keshimur.[90]

CHAPTER 31

Of the PROVINCE of KESHIMUR

KESHIMUR IS A province that is also inhabited by a people who are idolaters and have a language of their own. They have an astonishing acquaintance with the devilries of enchantment; insomuch as they make their idols speak. They can also by their sorceries bring on changes of weather and produce darkness, and do a number of things so extraordinary that no one without seeing them would believe them. Indeed, this country is the very original source from which idolatry has spread abroad.[91] In this direction you can proceed further until you come to the Sea of India.[92]

The men are brown and lean, but the women, taking them as brunettes, are very beautiful. The food of the people is flesh, milk and rice.[93] The clime is finely tempered, being neither very hot nor very cold. There are numbers of towns and villages ... but also forests and desert tracts, and strong passes, so that the people have no fear of anybody, and keep their independence, with a king of their own ....

There are in this country those who dwell in seclusion and practise great abstinence in eating and drinking. They observe strict chastity, and keep from all sins forbidden in their law, so that they are regarded by their own folk as very holy persons. They live to a very great age. There are also a number of idolatrous abbeys and monasteries.... The coral which is carried from our parts of the world has a better sale there than in any other country.

Now we will quit this country.... Let us go back ... to Badashan, for we cannot otherwise proceed on our journey.

CHAPTER 32

Of the GREAT RIVER of BADASHAN

IN LEAVING BADASHAN you ride twelve days between east and

northeast, ascending a river that runs through land belonging to a brother of the prince of Badashan, and containing a good many towns and villages and scattered habitations. The people are Muslims, and valiant in war. At the end of those twelve days you come to a province of no great size, extending no more than three days' journey in any direction, which is called Vokhan. The people are Muslims, and they have a peculiar language. They are gallant soldiers, and they have a chief whom they call *none*, which is as much as to say count, and they are liegemen to the prince of Badashan.

There are numbers of wild beasts of all sorts in this region. And when you leave this little country, and ride three days northeast, always among mountains, you get to such a height that 'tis said to be the highest place in the world! And when you have got to this height you find a great lake between two mountains, and out of it a fine river running through a plain clothed with the finest pasture in the world; insomuch that a lean beast there will fatten to your heart's content in ten days. There are great numbers of all kinds of wild beasts; among others, wild sheep of great size, whose horns are a good six palms in length. From these horns the shepherds make great bowls to eat from, and they use the horns also to enclose folds for their cattle at night.[94]

The plain is called Pamier, and you ride across it for twelve days together, finding nothing but a desert without habitations or any green thing, so that travellers are obliged to carry with them whatever they have need of. The region is so lofty and cold that you do not even see any birds flying. And I must notice also that because of this great cold, fire does not burn so brightly, nor give out so much heat as usual, nor does it cook food so effectually.[95]

Now, if we go on with our journey toward the east–northeast, we travel a good forty days, continually passing over mountains and hills, or through valleys, and crossing many rivers and tracts of wilderness. And in all this way you find neither habitation of man, nor any green thing, but must carry with you whatever you require. The country is called Bolor. The people dwell high up in the mountains, and are savage idolaters, living only by the chase, and clothing themselves in the skins of beasts.

CHAPTER 33

Of the KINGDOM of CASCAR

CASCAR IS A region lying between northeast and east, and constituted a kingdom in former days, but now it is subject to the Great Khan.[96] The people are Muslims. There are a good number of towns and villages, but the greatest and finest is Cascar itself. The inhabitants live by trade and handicrafts; they have beautiful gardens and vineyards, and fine estates, and grow a great deal of cotton. From this country many merchants go forth about the world on trading journeys. The natives are a wretched, niggardly set of people; they eat and drink in miserable fashion. There are in the country many Nestorian Christians, who have churches of their own. The people of the country have a peculiar language, and the territory extends for five days' journey.

CHAPTER 34

Of the GREAT CITY of SAMARKAND

SAMARKAND IS A great and noble city toward the northwest, inhabited by both Christians and Muslims, who are subject to the Great Khan's nephew, Caidu …; he is, however, at bitter enmity with the *khan*. I will tell you of a great marvel that happened at this city.[97]

It is not a great while ago that Chagatai, own brother to the Great Khan, who was lord of this country and of many a one besides, became a Christian.[98] The Christians rejoiced greatly at this, and they built a great church in the city, in honour of John the Baptist; and by his name the church was called. And they took a very fine stone, which belonged to the Muslims, and placed it as the pedestal of a column in the middle of the church, supporting the roof. It came to pass, however, that Chagatai died. Now the Muslims were full of rancour about that stone that had been theirs, and which had been set up in the church of the Christians; and when they saw that the prince was dead, they said ... that now was the time to get back their stone, by fair means or by foul. And that they might do, for they were ten times as many as the Christians. So they got together and went to the church and said that the stone they must and would have. The Christians acknowledged that it was theirs indeed, but offered to pay ... compensation. The others replied that they would not give up the stone for anything in the world. And feelings ran so high that the prince heard about it and ordered the Christians to arrange to satisfy the Muslims, either with money, if needs be, or by restoring the stone. And he allowed them three days to do the one thing or the other.

What shall I tell you? Well, the Muslims would on no account agree to leave the stone where it was, and this out of pure spite ... for they knew well enough that if the stone were stirred the church would come down. So the Christians were in great trouble and knew not what to do. But they did do the best thing possible; they besought Jesus Christ that he would consider their case, so that the holy church should not come to destruction, nor the name of its patron saint, John the Baptist, be tarnished by its ruin. And so when the day fixed by the prince came round, they went to the church in the morning, and lo, they found the stone removed from under the column; the foot of the column was without support, and yet it bore the load as stoutly as before! Between the foot of the column and the ground there was a space of three palms. So the Muslims had away their stone, and mighty little joy withal. It was a glorious miracle, nay, it *is* so, for the column still so standeth, and will stand as long as God pleaseth.[99]

Now let us quit this and continue our journey.

CHAPTER 35

Of the PROVINCE *of* YARCAN

YARCAN IS A province five days' journey in extent.[100] The people follow Islam, but there are also Nestorian and Jacobite Christians.

They are subject to the ... Great Khan's nephew. They have plenty of everything ... particularly of cotton. The inhabitants are also great craftsmen, but a large proportion of them have swollen legs and tumours in the throat, which arise from some quality in their drinking-water. As there is nothing else worth telling we may pass on.[101]

CHAPTER 36

Of a PROVINCE *called* COTAN

COTAN IS A province lying between northeast and east, and is eight days' journey in length. The people are subject to the Great Khan, and are all Muslims. There are numerous towns and villages in the country, but Cotan, the capital, is the most noble of all, and gives its name to the kingdom.[102] Everything is to be had there in plenty, including an abundance of cotton (with flax, hemp, wheat, wine and the like). The people have vineyards and gardens and estates. They live by commerce and manufactures, and are no soldiers.

CHAPTER 37

Of the PROVINCE *of* PEIN

PEIN IS A province five days in length, lying between east and northeast. The people are Muslims, and subjects of the Great Khan. There are a good number of towns and villages, but the most noble is Pein, the capital of the kingdom.[103] There are rivers in this country, in which quantities of jasper and chalcedony are found.[104] The people have plenty of all products, including cotton. They live by manufactures and trade. But they have a custom that I must relate. If the husband of any woman goes away on a journey and remains away for more than twenty days, as soon as that term has passed the woman may marry another man, and the husband also may then marry whom he pleases.

I should tell you that all the provinces that I have been speaking of, from Cascar forward,[105] and those I am going to mention (as far as the city of Lop) belong to Great Turkey.[106]

Of the PROVINCE *of* CHARCHAN

CHARCHAN IS A province of Great Turkey, lying between northeast and east.[107] The people are Muslim. There are numerous towns and villages, and the chief city of the kingdom bears its name, Charchan. The province contains rivers which bring down jasper and chalcedony, and these are carried for sale into Cathay, where they fetch great prices. The whole of the province is sandy, and so is the road all the way from Pein, and much of the water that you find is bitter and bad. However, at some places you do find fresh and sweet water. When an army passes through the land, the people escape with their wives, children and cattle a distance of two or three days' journey into the sandy waste; and, knowing the spots where water is to be had, they are able to live there, and to keep their cattle alive, while it is impossible to discover them because the wind immediately blows the sand over their tracks.

... And now I will tell you of a province called Lop, in which there is a city, also called Lop, which you come to at the end of five days. It is on the border of the great desert, and it is here that travellers repose before entering the desert.[108]

CHAPTER 39

Of the CITY *of* LOP *and the* GREAT DESERT

LOP IS A large town situated between east and northeast at the edge of the desert called the Desert of Lop. It belongs to the Great Khan, and the people are Muslim. Those travellers who intend to cross the

desert take a week's rest in this town to refresh themselves and their cattle; and then they make ready for the journey, taking with them a month's supply for man and beast. …

The length of this desert is so great that 'tis said it would take a year and more to ride from one end of it to the other. And here, where its breadth is least, it takes a month to cross it. 'Tis all composed of hills and valleys of sand, and not a thing to eat is to be found. But after riding for a day and a night you find fresh water, enough for some fifty or 100 persons with their beasts, but not for more. And all across the desert you will find water in like manner, that is to say, in some twenty-eight places altogether you will find good water, but in no great quantity; and in four places also you find brackish water.

Beasts there are none; for there is nought for them to eat. But there is a marvellous thing related in respect of this desert, which is that when travellers are on the move by night, and one of them chances to lag behind or to fall asleep or the like, when he tries to gain his company again he will hear spirits talking, and will suppose them to be his comrades. Sometimes the spirits will call him by name; and thus shall a traveller many times be led astray so that he never finds his party. And in this way many have perished.[109]

Even in the daytime one hears those spirits talking. And sometimes you shall hear the sound of a variety of musical instruments, and still more commonly the sound of drums. (Hence in making this journey 'tis customary for travellers to keep close together. All the animals too have bells at their necks, so that they cannot easily get astray. And at sleeping-time a signal is put up to show the direction of the next march.)

So thus it is that the desert is crossed.

CHAPTER 40

CONCERNING *the* GREAT PROVINCE *of* TANGUT

AFTER YOU HAVE travelled thirty days through the desert, as I have described, you come to a city called Sachiu, lying between northeast and east; it belongs to the Great Khan, and is in a province called Tangut.[110] The people are for the most part idolaters, but there are also some Nestorian Christians and some Muslims. The idolaters have a peculiar language, and are no traders, but live by their agriculture.[111] They have a great many abbeys and minsters full of idols of sundry fashions, to which they pay great honour and reverence, worshipping them and sacrificing to them with much ado. For example, those with children will feed up a sheep in honour of the idol, and at the New Year, or on the day of the idol's feast, they will take their children and the sheep along with them into the presence of the idol with great ceremony. Then they will have the sheep slaughtered and cooked, and again present it before the idol with like reverence, and leave it there before him, whilst they are reciting the offices of their worship and their prayers for the idol's blessing on their children. And, if you will believe them, the idol feeds on the meat that is set before it!

After these ceremonies they take up the flesh and carry it home, and call together all their kindred to eat it with them in great festivity .... After they have eaten, they collect the bones that are left and store them carefully in a hutch.

And you must know that all the idolaters in the world burn their dead. And when they are going to carry a body to the burning, the kinsfolk build a wooden house on the way to the spot, and drape it with cloths of silk and gold. When the body is going past this building they call a halt and set before it wine and meat and other eatables; and this they do with the assurance that the defunct will be received with the like attentions in the other world. All the minstrelsy in the town goes playing before the body; and when it reaches the burning-place the kinsfolk are prepared with figures cut out of parchment and paper in the shape of men and horses and camels, and also with round pieces of paper like gold coins, and all these they burn along with the corpse. For they say that in the other world the defunct will be provided with slaves and cattle and money, just in proportion to the amount of such pieces of paper that has been burnt along with him.[112]

But they never burn their dead until they have sent for the astrologers, and told them the year, the day, and the hour of the deceased person's birth, and when the astrologers have ascertained under what constellation, planet and sign he was born, they declare the day on which, by the rules of their art, he ought to be burnt. And until that day arrives they keep the body, so that 'tis sometimes a matter of six months, more or less, before it comes to be burnt.[113]

Now the way they keep the body in the house is this: They make a coffin .... This they fill up with camphor and spices ... and then they cover it with a cloth. For every day that the body is kept, they set a table before the dead ... and they will have it that the soul comes and eats and drinks.

Sometimes those soothsayers shall tell them that 'tis not good luck to carry out the corpse by the door, so they have to break a hole in the wall, and lo draw it out that way when it is taken to the burning.[114] And these, I assure you, are the practices of all the idolaters of those countries.

However, we will quit this subject, and I will tell you of another city which lies toward the northwest at the extremity of the desert.

CHAPTER 41

Of the PROVINCE of CAMUL

CAMUL IS A province which in former days was a kingdom. It contains numerous towns and villages, but the chief city bears the name of Camul. The province lies between the two deserts; for on the one side is the great Desert of Lop, and on the other side is a small desert of three days' journey in extent.[115] The people are all idolaters, and have a peculiar language. They live by the fruits of the earth, which they have in plenty, and dispose of to travellers. They are a people who take things very easily, for they mind nothing but playing and singing, and dancing and enjoying themselves.

And it is the truth that if a foreigner comes to the house of one of these people to lodge, the host is delighted, and desires his wife to put herself entirely at the guest's disposal, whilst he himself gets out of the way, and comes back no more until the stranger shall have departed. The guest may stay and enjoy the wife's society, whilst the husband has no shame in the matter, but indeed considers it an honour. And all the men of this province are made cuckolds of by their wives in this way. The women themselves are fair and wanton.[116]

Now it came to pass during the reign of Mangku Khan, that as lord of this province he came to hear of this custom, and he sent forth an order commanding them under grievous penalties to do so no more .... And when they heard this order they were much vexed. For about three years' duration they carried it out. But then they found that their lands were no longer fruitful ... So they petitioned their lord to let them retain the custom inherited from their ancestors; for it was by reason of this usage that their gods bestowed upon them all the good things that they possessed, and without it they saw not how they could continue to exist.

When the prince had heard the petition his reply was "Since you

must needs keep your shame, keep it then", and so he left them at liberty to maintain their naughty custom. And they always have kept it up, and do so still.

Now let us quit Camul, and I will tell you of another province which lies between northwest and north, and belongs to the Great Khan.

CHAPTER 42

Of the PROVINCE *of* CHINGINTALAS

CHINGINTALAS IS ALSO a province at the verge of the desert, and lying between northwest and north. It has an extent of sixteen days' journey ... and contains numerous towns and villages. There

are three different races of people in it – idolaters, Muslims and some Nestorian Christians.[117] At the northern extremity … there is a mountain in which are excellent veins of steel and *ondanique*. And you must know that in the same mountain there is a vein of the substance from which salamander is made.[118] For the real truth is that the salamander is no beast, as they allege in our part of the world, but is a substance found in the earth …

Everybody must be aware that it can be no animal's nature to live in fire, seeing that every animal is composed of all the four elements. Now I, Marco Polo, had a Turkish acquaintance of the name of Zurficar, and he was a very clever fellow. And this Turk related how he had lived three years in that region on behalf of the Great Khan, in order to procure those salamanders for him. He said that the way they got them was by digging in that mountain until they found a certain vein. The substance of this vein was then taken and crushed, and when so treated it divides as it were into fibres of wool, which they set forth to dry.

When dry, these fibres were pounded in a great copper mortar, and then washed, so as to remove all the earth and to leave only the wool-like fibres. These were then spun and made into napkins. When first made these napkins are not very white, but by putting them into the fire for a while they come out as white as snow. And so again whenever they become dirty they are bleached by being put in the fire.

Now this, and nought else, is the truth about the salamander, and the people of the country all say the same. Any other account of the matter is fabulous nonsense. And I may add that they have at Rome a napkin of this stuff, which the Great Khan sent to the pope to make a wrapper for the holy *sudarium* of Jesus Christ.[119]…

CHAPTER 43

Of the PROVINCE *of* SUKCHUR

ON LEAVING THE province of which I spoke before you ride ten days between northeast and east, and in all that way you find no human dwelling, or next to none, so that there is nothing for our book to speak of. At the end of those ten days you come to another province called Sukchur, in which there are numerous towns and villages. The chief city is called Sukchu.[120] The people are partly Christians and partly idolaters, and all are subject to the Great Khan.

The great province to which all these three belong is called Tangut.

Over all the mountains of this province rhubarb is found in great abundance, and thither merchants come to buy it, and carry it thence all over the world. Travellers, however, dare not visit those mountains with any cattle but those of the country, for a certain plant grows there which is so poisonous that cattle which eat it lose their hoofs. The cattle of the country know it and eschew it. The people live by agriculture, and have not much trade. The people are of a brown complexion. The whole of the province is healthy.

CHAPTER 44

Of the CITY *of* CAMPICHU

CAMPICHU IS ALSO a city of Tangut, and a very great and noble one. Indeed it is the capital and place of government of the whole province of Tangut.[121] The people are idolaters, Muslims, and Christians, and the latter have three very fine churches in the city,[122] whilst the idolaters have many monasteries after their fashion. In these they have an enormous number of idols, both small and great … They are all highly polished, and then covered with gold. The great idols of which I speak lie at length.[123] And round about them there are other figures of considerable size, as if adoring and paying homage before them.

Now, as I have not yet given you particulars about the customs of these idolaters, I will proceed to tell you …

You must know that there are among them certain religious recluses who lead a more virtuous life than the rest. These abstain from sex, though they do not regard unlicensed sexual activity as a deadly sin. They have an ecclesiastical calendar as we have; and there are five days in the month that they observe particularly; and on these five days they will not slaughter any animal or eat flesh meat. On those days, moreover, they observe greater abstinence than on other days.[124]

Among these people a man may take thirty wives, more or less, if he can but afford to do so, each having wives in proportion to his wealth and means; but the first wife is always held in highest consideration. The men endow their wives with cattle, slaves and money, according to their ability. And if a man dislikes any one of his wives, he just turns her out and takes another. They take as wives their cousins' and their fathers' widows (always excepting the man's own mother), holding to be no sin many things that we think grievous sins.[125]

Messer Maffeo and Messer Marco Polo dwelt a whole year in this city when on a mission.[126]

Now we will leave this and tell you about other provinces toward the north, for we are going to take you a sixty days' journey in that direction.

CHAPTER 45

Of the CITY *of* ETZINA

WHEN YOU LEAVE the city of Campichu you ride for twelve days, and then reach a city called Etzina, which is toward the north on the verge of the Sandy Desert; it belongs to the province of Tangut.[127] The people are idolaters, and possess plenty of camels and cattle, and the country produces a number of good falcons, both sakers and lanners. The inhabitants live by their cultivation and their cattle, for they have no trade. At this city you must lay in victuals for forty days, because when you quit Etzina, you enter a desert that extends forty days' journey to the north, and on which you meet with no habitation nor baiting-place. In the summertime you will fall in with people, but in the winter the cold is too great. You also meet with wild beasts (for there are some small pinewoods here and there), and with numbers of wild asses.[128] When you have travelled these forty days ... you come to a certain province lying to the north. Its name you shall hear presently.

CHAPTER 46

Of the CITY of CARACORON

CARACORON IS A city of some three miles in circuit. It is surrounded by a strong earthen rampart, for stone is scarce there. And beside it there is a great citadel, which has a fine palace where the governor resides. 'Tis the first city that the Tartars possessed after they emerged from their own country. And now I will tell you all about how they first acquired dominion and spread over the world.[129]

Originally the Tartars[130] dwelt in the north on the borders of Chorcha.[131] Their country was one of great plains; and there were no towns or villages in it, but excellent pasture lands, with great rivers and many sheets of water; in fact it was a very fine and extensive region. But there was no sovereign in the land. They did, however, pay tax and tribute to a great prince who was called in their tongue *un-khan*, the same that we call Prester John, him in fact about whose great dominion all the world talks.[132] The tribute he had of them was one beast out of every ten, and also a tithe of all their other gear.

Now it came to pass that the Tartars multiplied exceedingly. And when Prester John saw how great a people they had become, he began to fear that he should have trouble from them. So he made a scheme to distribute them over sundry countries, and sent one of his barons to carry this out. When the Tartars became aware of this ... [they] left their country and went off across a desert to a distant region toward the north, where Prester John could not annoy them.

Thus they revolted from his authority and paid him tribute no longer. And so things continued for a time.

CHAPTER 47

Of GENGHIS, and HOW he BECAME
the FIRST KHAN of the TARTARS

NOW IT CAME to pass in the year of Christ's incarnation 1187 that the Tartars elected a king whose name was Genghis Khan.[133] He was a man of great integrity, wisdom, eloquence and valour. And as soon as the news that he had been chosen was spread through those countries, all the Tartars in the world came to him and owned him for their lord. And right well did he maintain the sovereignty they had given him. What shall I say? The Tartars gathered to him in astonishing multitude, and when he saw such numbers he asked them to equip themselves with spears, bows and arrows and such other arms as they used, and set about the conquest of all those regions until he had conquered eight provinces. When he conquered a province he did no harm to the people or their property, but merely established some of his own men in the country along with a proportion of theirs, whilst he led the remainder to the conquest of other provinces.

And when those whom he had conquered became aware how well and safely he protected them against all others, and how they suffered no ill at his hands, and saw what a noble prince he was, then they joined him heart and soul and became his devoted followers. And when he had thus gathered such a multitude that they seemed to cover the earth, he began to think of conquering a great part of the world. Now in the year of Christ 1200 he sent an embassy to Prester John, demanding to have his daughter in marriage. But when Prester John heard this he said indignantly to the envoys, "What impudence is this, to ask for my daughter as his wife! Doesn't he know well that he was my liegeman and serf? Go back and tell him that I would rather set my daughter on fire than give her in marriage to him, and that he deserves to die at my hand, rebel and traitor that he is!" The envoys … made haste to their master, relating everything that Prester John had ordered them to say and keeping nothing back.[134]

CHAPTER 48

How GENGHIS MUSTERED HIS PEOPLE
to MARCH AGAINST PRESTER JOHN

WHEN GENGHIS KHAN heard the brutal message that Prester John had sent him, such rage seized him that his heart came close to bursting. At last he spoke, and so loud that all who were present could hear him. He would not be worthy of being a prince any longer if he did not take revenge for the brutal message – and before long Prester John would know whether Genghis were his serf or not.

So then Genghis ... levied such a host as never before was seen or heard of, sending word to Prester John to be on his defence. And when Prester John had confirmation that Genghis really was coming against him with a multitude, he still treated it as a trifle, jesting that "these be no soldiers". Nonetheless he marshalled his forces and made preparations, in order that if Genghis did come, he might capture him and put him to death. In fact he assembled such a host of many different nations that it was a wonder of the world.

And so both sides got ready to battle. And why should I make a long story of it? Genghis Khan ... arrived at a vast and beautiful plain ... called Tanduc, belonging to Prester John, and there he pitched his camp.[135] ... And when he heard that Prester John was coming, he rejoiced, for the site afforded a fine and ample battleground, so he was glad to wait there....

CHAPTER 49

How PRESTER JOHN
MARCHED *to* MEET GENGHIS

NOW THE STORY goes that when Prester John became aware that Genghis ... was marching against him, he ... advanced until he reached the same plain of Tanduc, and pitched his camp opposite

that of Genghis Khan at a distance of 20 miles. And then both armies remained at rest for two days that they might be fresher and heartier for battle.

So when the two great hosts were pitched ... Genghis Khan summoned his astrologers, both Christians and Muslims, and asked them which of the two armies would win. The Muslims tried to ascertain, but were unable to give a true answer. The Christians, however, did give a true answer, and showed manifestly beforehand how the event should be. For they got a cane and split it lengthwise, and laid one half on this side and one half on that, allowing no one to touch the pieces. And one piece of cane they marked Genghis Khan, and the other piece they marked Prester John. And then they said to Genghis: "Now watch and you will see the course of the battle, and who shall have the best of it; for whoever has the cane that gets on top of the other shall achieve the victory." He asked them to begin. Then the Christian astrologers read a psalm out of the psalter, and went through other incantations. And while everyone watched, the cane that bore the name of Genghis Khan, without being touched by anybody, advanced to the one that bore the name of Prester John, and got on top of it. When the prince saw that he was greatly delighted, and because he believed the Christians had revealed the truth, he always treated them with great respect and held them to be men of truth for ever after.[136]

CHAPTER 50

The BATTLE BETWEEN GENGHIS KHAN *and* PRESTER JOHN

AND AFTER BOTH sides had rested well those two days, they armed for the fight and engaged in desperate combat. It was the greatest battle that ever was seen. Great numbers were slain on both sides, but in the end Genghis Khan obtained the victory. And in the battle Prester John was slain. And from that time forward, day by day, his kingdom passed into the hands of Genghis Khan until the whole of it was conquered.[137]

… Genghis Khan reigned six years after this battle, engaged continually in conquest, and took many a province and city and stronghold. But at the end of those six years he went against a certain castle … called Caaju, and there he was shot with an arrow in the knee, so that he died of his wound. A great pity it was, for he was a valiant and a wise man.[138]

CHAPTER 51

Of THOSE WHO DID REIGN AFTER GENGHIS KHAN, *and of the* CUSTOMS *of the* TARTARS

NOW THE NEXT that reigned after Genghis Khan, their first lord, was Cuy Khan, and the third prince was Batuy Khan, and the fourth was Alacou Khan, the fifth Mangku Khan, the sixth Kublai Khan, who is the sovereign now reigning, and is more potent than any of

the five who went before him; in fact, if you were to take all those five together, they would not be so powerful as he is.[139] Nay, I will say yet more; for if you were to put together all the Christians in the world, with their emperors and their kings, the whole of these Christians – aye, and throw in the Muslims to boot – would not have such power, or be able to do so much, as this Kublai, who is the lord of all the Tartars in the world, those of the Levant and of the Ponent; for these are all his liegemen and subjects. I mean to show you all about this great power of his in this book.[140]

You should be told also that all the Great Khans, and all the descendants of Genghis their first lord, are carried to a mountain called Altay to be interred. Wheresoever the sovereign may die, he is carried to his burial ... with his predecessors; no matter if the place of his death were 100 days' journey distant, thither must he be carried to his burial.[141]

Let me tell you a strange thing too. When they are carrying the body of any emperor to be buried with the others, the convoy that goes with the body puts to the sword all whom they encounter on the road ... For they truly believe that all those they slay in this manner go to serve their lord in the other world. They do the same too with horses; for when the emperor dies, they kill all his best horses in order that he may have the use of them in the other world, as they believe. And I tell you as a certain truth that when Mangku Khan died, more than 20,000 persons, who chanced to meet the body on its way, were slain in the manner I have told.

CHAPTER 52

CONCERNING *the* CUSTOMS
of the TARTARS

NOW THAT WE have begun to speak of the Tartars, I have plenty to tell you on that subject. The Tartar custom is to spend the winter in warm plains, where they find good pasture for their cattle, whilst in summer they take themselves to a cool climate among the mountains and valleys, where water is to be found as well as woods and pastures.

Their houses are circular, and are made of wands covered with felts.[142] These are carried with them wherever they go; for the wands are so strongly bound together, and likewise so well combined, that the frame can be made very light. Whenever they erect these huts the door is always to the south. They also have waggons covered with black felt so efficaciously that no rain can get in. These are drawn by oxen and camels, and the women and children travel in them. The women do … whatever is necessary to provide for the husband and household; for the men all lead the life of gentlemen, troubling themselves about nothing but hunting and hawking … unless it be the practice of warlike exercises.

They live on the milk and meat which their herds supply, and on the produce of the chase; and they eat all kinds of flesh, including that of horses and dogs, and pharaoh's rats, of which last there are great numbers in burrows on those plains.[143] Their drink is mare's milk.

They are very careful not to meddle with each other's wives, and will not do so on any account, holding that to be an abominable thing. The women too are very good and loyal to their husbands, and notable housewives.

The marriage customs of Tartars are as follows. Any man may take 100 wives if he so pleases, and if he be able to keep them. But the first wife is always held in the greatest honour, and is the most legitimate (and the same applies to the sons whom she may bear). The husband gives a marriage payment to his wife's mother, and the wife brings nothing to her husband. They have more children than other people, because they have so many wives. They may marry their cousins, and if a father dies, his son may take any of the wives, his own mother always excepted; that is to say, the eldest son may do this, but no other. A man may also take the wife of his own brother after the latter's death....

CHAPTER 53

CONCERNING *the* GOD *of the* TARTARS

THIS IS THE fashion of their religion. They say there is a Most High God of Heaven, whom they worship daily with incense, but they pray to Him only for health of mind and body. But they have also a certain [other] god of theirs called Natagai, and they say he is the god of the Earth, who watches over their children, cattle and crops. They show him great worship and honour, and every man has a figure of him in his house, made of felt and cloth; and they also make in the same manner images of his wife and children. The wife they put on the left hand, and the children in front. And when they eat, they take the fat of the meat and grease the god's mouth with it, as well as the mouths of his wife and children. Then they take the broth and sprinkle it before the door of the house; and, that done, they deem that their god and his family have had their share of the dinner.[144]

Their drink is mare's milk, prepared in such a way that you would take it for white wine; and a right good drink it is, called by them *kemiz*.[145]

The clothes of the wealthy Tartars are for the most part of gold and silkstuffs, lined with costly furs, such as sable and ermine, squirrel and fox, in the richest fashion.

C H A P T E R 5 4

CONCERNING *the* TARTAR
CUSTOMS *of* WAR

ALL THEIR HARNESS of war is excellent and costly. Their arms are bows and arrows, sword and mace; but above all the bow, for they are great archers – indeed, the best that are known. On their backs they wear armour prepared from buffalo and other hides, which is very strong.[146] They are excellent soldiers, and valiant in battle. They are also more capable of hardships than other nations ... if need be, they will go for a month ... living only on the milk of their mares and on such game as their bows may win them. Their horses, too, will subsist entirely on the grass of the plains, so that there is no need to carry a store of barley or straw or oats; and they are very docile to their riders, who, in case of need, will stay on horseback all night long, armed at all points, while the horse will be continually grazing.

Of all the troops in the world these endure the greatest hardship and fatigue, and cost the least; and they are the best of all for conquering great portions of country. And this you will perceive from what you have heard and shall hear in this book; and (as a fact) there can be no ... doubt that now they are the masters of the biggest half of the world. Their troops are admirably ordered in the manner that I shall now relate.

You see, when a Tartar prince goes forth to war, he takes with him, say, 100,000 horse. Well, he appoints an officer to every ten men, one to every 100, one to every 1,000, and one to every 10,000, so that his own orders have to be given to ten persons only, and each of these ten persons has to pass the orders only to another ten, and so on; no one having to give orders to more than ten. And every one in turn is responsible only to the officer immediately over him; and the discipline and order that comes of this method is marvellous, for they are a people very obedient to their chiefs....[147] And when the army is on the march they have always 200 horsemen ... who are sent a distance of two marches in advance to reconnoitre, and these always keep ahead. They have a similar party detached in the rear, and on either flank, so that there is a good lookout kept on all sides …. When they are going on a distant expedition they take no gear with them except two leather bottles for milk; a little earthenware pot to cook their meat in, and a little tent to shelter them from rain. And in case of great urgency they will ride ten days on end without lighting a fire or taking a meal. On such an occasion they will sustain themselves on the blood of their horses, opening a vein and … drinking until they have had enough, and then staunching it.

They also have milk dried into a kind of paste to carry with them; and when they need food they put this in water, and beat it so that it dissolves, and then drink it.[148]

When they come to an engagement with the enemy, they will win … in the following fashion. They never let themselves get into a regular medley, but keep perpetually riding round and shooting into the enemy. And as they do not count it any shame to run away

in battle, they will sometimes pretend to do so, and in running away they turn in the saddle and shoot hard and strong at the foe, and in this way cause great havoc.

Their horses are trained so perfectly that they will double hither and thither, just like a dog, in a way that is quite astonishing. Thus they fight to as good a purpose in running away as if they had stood and faced the enemy, because of the vast volleys of arrows that they shoot … upon their pursuers, who fancy that they have won the battle. But once the Tartars see that they have killed and wounded many horses and men, they wheel round bodily and return to the charge in perfect order … and in a very short time the enemy is routed. In truth they are stout and valiant soldiers, and inured to war. And you perceive that it is just when the enemy sees them run, and imagines that it has gained the battle, that it has in reality lost – for the Tartars wheel round in a moment, when they judge the right time has come, and in this fashion they have won many a fight.[149]

All this that I have been telling you is true of the manners and customs of the genuine Tartars. But I must add also that in these days they are greatly degenerated; for those who are settled in Cathay have taken up the practices of the idolaters of the country, and have abandoned their own institutions; whilst those who have settled in the Levant have adopted the customs of the Muslims.[150]

C H A P T E R   5 5

CONCERNING *the* ADMINISTERING
of JUSTICE AMONG *the* TARTARS

THE WAY THEY administer justice is in the following manner. When anyone has committed a petty theft, they give him seven blows of a stick, or seventeen, or twenty-seven, or thirty-seven, or forty-seven, and so forth, always increasing by tens in proportion to the injury done, and running up to 107. Some die of these beatings. But if the offence be horse-stealing, or some other great matter, they cut the thief in two with a sword. However, if he is able to ransom himself

by paying nine times the value of the thing stolen, he is let off. Every lord or other person who possesses beasts has them marked with his peculiar brand, be they horses, mares, camels, oxen, cows or other great cattle, and then they are sent abroad to graze over the plains without any keeper. They get all mixed together, but eventually every beast is recovered by means of its owner's brand, which is known. For their sheep and goats they have shepherds. All their cattle are remarkably fine, big, and in good condition.[151]

They have another notable custom, which is this: if any man has a daughter who dies before marriage, and another man has had a son die before marriage, the parents of the two arrange a wedding between the dead lad and lass. And marry them they do, making a regular contract! And when the contract papers are made out they put them in the fire, in order (as they will have it) that the smoke can make the fact known to the parties in the other world.... And the parents thenceforward consider themselves related to each other, just as if their children had lived and married....

Now I have told you all about the manners and customs of the Tartars; but you have heard nothing yet of the great state of the Great Khan, who is the lord of all the Tartars and of the Supreme Imperial Court. All that I will tell you in this book in the proper time and place, but meanwhile I must return to my story which I left off in that great plain when we began to speak of the Tartars.

CHAPTER 56

SUNDRY PARTICULARS *of the*
PLAIN BEYOND CARACORON

AND WHEN YOU leave Caracoron and the Altay, in which they bury the bodies of the Tartar sovereigns, as I told you, you go north for forty days till you reach a country called the Plain of Bargu.[152] The people there are called Mescript; they are a wild race and live by their cattle ... Their customs are like those of the Tartars, and they are subject to the Great Khan. They have neither corn nor wine. They get birds for food, for the country is full of lakes and pools and marshes, which are much frequented by the birds when they are moulting – and when they have quite cast their feathers and can't fly, those people catch them. They also live partly on fish.[153]

And when you have travelled forty days over this great plain you come to the ocean, at the place where the mountains are in which the peregrine falcons have their nests. And in those mountains it is so cold that you find neither man or woman, nor beast nor bird, except one kind of bird called *barguerlac*, on which the falcons feed. They are as big as a partridge, and have feet like those of a parrot and a tail like a swallow, and are very strong in flight. And when the Great Khan wants peregrines from the nest, he sends thither to procure them.[154] It is also on islands in that sea that the gerfalcons are bred. You must know that the place is so far to the north that you leave the North Star somewhat behind you toward the south! The gerfalcons are so abundant there that the emperor can have as many as he likes to send for. And you must not suppose that those gerfalcons which the Christians carry into the Tartar dominions go to the Great Khan; they are carried only to the prince of the Levant.[155]

Now I have told you all about the provinces northward as far as the ocean, beyond which there is no more land at all; so I shall proceed to tell you of the other provinces on the way to the Great Khan. Let us, then, return to that province of which I spoke before, called Campichu.

CHAPTER 57

Of the KINGDOM *of* ERGUIUL, *and* PROVINCE *of* SINJU

ON LEAVING CAMPICHU you travel five days across a tract in which many spirits are heard speaking at night; and at the end of those marches, toward the east, you come to a kingdom called Erguiul, belonging to the Great Khan. It is one of several kingdoms which make up the province of Tangut. The people consist of Nestorian Christians, idolaters and Muslims.

There are plenty of cities in this kingdom, but the main one is Erguiul. You can travel in a southeasterly direction from this place into the province of Cathay. Should you follow that road to the southeast, you come to a city called Sinju, belonging also to Tangut, and subject to the Great Khan, which has under it many towns and villages.[156] The population is composed of idolaters and Muslims, but there are some Christians also. There are wild cattle in that country [almost] as big as elephants – splendid creatures, covered everywhere but on the back with shaggy hair a good four palms long.

They are partly black, partly white, and really wonderfully fine creatures; the hair or wool is extremely fine and white – finer and whiter than silk…. They also cross these with the common cow, and the cattle from this cross are wonderful beasts, and better for work than other animals. These the people use … for burden and general work, and for ploughing too; and at the latter they will do twice as much work as any other cattle, being such very strong beasts.[157]

In this country too is found the best musk in the world; and I will tell you how 'tis produced. There exists in that region a kind of wild animal like a gazelle. It has feet and tail like the gazelle's, and stag's hair of a very coarse kind, but no horns. It has four tusks, two below and two above, about three inches long, and slender in form, one pair growing upward, and the other downward. It is a very pretty creature. The musk is found in this way: when the creature has been taken, they find at the navel between the flesh and the skin something like a pod full of blood, which they cut out and remove with all the skin attached to it. And the blood inside this pod is the musk that produces that powerful perfume. There is an immense number of these beasts in the country we are speaking of.[158]

The people are traders and artisans, and also grow an abundance of corn. The province has an extent of twenty-six days' journey. Pheasants are found there twice as big as ours, indeed nearly as big as a peacock, and with tails of seven to ten palms in length; and besides them other pheasants in aspect like our own, and birds of many other kinds, and of beautiful variegated plumage.[159] The people, who are idolaters, are fat folks with little noses and black hair, and no beard, except a few hairs on the upper lip. The women too have very smooth and white skins, and in every respect are pretty creatures. The men are very sensual, and marry many wives, which is not forbidden by their religion. No matter how poor a woman's background may be, if she has beauty she may find a husband among the greatest men in the land, the man paying the girl's father and mother a great sum of money, according to the bargain that may be made.

CHAPTER 58

Of the KINGDOM of EGRIGAIA

STARTING AGAIN FROM Erguiul you ride eastward for eight days, and then come to a province called Egrigaia, containing numerous cities and villages, and belonging to Tangut. The capital city is called Calachan.[160] The people are chiefly idolaters, but there are fine churches belonging to the Nestorian Christians. They are all subjects of the Great Khan. They make in this city great quantities of camlets of camel's wool, the finest in the world; and some of the camlets that they make are white, for they have white camels, and these are the best of all. Merchants purchase these things here and carry them all over the world for sale.[161]

CHAPTER 59

CONCERNING the PROVINCE of TANDUC, and the DESCENDANTS of PRESTER JOHN[162]

TANDUC IS A province which lies toward the east, and contains numerous towns and villages; among which is the chief city, also called Tanduc. The king of the province is of the lineage of Prester

John, George by name, and he holds the land under the Great Khan; not that he holds anything like the whole of what Prester John possessed. It is a custom, I may tell you, that these kings of the lineage of Prester John always obtain as a wife either daughters of the Great Khan or other princesses of his family.

In this province is found the stone from which azure is made. It is obtained from a ... vein in the earth, and is of fine quality. There is also a great manufacture of fine camlets of different colours from camel's hair. The people get their living by their cattle and tillage, as well as by trade and handicraft.

The rule of the province is in the hands of the Christians but there are also plenty of idolaters and Muslims. And there is also here a class of people called Argons, because they are sprung from two different races: the idolaters of Tanduc and the Muslims. They are more handsome men than the other natives ... and because they have more ability, they come to have authority; and they are also first-class merchants.[163]

You must know that it was in this same ... Tanduc that Prester John had the seat of his government when he ruled over the Tartars, and his heirs still abide there; for, as I have told you, this King George is of his line, in fact, he is the sixth in descent from Prester John.

Here also is what we call the country of Gog and Magog; *they*, however, call it Ung and Mungul, after the names of two races of people that existed in that province before the migration of the Tartars. Ung was the title of the people of the country, and Mungul a name sometimes applied to the Tartars.[164]

And when you have ridden seven days eastward through this province you get near the provinces of Cathay. You find throughout those seven days' journey plenty of towns and villages, the inhabitants of which are Muslims, but with a mixture also of idolaters and Nestorian Christians. They get their living by trade and manufactures; weaving those fine cloths of gold which are called *nasich* and *naques*, besides silkstuffs of many kinds. For just as we have cloths of wool in our country, manufactured in a great variety of kinds, so in those regions they have stuffs of silk and gold in like variety.[165]

All this region is subject to the Great Khan. There is a city you come to called Sindachu, where they carry on a great many crafts such as provide for the equipment of the emperor's troops. In a mountain of the province there is a very good silver mine: the place is called Ydifu. The country is well stocked with game, both beast and bird.[166]

Now we will quit that province and go three days' journey forward.

CHAPTER 60

CONCERNING *the* KHAN'S PALACE
of CHAGAN NOR

AT THE END of those three days you find a city called Chagan Nor ... at which there is a great palace of the Great Khan's;[167] and he likes much to reside there on account of the lakes and rivers in the neighbourhood, which are the haunt of swans and of a great variety of other birds.

The adjoining plains abound with cranes, partridges, pheasants and other game birds, so that the emperor takes all the more delight in staying there, in order to go hawking ... a sport of which he is very fond.

There are five different kinds of cranes found in those tracts, as I shall tell you. First, there is one which is very big and as black as a crow; the second kind is all white, and is the biggest of all – its wings are really beautiful, for they are adorned with round eyes like those of a peacock, but of a resplendent golden colour, whilst the head is red and black on a white ground. The third kind is the same as ours. The fourth is a small kind, having at the ears beautiful long pendent feathers of red and black. The fifth kind is grey all over and of great size, with a handsome head, red and black.[168]

Near this city there is a valley in which the emperor has had several little houses erected in which he keeps partridges. You would be astonished to see what a quantity there are, with men to take charge of them. So whenever the Great Khan visits the place he is furnished with as many as he wants.

CHAPTER 61

Of the CITY of CHANDU, and the KHAN'S PALACE THERE

AND WHEN YOU have ridden three days from the city last mentioned, between northeast and north, you come to … Chandu,[169] which was built by the *khan* now reigning. There is … a very fine marble palace, the rooms of which are all gilt and painted with figures of men and beasts and birds, and with a variety of trees and flowers, all executed with such exquisite art that you regard them with delight and astonishment.

Round this palace a wall is built, 16 miles in circumference, and inside the park there are fountains and rivers and brooks, and beautiful meadows, with all kinds of wild animals (excluding such as are of a ferocious nature), which the emperor has procured and placed there to supply food for his gerfalcons and hawks, which he keeps there. Of these there are more than 200 gerfalcons alone, without counting the other hawks. The *khan* himself goes every week to see his birds, and sometimes he rides through the park with a leopard behind him on his horse's croup; and then if he sees any animal that takes his fancy, he slips his leopard at it, and the game when taken is used to feed the hawks. This he does for diversion.

Moreover (at a spot in the park where there is a charming wood) he has another palace built of cane, of which I must give you a description. It is gilt all over, and most elaborately finished inside. It has gilt and lacquered columns, on each of which is a dragon all gilt, the tail of which is attached to the column whilst the head supports the architrave, and the claws likewise are stretched out ... to support the architrave. The roof, like the rest, is formed of canes, covered with a varnish so strong and excellent that no amount of rain will rot them. These canes are a good three palms in girth, and from ten to fifteen paces in length.... In short, the whole palace is built of these canes, which (I may mention) serve also for a great variety of other useful purposes. The construction of the palace is so devised that it can all be taken to pieces and removed to wherever the emperor may command. When erected, it is braced against mishaps from the wind by more than 200 cords of silk.[170]

The lord abides at this park of his, dwelling sometimes in the Marble Palace and sometimes in the Cane Palace for three months of the year, to wit, June, July, and August; preferring this residence because it is ... a very cool place. When the twenty-eighth day of (the moon of) August arrives he takes his departure, and the Cane Palace is taken to pieces.[171] But I must tell you what happens when he goes away from this palace every year on the twenty-eighth of the August (moon).

You must know that the *khan* keeps an immense stud of white horses and mares; in fact more than 10,000 of them, and all pure white without a speck. The milk of these mares is drunk by himself and his family, and by none else, except by those of one great tribe that have also the privilege of drinking it. This privilege was granted them by Genghis Khan, on account of a certain victory that they helped him to win long ago. The name of the tribe is Horiad.[172]

Now when these mares are passing across the country, and anyone falls in with them, be he the greatest lord in the land, he must not presume to pass until the mares have gone by; he must either delay where he is, or go a half-day's journey round if need so be, so as not to go near them; for they are to be treated with the greatest respect. Well, when the lord sets out from the park on the twenty-eighth of August, as I told you, the milk of all those mares is taken and sprinkled on the ground. And this is done on the injunction of the idolaters and idol-priests, who say that it is an excellent thing to sprinkle that milk on the ground every twenty-eighth of August, so

that the earth and the air and the false gods shall have their share of it, and the spirits likewise that inhabit the air and the earth. And thus those beings will protect and bless the *khan* and his children and his wives and his folk and his gear, and his cattle and his horses, his corn and all that is his. After this is done, the emperor is off and away.[173]

But I must now tell you a strange thing that hitherto I have forgotten to mention. During the three months of every year that the lord resides at that place, if it should happen to be bad weather, there are certain enchanters and astrologers in his entourage who are such adepts in necromancy and the diabolic arts that they are able to prevent any cloud or storm from passing over the spot on which the emperor's palace stands. The sorcerers who do this are called Tibet and Keshimur, which are the names of two nations of idolaters. Whatever they do in this way is by the help of the Devil, but they make those people believe that it is compassed by dint of their own sanctity and the help of God.[174]

These people also have a custom which I must tell you. If a man is condemned to death and executed by the lawful authority, they take his body and cook and eat it. But if anyone die a natural death then they will not eat the body.[175]

There is another marvel performed by those of whom I have been speaking as knowing so many enchantments. For when the Great Khan is in his palace, seated at his table, which stands on a platform some eight cubits above the ground, his cups are set before him (on a great buffet) in the middle of the hall pavement, at a distance of some ten paces from his table, and filled with wine, or other good spiced liquor such as they use. Now when the lord desires to drink, these enchanters cause the cups to move ... without being touched by anybody, and to present themselves to the emperor! This everyone present may witness, and there are oft times more than 10,000 persons are present. 'Tis a truth and no lie! And so will tell you the sages of our own country who understand necromancy, for they also can perform it.[176]

And when the idol festivals come round, these necromancers request things with which to "perform a solemn service and a great sacrifice to our idols"....

... Thus it is that they keep their festivals. You must know that each of the idols has a name of his own, and a feast day, just as our saints have their anniversaries.

They have also immense minsters and abbeys, some of them as big as a small town, with more than 2,000 monks ... in a single abbey. These monks ... have the head and beard shaven. There are some among them who are allowed by their rule to take wives, and who have plenty of children.[177]

Then there is another kind of devotees called *sensin*, who are men of extraordinary abstinence, and lead a life of such hardship as I will describe. All their life long they eat nothing but bran,[178] which they take mixed with hot water. That is their food: bran, and nothing but bran; and water for their drink. 'Tis a lifelong fast – such that I may well say their life is one of extraordinary asceticism. They have great idols, and plenty of them; but they sometimes also worship fire. The other idolaters who are not of this sect call these people heretics because they do not worship their idols in their own fashion. Those of whom I am speaking would not take a wife on any consideration. They wear dresses of hempen stuff, black and blue, and sleep upon mats; in fact their asceticism is something astonishing. Their idols are all feminine, that is to say, they have women's names.[179]

Now let us have done with this subject, and let me tell you of the great state and wonderful magnificence of the great lord of lords; I mean that great prince who is the sovereign of the Tartars, Kublai by name, that most noble and powerful lord.

THE
GREAT KHAN,
HIS COURT AND
CAPITAL

CHAPTER 1

Of KUBLAI KHAN, *the* GREAT KHAN NOW
REIGNING, *and of* HIS GREAT POWER[1]

NOW AM I come to that part of our book in which I shall tell you of
the … magnificence of the Great Khan now reigning, by name Kublai
Khan; *khan* being a title which signifies "the great lord of lords", or
emperor.[2] And he has good right to such a title, for all men know
… that he is the most potent man, as regards forces and lands and
treasure, that exists in the world, or ever has existed from the time

of our first father Adam until this day. All this I will make evident to you in this book of ours .... And now you shall hear how.

CONCERNING *the* REVOLT *of* NAYAN, WHO WAS UNCLE *to the* GREAT KHAN KUBLAI

NOW THIS KUBLAI Khan is of the right imperial lineage, being descended from Genghis Khan, the first sovereign of all the Tartars. And he is the sixth lord in that succession, as I have already told you in this book. He came to the throne in the year of Christ 1256 and the empire fell to him because of his ability, valour and great worth, as was right and reason.[3] His brothers, indeed, and other kinsmen disputed his claim, but his it remained ....

Up to the year of Christ now running, to wit 1298, he has reigned two-and-forty years, and his age is about eighty-five, so that he must have been about forty-three years of age when he first came to the throne.[4] Before that time he had often been to war and had shown himself a gallant soldier and an excellent captain. But after coming to the throne he never went to war in person save once.[5] This happened in the year of Christ 1286 and I will tell you why he went.

There was a great Tartar chief whose name was Nayan,[6] a young man [of thirty], lord over many lands and many provinces; and he was uncle to the emperor Kublai Khan .... he could bring into the field 300,000 horsemen, though all the time he was liegeman to his nephew .... Seeing then what great power he had, he took it into his head that he would be the Great Khan's vassal no longer ... So this Nayan sent envoys to another prince called Caidu, also a potent lord, who was a kinsman of his, and who was a nephew of the Great Khan and his lawful liegeman also, though he was in rebellion .... The message that Nayan sent was this: That he himself was making ready to march against the Great Khan with all his forces (which were great), and he begged Caidu to do likewise from his side, so that by attacking Kublai on two sides at once with such great forces they would be able to wrest his dominion from him.

And when Caidu heard the message of Nayan, he was glad, and thought the time was come at last to gain his object. So he sent back the answer that he would do as requested; and got ready his host, which mustered a good 100,000 horsemen.

CHAPTER 3

How the GREAT KHAN MARCHED against NAYAN

WHEN THE GREAT Khan heard what was afoot, he made his preparations in right good heart. Confident in his own conduct and prowess, he ... vowed that he would never wear the crown again if he did not bring those two traitorous ... chiefs to an ill end. So swiftly and secretly were his preparations made, that no one knew of them but his privy council, and all were completed within ten or twelve days. In that time he had assembled 360,000 horsemen and 100,000 footmen – but a small force indeed for him .... For the rest of his vast forces were too far off to answer so hasty a summons, being engaged ... on distant expeditions to conquer assorted countries and provinces. If he had waited to summon all his troops, the multitude assembled would have been past all counting. In fact, those 360,000 horsemen ... consisted merely of the falconers and whippers-in that were about the court![7]

And when he had got ready this handful (as it were) of his troops ... his astrologers ... told him ... he would conquer and gain a glorious victory: whereat he greatly rejoiced.

So he marched with his army, and after advancing for twenty days they arrived at a great plain where Nayan lay with all his host, amounting to some 400,000 horse.

Now the Great Khan's forces arrived so fast and so suddenly that the others knew nothing of the matter. For the *khan* had caused such strict watch to be made in every direction for scouts that every one that appeared was instantly captured. Thus Nayan had no warning of his coming and was completely taken by surprise; insomuch that when the Great Khan's army came up, he was asleep in the arms of a wife of his of whom he was extravagantly fond. So thus you see why it was that the emperor equipped his force with such speed and secrecy.

CHAPTER 4

Of the BATTLE *that the* GREAT KHAN
FOUGHT *with* NAYAN

WHAT SHALL I say about it? When day had broken, there was the *khan* with his host upon a hill overlooking the plain where Nayan lay in his tent ... without the slightest thought of anyone coming to do him harm. In fact, [his] confidence was such that he kept no vedettes,[8] whether in front or in rear....

And what shall I tell you next? The *khan* was there on the hill, mounted on a great wooden bartizan,[9] which was borne by four well-trained elephants, and over him was hoisted his standard .... His

troops were ordered in battles of 30,000 men apiece ... and the whole plain seemed to be covered with his forces.... When Nayan and his people saw what had happened, they were sorely confounded, and rushed in haste to arms. Nevertheless they ... formed their troops in an orderly manner. And when all were in battle array on both sides ... then might you have heard a sound arise of many instruments ... and of the voices of the whole of the two hosts loudly singing. For this is a custom of the Tartars, that before they join battle they all unite in singing and playing on a certain two-stringed instrument of theirs, a thing right pleasant to hear. And so they continue in their array of battle, singing and playing in this pleasing manner, until the great *naccara* ... is heard to sound....[10]

... thenceforward the din of battle began to be heard loudly from this side and from that. And they rushed to work so doughtily with their bows and their maces, with their lances and swords, and with the arblasts of the footmen, that it was a wondrous sight to see. Now might you behold such flights of arrows from this side and from that, that the whole heaven was canopied with them and they fell like rain. Now might you see on this side and on that ... many a cavalier and man-at-arms fall slain, insomuch that the whole field seemed covered with them. From this side and from that such cries arose from the crowds of the wounded and dying that had God thundered you would not have heard Him! For fierce and furious was the battle, and quarter there was none given.[11]

But why should I make a long story of it? You must know that it was the most ... fierce and fearful battle that ever has been fought in our day. Nor have there ever been such forces in the field ... for, taking both sides, there were not fewer than 760,000 horsemen .... And that without reckoning the footmen, who were also very numerous. The battle endured with various fortune on this side and on that from morning until noon. But at the last ... the Great Khan had the victory, and Nayan ... was utterly routed. For the army of the Great Khan performed such feats of arms that Nayan and his host could stand against them no longer, so they turned and fled. But this availed nothing for Nayan; for he and all the barons with him were taken prisoners, and had to surrender to the *khan* with all their arms.

CHAPTER 5

HOW *the* GREAT KHAN CAUSED NAYAN
to BE PUT *to* DEATH

AND WHEN THE Great Khan learnt that Nayan was taken prisoner he was delighted, and commanded that he should be put to death straightaway and in secret, lest endeavours should be made to obtain pity and pardon for him, because he was of the *khan's* own flesh and blood. And this was the way in which he was put to death: he was wrapped in a carpet, and tossed to and fro so mercilessly that he died. And the *khan* caused him to be put to death in this way because he would not have the blood of his imperial line spilled upon the ground or exposed in the eye of heaven and before the sun.[12]

And when the Great Khan had won this battle, as you have heard, all the barons and people of Nayan's provinces renewed their fealty to the *khan*. Now these provinces that had been under the lordship of Nayan were four in number; to wit, the first called Chorcha; the second Cauly; the third Barscol; the fourth Sikintinju. It was a very great dominion.[13]

And after the Great Khan had conquered Nayan, as you have heard, it came to pass that the different kinds of people who were present, Muslims and idolaters and Jews, and many others that believed not in God, did gibe those that were Christians because of the Cross that Nayan had borne on his standard.[14] ... And such a din arose about the matter that it reached the Great Khan's own ears. When it did so, he sharply rebuked those who cast these gibes; and he also bade the Christians be of good heart, for "if the Cross had rendered no help to Nayan, the Cross had done right well; nor could that which was good, as it was, have done otherwise; for Nayan was a disloyal and traitorous rebel against his lord, and well deserved that which had befallen him. Wherefore the Cross of your God did well, in that it gave him no help against the right." And this he said so loud that everybody heard him....

And so thenceforward no more was heard of the floutings of the unbelievers against the Christians; for they heard very well what the sovereign said to the latter about the Cross on Nayan's banner, and its giving him no help.

CHAPTER 6

HOW *the* GREAT KHAN WENT BACK
to the CITY *of* CAMBALUC

AND AFTER THE Great Khan had defeated Nayan he went back to his capital city of Cambaluc, taking his ease and making festivity.[15] And the other Tartar lord called Caidu was greatly troubled when he heard of the defeat and death of Nayan, and held himself in readiness for war; but he stood greatly in fear of being handled as Nayan had been.

I told you that the Great Khan never went on a campaign but once, and it was on this occasion; in all other cases of need he sent his sons or his barons into the field. But this time he would have none go in command but himself, for he regarded the presumptuous rebellion of Nayan as far too serious and perilous an affair to be otherwise dealt with.

CHAPTER 7

HOW *the KHAN* REWARDED
the VALOUR *of* HIS CAPTAINS

SO WE WILL have done with this matter of Nayan, and go on with our account of the great state of the Great Khan. We have already told you of his lineage and of his age; but now I must tell you what he did after his return, in regard to those barons who had behaved well in the battle. Him who was before captain of 100 he made captain of 1,000; and him who was captain of 1,000 men he made to be captain of 10,000, advancing every man according to his deserts and to his previous rank. Besides that, he also made them presents of fine silver plate and other rich appointments; gave them tablets of authority[16] of a higher degree than they held before; and bestowed upon them fine jewels of gold and silver, and pearls and precious stones; insomuch that the amount that fell to each of them was something astonishing. And yet 'twas not so much as they had deserved; for never were men seen who did such feats of arms for the love and honour of their lord as these had done on that day of the battle ....

CHAPTER 8

CONCERNING *the* PERSON *of the* GREAT KHAN

THE PERSONAL APPEARANCE of the Great Khan, lord of lords, whose name is Kublai, is such as I shall now tell you. He is of a good stature, neither tall nor short, but of a middle height. He has a becoming amount of flesh, and is very shapely in all his limbs. His complexion is white and red, the eyes black and fine, the nose well formed and well set on.[17] He has four wives, whom he retains permanently as his legitimate consorts; and the eldest of his sons by those four wives ought by rights to be emperor – I mean when his father dies. Those four ladies are called empresses, but each is distinguished also by her proper name. And each of them has a special court of her own ... no one of them having fewer than 300 fair damsels. They have also many pages and eunuchs, and a number of other attendants of both sexes; so that each of these ladies has not fewer than 10,000 persons attached to her court.[18]

When the emperor desires the society of one of these four consorts, he will sometimes summon the lady to his apartment and sometimes visit her at her own. He has also a great number of concubines, and I will tell you how he obtains them.

You must know that there is a tribe of Tartars called Ungrat, who are noted for their beauty.[19] Now every year 100 of the most beautiful maidens of this tribe are sent to the Great Khan, who commits them

to the charge of certain elderly ladies in his palace. And these old
ladies make the girls sleep with them, in order to ascertain if they
have sweet breath ... and are sound in all their limbs. Then such
of them as are of approved beauty, and are good and sound in all
respects, are appointed to attend on the emperor by turns. Thus
six of these damsels take their turn for three days and nights ... to
serve him in any way, and to be entirely at his orders. At the end
of the three days and nights they are relieved by another six. And
so throughout the year, there are reliefs of maidens by six and six,
changing every three days and nights.

CHAPTER 9

CONCERNING *the* GREAT KHAN'S SONS

THE EMPEROR HAS, by those four wives of his, twenty-two male children; the eldest of whom was called Chinkin for the love of the good Genghis Khan, the first lord of the Tartars. And this Chinkin, as the eldest son of the *khan*, was to have reigned after his father's death; but, as it came to pass, he died. He left a son behind him, however, whose name is Temur, and he is to be the Great Khan and

emperor after the death of his grandfather, as is but right; he being the child of the Great Khan's eldest son. And this Temur is an able and brave man, as he has already proven on many occasions.[20]

The Great Khan also has twenty-five other sons by his concubines; and these are good and valiant soldiers, and each of them is a great chief. I tell you moreover that of his children by his four lawful wives there are seven who are kings of vast realms or provinces, and govern them well....[21]

CONCERNING *the* PALACE *of the* GREAT KHAN

YOU MUST KNOW that for three months of the year, to wit December, January, and February, the Great Khan resides in the capital city of Cathay, which is called Cambaluc .... In that city stands his great palace, and now I will tell you what it is like.

It is enclosed all round by a great wall forming a square, each side of which is a mile in length ... it is also very thick, and a good ten paces in height, whitewashed and loopholed all round. At each angle of the wall there is a ... palace in which the war-harness of the emperor is kept, such as bows and quivers, saddles and bridles, and bowstrings, and everything needed by an army. Also midway between every two of these corner palaces there is another of the like; so that taking the whole compass of the enclosure you find eight vast palaces stored with the great lord's harness of war.[22] And you must understand that each palace is assigned to only one kind of article; thus one is stored with bows, a second with saddles, a third with bridles, and so on in succession right round.[23]

The great wall has five gates on its southern face, the middle one being the great gate, which is never opened on any occasion except when the Great Khan himself goes forth or enters. Close on either side of this great gate is a smaller one by which all other people pass; and then toward each angle is another great gate, also open to people in general; so that on that side there are five gates in all.[24]

Inside of this wall there is a second, enclosing a space that is somewhat greater in length than in breadth.... In the middle of the second enclosure is the lord's Great Palace, and I will tell you what it is like.

... The palace ... has no upper storey, but is all on the ground floor; only the basement is raised some ten palms above the surrounding soil, and this elevation is retained by a wall of marble raised to the level of the pavement ... projecting beyond the base of the palace so as to form a kind of terrace-walk, by which people can pass round the building, and which is exposed to view .... The roof is very lofty, and the walls of the palace are all covered with gold and silver. They are also adorned with representations of dragons (sculptured and gilt), beasts and birds, knights and idols, and sundry other subjects. And on the ceiling too you see nothing but gold and silver and painting. On each of the four sides there is a great marble staircase leading to the top of the marble wall, and forming the approach to the palace.

The hall of the palace is so large that it could easily dine 6,000 people; and it is quite a marvel to see how many rooms there are besides. The building is altogether so vast, so rich, and so beautiful, that no man on earth could design anything superior to it. The outside of the roof also is all coloured with vermilion and yellow and green and blue and other hues, which are fixed with a varnish so fine and exquisite that they shine like crystal, and lend a resplendent lustre to the palace as seen for a great way round. This roof is made too with such strength and solidity that it is fit to last for ever.

Between the two walls of the enclosure ... there are fine parks and beautiful trees bearing a variety of fruits. There are beasts also of sundry kinds, such as white stags and fallow deer, gazelles and roebucks, and fine squirrels of various sorts, with numbers also of the animal that gives the musk, and all manner of other beautiful creatures, insomuch that the whole place is full of them, and no spot remains void except where there is traffic of people going and coming.

From that corner of the enclosure which is toward the northwest there extends a fine lake, containing ... fish of different kinds which the emperor has caused to be put in there, so that whenever he desires any he can have them at his pleasure.... Moreover on the north side of the palace, about a bow-shot off, there is a hill which has been made from the earth dug out of the lake .... This hill is entirely covered with trees that never lose their leaves, but remain ever green. And I assure you that wherever a beautiful tree may exist, and the emperor gets news of it, he sends for it and has it transported bodily with all its roots and the earth attached to them, and planted on that hill of his.... and in this way he has got together the most beautiful collection of trees in all the world. And he has also caused the whole hill to be covered with the ore of azure,[25] which is very green. And thus not only are the trees all green, but the hill itself is all green likewise; and there is nothing to be seen on it that is not green; and hence it is called the Green Mount; and in good sooth 'tis named well.

 ... Now I am going to tell you of the chief city of Cathay ... and why it was built, and how.

CHAPTER 11

CONCERNING *the* CITY *of* CAMBALUC

NOW THERE WAS on that spot in old times a great and noble city called Cambaluc, which is as much as to say in our tongue "The city of the Emperor."[26] But the Great Khan was informed by his astrologers that this city would prove rebellious... So he caused the present city to be built close beside the old one, with only a river between them.[27] And he caused the people of the old city to be removed to the new town that he had and this is called Taidu.

 As regards the size of this (new) city you must know that ... each side of it has a length of six miles, and it is four-square. And it is all walled round with walls of earth which have a thickness of fully ten paces at the bottom, and a height of more than ten paces... And they are provided throughout with loopholed battlements, which are all whitewashed.

There are twelve gates, and over each gate there is a great and handsome palace, so that there are on each side of the square three gates and five palaces; for (I ought to mention) there is at each angle also a great and handsome palace ... in which are kept the arms of the city garrison.[28]

The streets are so straight and wide that you can see right along them from end to end and from one gate to the other. And up and down the city there are beautiful palaces, and many great and fine hostelries, and fine houses in great numbers. All the plots of ground on which the houses ... are built are four-square, and laid out with straight lines.... Each square plot is encompassed by handsome streets for traffic; and thus the whole city is arranged in squares just like a chessboard, and disposed in a manner so perfect and masterly that it is impossible to give a description that should do it justice.

Moreover, in the middle of the city there is a great clock – that is to say, a bell, which is struck at night. And after it has struck three times no one must go out in the city, unless it be for the needs of a woman in labour, or of the sick.[29] And those who go about on such errands are bound to carry lanterns with them. Moreover, the established guard at each gate of the city is 1,000 armed men ... kept up ... as a guard of honour for the sovereign, who resides there, and to prevent thieves from doing mischief in the town.

CHAPTER 12

HOW *the* GREAT KHAN MAINTAINS *a* GUARD *of* 12,000 HORSE, *which are called* KESHICAN

YOU MUST KNOW that the Great Khan ... has a guard of 12,000 horsemen, who are styled *keshican*, which is as much as to say "knights devoted to their lord". Not that he keeps these for fear of any man whatever, but merely because of his own exalted dignity. These 12,000 men have four captains, each of whom is in command of 3,000 and each body of 3,000 takes a turn of three days and nights to guard the palace, where they also take their meals. After three days and nights have expired they are relieved by another 3,000, who mount guard for the same space of time, and then another body takes its turn, so that there are always 3,000 on guard. Thus it goes until the whole 12,000 have been on duty, and then the tour begins again, and so runs on from year's end to year's end.

CHAPTER 13

The FASHION of the GREAT KHAN'S TABLE at his HIGH FEASTS

AND WHEN THE Great Khan sits at table on any great court occasion, it is in this fashion. His table is elevated a good deal above the others, and he sits at the north end of the hall, looking toward the south, with his chief wife beside him on the left. On his right sit his sons and his nephews, and other kinsmen of the blood imperial, but lower, so that their heads are on a level with the emperor's feet. And then the other barons sit at other tables lower still. So also with the women; for all the wives of the lord's sons, and of his nephews and other kinsmen, sit at the lower table to his right; and below them again the ladies of the other barons and knights, each in the place assigned by the lord's orders. The tables are so disposed that the emperor can see the whole of them from end to end, many as they are.... Outside the hall will be found more than 40,000 people; for there is a great concourse of folk bringing presents to the lord, or come from foreign countries with curiosities.

In ... the hall near where the Great Khan holds his table, there stands a great vessel of pure gold, holding as much as an ordinary butt; and at each corner of the great vessel is one of smaller size, and from the former the wine or beverage flavoured with fine and costly spices is drawn off into the latter. And on the buffet aforesaid are set all the lord's drinking vessels, among which are certain pitchers of the finest gold ... one of these is put between every two persons, besides a couple of golden cups with handles, so that every man helps himself from the pitcher that stands between him and his neighbour.

And the ladies are supplied in the same way. The value of these pitchers and cups is something immense; in fact, the Great Khan has such a quantity of this kind of plate, and of gold and silver in other shapes, as no one ever before saw or heard tell of, or could believe.

And you must know that those who wait upon the Great Khan … are some of the great barons. They have the mouth and nose muffled with fine napkins of silk and gold, so that no breath nor odour from their persons should taint the dish or the goblet presented to the lord. And when the emperor is going to drink, all the musical instruments, of which he has vast store of every kind, begin to play. And when he takes the cup all the barons and the rest of the company drop on their knees and make the deepest obeisance before him, and then the emperor doth drink. But each time that he does so the whole ceremony is repeated.

… when all have dined and the tables have been removed, then come in a great number of players and jugglers … and perform before the emperor and the rest of the company, creating great diversion and mirth, so that everybody is full of laughter and enjoyment. And when the performance is over, the company breaks up and everyone goes to his quarters.

CHAPTER 14

CONCERNING *the* GREAT FEAST *held by the* GREAT KHAN EVERY YEAR *on his* BIRTHDAY

YOU MUST KNOW that the Tartars celebrate yearly on their birthday. And the Great Khan was born on the twenty-eighth day of the September moon, so on that day is held the greatest feast of the year at the *khan's* court, always excepting that which he holds on New Year's Day, of which I shall tell you afterwards.[30] Now, on his birthday, the Great Khan dresses in the best of his robes, all wrought with beaten gold; and fully 12,000 barons and knights come forth dressed in robes … precisely like those of the Great Khan, except that they are not so costly; but still they are … also of silk and gold.

Every man so clothed has also a girdle of gold; and this, as well as the dress, is given to him by the sovereign. And I will aver that ... some of these suits decked with so many pearls and precious stones ... shall be worth 10,000 golden bezants.[31]

And of such raiment there are several sets. For you must know that the Great Khan, thirteen times in the year, presents to his barons and knights such suits.[32] ... And on each occasion they wear the same colour that he does, a different colour being assigned to each festival. Hence you may see what a huge business it is, and that there is no prince in the world but he alone who could keep up such customs as these. On his birthday also, all the Tartars in the world, and all the countries and governments that owe allegiance to the *khan*, offer him great presents .... And many other persons also come with great presents to the *khan*, in order to beg for some employment from him. And the Great Khan has chosen twelve barons on whom is laid the charge of assigning to each of these supplicants a suitable answer.

On this day likewise all the idolaters, all the Muslims, and all the Christians and other descriptions of people make great and solemn devotions ... each to the God whom he doth worship, praying that He would save the emperor, and grant him long life and health and happiness. And thus, as I have related, is celebrated the joyous feast of the Great Khan's birthday. Now I will tell you of ... the White Feast.

CHAPTER 15

Of the GREAT FESTIVAL *which the* KHAN HOLDS *on* NEW YEAR'S DAY

THE BEGINNING OF their New Year is the month of February, and on that occasion the Great Khan and all his subjects made such a feast as I now shall describe.

It is the custom that on this occasion the *khan* and all his subjects should be clothed entirely in white ... for they deem that white clothing is lucky.[33] On that day also all the people of all the provinces and governments and kingdoms and countries that owe allegiance to the *khan* bring him great presents of gold and silver, and pearls and gems, and rich textures .... And the people also make presents to each other of white things, and embrace and kiss and make merry, and wish each other happiness and good luck for the coming year. On that day, I can assure you, among the customary presents there shall be offered to the *khan* from various quarters more than 100,000 white horses, beautiful animals, and richly caparisoned.

On that day also, the whole of the *khan*'s elephants, amounting to 5,000 in number, are exhibited, all covered with rich ... housings of inlaid cloth representing beasts and birds, whilst each of them carries on his back two splendid coffers; all of these being filled with the emperor's plate and other costly furniture required for the court on the occasion of the White Feast. And these are followed by a vast number of camels, which are likewise covered with rich housings and laden with things needful for the feast. All these are paraded before the emperor, and it makes the finest sight in the world.

Moreover, on the morning of the feast, before the tables are set, all the kings, dukes, marquesses, counts, barons, knights, and astrologers, and philosophers, and leeches, and falconers, and other officials of sundry kinds from all the places round about, present themselves in the Great Hall before the emperor.... And when they are all seated, each in his proper place, then a great prelate rises and says with a loud voice: "Bow and adore!" And as soon as he has said this, the company bow down until their foreheads touch the earth in adoration toward the emperor as if he were a god. And this adoration they repeat four times, and then go to a highly decorated altar, on which is a vermilion tablet with the name of the Great Khan inscribed thereon, and a beautiful censer of gold. So they incense the tablet and the altar with great reverence, and then return each man to his seat.[34]

When all have performed this, then the presents are offered. And after all have been seen by the emperor, the tables are set, and all take their places at them with perfect order as I have already told you. And after dinner the jugglers come in and amuse the court as you have heard before; and when that is over, every man goes to his quarters.

C H A P T E R   1 6

CONCERNING *the* 12,000 BARONS *who* RECEIVE ROBES *of* CLOTH *of* GOLD *from the* EMPEROR *on the* GREAT FESTIVALS, THIRTEEN CHANGES APIECE

... THE GREAT KHAN has set apart 12,000 of his men ... as I have told you before ... and on each ... he bestows thirteen changes of raiment.... These robes are garnished with ... precious things in a ... costly manner.[35] And ... he bestows on each of those 12,000 barons a fine golden girdle of great ... value, and likewise a pair of boots ... curiously wrought with silver thread; insomuch that when they are clothed ... every man of them looks like a king![36] And there is an order as to which dress is to be worn at each of those thirteen feasts. The emperor himself also has his thirteen suits corresponding to those of his barons; in *colour*, I mean (though his are grander, richer, and costlier), so that he is always arrayed in the same colour as his barons, who are, as it were, his comrades. And you may see that all this costs an amount which it is scarcely possible to calculate.

... And now I must mention another thing that I had forgotten, but which you will be astonished to learn from this book. You must know that on the feast day a great lion is led to the emperor's presence, and as soon as it sees him it lies down before him with every sign of the greatest veneration, as if it acknowledged him for its lord; and it remains there lying before him, and entirely unchained. Truly this must seem a strange story to those who have not seen the thing!

CHAPTER 17

HOW *the* GREAT KHAN ENJOINETH HIS PEOPLE *to* SUPPLY HIM *with* GAME

THE THREE MONTHS of December, January and February, during which the emperor resides at his capital, are assigned for hunting and fowling ... and it is ordained that the larger game taken be sent to the court. To be more particular: of all the larger beasts of the chase, such as boars, roebucks, bucks, stags, lions, bears, and so on, the greater part of what is taken has to be sent, and feathered game likewise. The animals are gutted and sent to the court on carts. This is done by all the people within twenty or thirty days' journey, and the quantity so sent is immense.

CHAPTER 18

Of the LIONS *and* LEOPARDS *and* WOLVES
that the KHAN *keeps for the* CHASE

THE EMPEROR HAS numbers of leopards trained to the chase,[37] and has also ... many lynxes taught in like manner to catch game, and which afford excellent sport. He has also several great lions, bigger than those of Babylonia, beasts whose skins are coloured in the most beautiful way, being striped all along the sides with black, red and white. These are trained to catch boars and wild cattle, bears, wild asses, stags, and other great or fierce beasts. And 'tis a rare sight, I can tell you, to see those lions giving chase to such beasts as I have mentioned! (They are obliged to approach the game against the

wind, otherwise the animals would catch the scent ... and be off.)[38] There are also a great number of eagles, all broken to catch wolves, foxes, deer, and wild goats, and they do catch them in great numbers. But those especially that are trained to wolf-catching are very large and powerful birds, and no wolf is able to get away from them.[39]

CHAPTER 19

CONCERNING *the* TWO BROTHERS *who* HAVE CHARGE *of the* KHAN'S HOUNDS

THE EMPEROR HAS two barons who are brothers, one called Baian and the other Mingan; and these two are styled *chinuchi* (or *cunichi*), which is ... "the keepers of the mastiff dogs."[40] Each ... has 10,000 men under his orders .... Out of each body of 10,000 there are 2,000 men who are each in charge of one or more great mastiffs, so that the whole number of these is very large. And when the prince goes a-hunting, one of those barons, with his 10,000 men and something like 5,000 dogs, goes toward the right, whilst the other goes toward the left ... in like manner. They move along, all abreast of one another, so that the whole line extends over a full day's journey, and no animal can escape them. Truly it is a glorious sight to see the working of the dogs and the huntsmen on such an occasion! And as the lord rides a-fowling across the plains, you will see these big hounds coming tearing up, one pack after a bear, another pack after a stag, or some other beast, and running the game down now on this side and now on that, so that it is really a most delightful sport and spectacle.

CHAPTER 20

HOW *the* EMPEROR GOES *on a* HUNTING EXPEDITION

AFTER HE HAS stopped at his capital city those three months that

I mentioned ... he starts off on the first day of March, and travels southward toward the Ocean Sea, a journey of two days.[41] He takes with him fully 10,000 falconers, and some 500 gerfalcons besides peregrines, sakers, and other hawks in great numbers; and goshawks also ....[42] And let me tell you when he goes thus a-fowling with his gerfalcons and other hawks, he is attended by fully 10,000 men who are disposed in couples; and these are called *toscaol*, which is as much as to say, "watchers". And the name describes their business.... Every man of them is provided with a whistle and hood, so as to be able to call in a hawk and hold it in hand. And when the emperor makes a cast, there is no need that he follow it up, for those men I speak of keep so good a lookout that they never lose sight of the birds, and if these have need of help they are ready to render it.

All the emperor's hawks, and those of the barons as well, have a little label attached to the leg to mark them, on which is written the names of the owner and the keeper of the bird. And in this way the hawk, when caught, is at once identified and handed over to its owner. But if not, the bird is carried to a certain baron, who is styled the *bularguchi*, which is as much as to say "the keeper of lost property". And I tell you that whatever may be found without a known owner, whether it be a horse, or a sword, or a hawk, or what not, it is carried to that baron straightaway, and he takes charge of it.... Likewise the loser of any article goes to the baron, and if the thing be in his hands it is immediately given up to the owner. Moreover, the said baron always pitches on the highest spot of the camp, with his banner displayed, in order that those who have lost or found anything may have no difficulty in finding their way to him. Thus nothing can be lost but it shall be incontinently found and restored.

And so the emperor follows this road that I have mentioned, leading along in the vicinity of the Ocean Sea (which is within two days' journey of his capital city, Cambaluc), and as he goes there is ... plenty of the very best entertainment in hawking; in fact, there is no sport in the world to equal it! ...

And when he has travelled until he reaches a place called Cachar Modun,[43] there he finds his tents pitched ... so that there shall be fully 10,000 tents in all …. The tent in which he holds his courts is large enough to give cover easily to 1,000 souls…. Immediately behind the great tent there is a fine large chamber where the lord sleeps; and there are also many other tents and chambers, but they are not in contact with the Great Tent as these are. The two audience-tents and the sleeping-chamber are constructed in this way. Each of the audience-tents has three poles, which are of spicewood, and are most artfully covered with lions' skins, striped with black and white and red, so that they do not suffer from any weather. All three apartments are also covered outside with similar skins of striped lions, a substance that lasts for ever. And inside they are all lined with ermine and sable, these two being the finest and most costly furs in existence. For a robe of sable, large enough to line a mantle, is worth 2,000 bezants of gold, or 1,000 at least, and this kind of skin is called by the Tartars "the king of furs". The beast itself is about the size of a marten. These two furs of which I speak are applied and inlaid so exquisitely, that it is really something worth seeing. All the tent-ropes are of silk. And in short I may say that those tents, to wit the two audience-halls and the sleeping-chamber, are so costly that not every king could pay for them.

Round about these tents are others, also fine ones and beautifully pitched ... so that altogether the number of tents there on the plain is something wonderful. ... you would take the camp for a big city....

The lord remains encamped there until the spring and all that time he does nothing but go hawking round about among the canebrakes along the lakes and rivers that abound in that region.... The other gentry of the camp also are never done with hunting and hawking, and every day they bring home great store of venison and feathered game of all sorts....

There is another thing I should mention; to wit, that for twenty days' journey round the spot nobody is allowed ... to keep hawks or hounds, though anywhere else whosoever may keep them. And furthermore throughout all the emperor's territories, nobody however audacious dares to hunt any of these four animals, to wit, hare, stag, buck and roe, from the month of March to the month of October. Anybody who should do so would rue it bitterly. But those people are so obedient to their lord's command, that even if a man were to find one of those animals asleep by the roadside he would not touch it for the world! And thus the game multiplies at such a rate that the whole country swarms with it, and the emperor gets as much as he could desire. Beyond the term I have mentioned, however, to wit that from March to October, everybody may take these animals.

After the emperor has tarried in that place, enjoying his sport as I have related, from March to the middle of May, he moves with all his people, and returns straight to his capital city ... but all the while continuing to take his diversion in hunting and hawking as he goes along.

CHAPTER 21

REHEARSAL *of the* WAY *the* YEAR *of* *the* GREAT KHAN *is* DISTRIBUTED

ON ARRIVING AT his capital of Cambaluc, he stays in his palace there three days and no more; during which time he has great court entertainments and rejoicings, and makes merry with his wives. He then quits his palace at Cambaluc, and proceeds to that city which he has built, as I told you before, and which is called Chandu, where he has that grand park and palace of cane, and where he keeps his gerfalcons. There he spends the summer, to escape the heat, for where it is situated is very cool. After stopping there from the beginning of May to the twenty-eighth of August, he ... returns to his capital Cambaluc. There he stops, as I have told you also, the month of September, to keep his Birthday Feast, and also throughout October, November, December, January and February, in which last month he keeps the grand feast of the New Year, which they call the White Feast, as you have heard already with all particulars. He then sets out on his march toward the Ocean Sea, hunting and hawking, and continues out from the beginning of March to the middle of May; and then comes back for three days only to the capital... and then he starts off again as you know.

So thus the whole year is spent; six months at the capital, three months in hunting, and three months at the palace of cane to avoid the heat. And in this way he passes his time with the greatest enjoyment; not to mention occasional journeys in this or that direction at his own pleasure.

CHAPTER 22

CONCERNING *the* CITY *of* CAMBALUC *and its* GREAT TRAFFIC *and* POPULATION

YOU MUST KNOW that the city of Cambaluc has such a multitude of houses, and such a vast population inside the walls and outside, that it seems quite past all possibility. There is a suburb outside each of the gates, which are twelve in number;[44] and these suburbs are so great that they contain more people than the city itself .... In those suburbs lodge the foreign merchants and travellers, of whom there are always great numbers who have come to bring presents to the emperor, or to sell articles at court, or because the city affords so good a mart to attract traders. (There are in each of the suburbs numerous fine hostelries for the lodgement of merchants from different parts of the world ....) And thus there are as many good houses outside of the city as inside, without counting those that belong to the great lords and barons, which are very numerous.

You must know that it is forbidden to bury any dead body inside the city. If the body be that of an idolater it is carried out beyond the city ... to a remote place assigned for the purpose, to be burnt. And if it be of one belonging to a religion the custom of which is to bury, such as the Christian, the Muslim, or what not, it is also carried out beyond the suburbs to a distant place assigned for the purpose. And thus the city is preserved in a better and more healthy state.

Moreover, no public woman[45] resides inside the city, but all such abide outside in the suburbs. And 'tis wonderful what a vast number of these there are for the foreigners; it is a certain fact that there are more than 20,000 of them living by prostitution. And that so many can live in this way will show you how vast is the population....

To this city also are brought articles of greater cost and rarity, and in greater abundance of all kinds, than to any other city in the world. For people of every description, and from every region, bring things (including all the costly wares of India, as well as the fine and precious goods of Cathay itself with its provinces) ....

As a sample, I tell you, no day in the year passes that there do not enter the city 1,000 cartloads of silk alone, from which are made quantities of cloth of silk and gold, and of other goods. And this is not to be wondered at; for in all the countries round about there is no flax, so that everything has to be made of silk. It is true, indeed, that in some parts of the country there is cotton and hemp, but not sufficient for their wants. This, however, is not of much consequence, because silk is so abundant and cheap, and is a more valuable substance than either flax or cotton.

Round about this great city of Cambaluc there are some 200 other cities at various distances, from which traders come to sell their goods and buy others for their lords; and all find means to make their sales and purchases, so that the traffic of the city is passing great.

CONCERNING *the* OPPRESSIONS *of* ACHMATH
the BAILO, *and the* PLOT *that was*
FORMED AGAINST HIM[46]

... THERE ARE TWELVE persons appointed who have authority to dispose of lands, offices and everything else at their discretion. Now one of these was a certain Muslim named Achmath, a shrewd, and able man, who had more power and influence with the Great Khan than any of the others; and the *khan* held him in such regard that he could do what he pleased. The fact was, as came out after his death, that Achmath had so wrought upon the *khan* with his sorcery, that the latter had the greatest faith and reliance on everything he said, and in this way did everything that Achmath wished him to do.

This person disposed of all governments and offices, and passed sentence on all malefactors; and whenever he desired to have anyone whom he hated put to death, whether with justice or without it, ... the lord would say "Do as you think right", and so he would have the man executed. Thus when people saw how unbounded were his powers, and how unbounded the reliance placed by the emperor on everything that he said, they did not venture to oppose him in anything. No one was so high in rank or power as to be free from the dread of him. If anyone was accused by him to the emperor of a capital offence, and desired to defend himself, he was unable to bring proofs in his own exculpation, for no one would stand by him, as no one dared to oppose Achmath. And thus the latter caused many to perish unjustly.[47]

Moreover, there was no beautiful woman whom he might desire, but he got hold of her.... Whenever he knew of anyone who had a pretty daughter, certain ruffians of his would go to the father, and say: "… give her in marriage to the *bailo* Achmath (for they called him "the *bailo*", or, as we should say, "the vice-regent")[48] and we will arrange for his giving you such … an office for three years." And so the man would surrender his daughter…. Thus either through the ambition of the parents, or through fear of the minister, all the beautiful women were at his beck, either as wives or mistresses. Also he had some twenty-five sons who held offices of importance, and some of these … committed scandals like his own, and many other abominable iniquities. This Achmath also had amassed great treasure, for everybody who wanted office sent him a heavy bribe.

In such authority did this man continue for twenty-two years. At last the people of the country, to wit the Cathayans, utterly wearied with the endless outrages and abominable iniquities … conspired to slay him and revolt …. Amongst the rest there was a certain Cathayan named Chenchu, a commander of 1,000, whose mother, daughter and wife had all been dishonoured by Achmath. Now this man, full of bitter resentment, entered into parley regarding the destruction of the minister with another Cathayan whose name was Wangchu, who was a commander of 10,000. They came to the conclusion that the time to do the business would be during the Great Khan's absence from Cambaluc. For after stopping there three months he used to go to Chandu and stop there three months; and at the same time his son Chinkin used to go away to his usual haunts, and this Achmath remained in charge of the city; sending to obtain the *khan's* orders from Chandu when any emergency arose.

So Wangchu and Chenchu … sent word to their friends in many other cities that they had determined on such a day, at the signal given by a beacon, to massacre all the men with beards, and that the other cities should stand ready to do the like on seeing the signal fires. The reason why they spoke of massacring the bearded men was that … beards are worn by the Tartars, Muslims and Christians…. all the Cathayans detested the Grand Khan's rule because he set over them governors who were Tartars, or still more frequently Muslims, and these they could not endure, for they were treated by them just like slaves. You see the Great Khan had not succeeded to the dominion of Cathay by hereditary right, but held it by conquest; and thus having no confidence in the natives, he put all authority into the hands of Tartars, Muslims or Christians who were attached to his household and devoted to his service, and were foreigners in Cathay.

Wherefore, on the day appointed, the aforesaid Wangchu and Chenchu having entered the palace at night, Wangchu ... sent a messenger to Achmath the *bailo* ... as if to summon him to the presence of Chinkin, the Great Khan's son, who (it was pretended) had arrived unexpectedly.

When Achmath heard this he ... made haste to go, for he feared the prince greatly. When he arrived at the gate he met a Tartar called Cogatai, who was captain of the ... standing garrison of the city; and the latter asked him whither he was bound so late? "To Chinkin, who is just arrived." Quoth Cogatai, "How can that be? How could he come so privily that I know nought of it?" So he followed the minister with a certain number of his soldiers. Now the notion of the Cathayans was that if they could make an end of Achmath, they would have nought else to be afraid of. So as soon as Achmath got inside the palace ... he bowed down before Wangchu, supposing him to be Chinkin, and Chenchu who was standing ready with a sword straightway cut his head off. As soon as Cogatai, who had halted at the entrance, beheld this, he shouted "Treason!" and instantly discharged an arrow at Wangchu and shot him dead as he sat. At the same time he called his people to seize Chenchu, and sent a proclamation through the city that anyone found in the streets would be instantly put to death. The Cathayans saw that the Tartars had discovered the plot, and ... they kept still in their houses, and were unable to pass the signal for the rising of the other cities.... Cogatai immediately dispatched messengers to the Great Khan giving an orderly report ... and the *khan* sent back orders for him to make a careful investigation, and to punish the guilty as their misdeeds deserved....

After the Great Khan had returned to Cambaluc he was very anxious to discover what had led to this affair, and he then learned all about the endless iniquities of ... Achmath and his sons.... The Great Khan then ordered all the treasure that Achmath had accumulated in the Old City to be transferred to his own treasury in the New City ....

He also ordered the body of Achmath to be dug up and cast into the streets for the dogs to tear; and commanded those of his sons that had followed the father's evil example to be flayed alive.

These circumstances called the *khan*'s attention to the accursed doctrines of the sect of the Muslims, which excuse every crime, even murder itself, when committed on such as are not of their religion. And seeing that this doctrine had led the accursed Achmath and his sons to act as they did without any sense of guilt, the *khan* was led to entertain the greatest disgust ... for it. So he summoned the Muslims and prohibited their doing many things that their religion enjoined.

Now when all this happened Messer Marco was on the spot.[49]

CHAPTER 24

HOW *the* GREAT KHAN CAUSETH *the* BARK
of TREES, *made into something like* PAPER,
to PASS FOR MONEY *over all his* COUNTRY

NOW THAT I have told you in detail of the splendour of this city of the emperor's, I shall proceed to tell you of the mint he has in the same city, in which he has his money coined and struck ... the way it is wrought is such that you might say he has the secret of alchemy in perfection, and you would be right! For he makes his money after this fashion.

He makes them take of the bark of a certain tree, in fact of the mulberry tree, the leaves of which are the food of the silkworms – these trees being so numerous that whole districts are full of them. What they take is a certain fine white bast or skin which lies between the wood of the tree and the thick outer bark, and this they make into something resembling sheets of paper, but black. When these sheets have been prepared they are cut up into pieces of different sizes. The smallest of these sizes is worth a half tornesel;[50] the next, a little larger, one tornesel; one, a little larger still, is worth half a silver groat of Venice; another a whole groat; others yet two groats, five groats and ten groats. There is also a kind worth one bezant of gold, and others of three bezants, and so up to ten. All these pieces of paper are issued with as much solemnity and authority as if they were of pure gold or silver; and on every piece a variety of officials ... have to write their names, and to put their seals. And when all is prepared duly, the chief officer deputed by the *khan* smears the seal entrusted to him with vermilion, and impresses it on the paper, so that the form of the seal remains printed upon it in red; the money is then authentic. Anyone forging it would be punished with death. And the *khan* causes every year to be made such a vast quantity of this money, which costs him nothing, that it must equal in amount all the treasure in the world.

With these pieces of paper ... he causes all payments on his own account to be made; and he makes them to pass current universally ... wherever his power and sovereignty extends. And nobody ... dares to refuse them on pain of death. And indeed everybody takes

them readily, for wherever a person may go throughout the *khan's* dominions he shall find these pieces of paper current, and shall be able to transact all sales and purchases of goods by means of them just as well as if they were coins of pure gold. And all the while they are so light that ten bezants' worth does not weigh one golden bezant.

Furthermore all merchants arriving from India or other countries, and bringing with them gold or silver or gems and pearls, are prohibited from selling to anyone but the emperor. He has twelve experts ... these appraise the articles, and the emperor then pays a liberal price for them in those pieces of paper. The merchants accept his price readily, for in the first place they would not get so good a price from anybody else, and secondly they are paid without any delay. And with this paper-money they can buy what they like anywhere in the empire, whilst it is also vastly lighter to carry about .... And it is a truth that the merchants will several times in the year bring wares to the amount of 400,000 bezants, and the grand sire pays for all in that paper. So he buys such a quantity of those precious things every year that his treasure is endless, whilst all the time the money he pays away costs him nothing at all....

When any of those pieces of paper are spoilt – not that they are so very flimsy neither – the owner carries them to the mint, and by paying three per cent on the value he gets new pieces in exchange. And if any baron, or anyone else, has need of gold or silver or gems or pearls, in order to make plate, or girdles, or the like, he goes to the mint and buys as much as he list, paying in this paper-money.[51]

... And now I will tell you of the great dignitaries which act in this city on behalf of the emperor.

CHAPTER 25

CONCERNING the TWELVE BARONS who are SET OVER ALL the AFFAIRS of the GREAT KHAN

YOU MUST KNOW that the Great Khan has chosen twelve great barons to whom he has committed all the necessary affairs of thirty-four great provinces; and now I will tell you particulars about them and their establishments.

... these twelve barons reside ... in a very rich and handsome palace, which is inside the city of Cambaluc, and consists of a variety of edifices, with many suites of apartments. To every province is assigned a judge and several clerks.... These ... administer all the affairs of the provinces to which they are attached, under the direction of the twelve barons. Howbeit, when an affair is of very great importance, the twelve barons lay in before the emperor, and he decides as he thinks best. But the power of those twelve barons is so great that they choose the governors for all those thirty-four great provinces that I have mentioned, and only after they have chosen do they inform the emperor of their choice. This he confirms, and grants to the person nominated a tablet of gold such as is appropriate to the rank of his government.

Those twelve barons also have such authority that they can dispose of the movements of the forces, and send them whither, and in such strength, as they please. This is done indeed with the emperor's cognizance, but still the orders are issued on their authority. They are styled *Shieng*, which is as much as to say "The Supreme Court", and the palace where they abide is also called *Shieng*. This body forms the highest authority at the court of the Great Khan ....[52]

HOW *the* KHAN'S POSTS *and* RUNNERS
are SPED THROUGH MANY LANDS
and PROVINCES

NOW YOU MUST know that from ... Cambaluc proceed many roads and highways leading to a variety of provinces ... and each road receives the name of the province to which it leads; and it is a very sensible plan. And the messengers of the emperor in travelling from Cambaluc, be the road whichsoever they will, find at every 25 miles of the journey a station which they call a *yamb*,[53] or, as we should say, the "horse-post-house". And at each of those stations ... there is a large and handsome building for them to put up at, in which they find all the rooms furnished with fine beds and all other necessary articles in rich silk, and where they are provided with everything they can want.

At some of these stations, moreover, there shall be posted some 400 horses standing ready for the use of the messengers; at others there shall be 200, according to the requirements, and to what the emperor has established in each case.... Even when the messengers have to pass through a roadless tract where neither house nor hostel exists, still there the station-houses have been established just the same, excepting that the intervals are somewhat greater, and the day's journey is fixed at 35 to 45 miles, instead of 25 to 30. But they are provided with horses and all the other necessaries just like those we have described, so that the emperor's messengers ... find everything ready for them.

... But now I will tell you another thing that I had forgotten, but which ought to be told whilst I am on this subject. You must know that by the Great Khan's orders there has been established between those posthouses, at every interval of three miles, a little fort with some forty houses round about it, in which dwell the people who act as the emperor's foot-runners. Every one of those runners wears a great wide belt set all over with bells, so that as they run the three miles from post to post their bells are heard jingling a long way off. And thus on reaching the post the runner finds another man similarly equipped, and all ready to take his place, who instantly takes over ... and runs his three miles. At the next station he finds his relief ready in like manner; and so the post proceeds, with a change at every three miles. And in this way the emperor, who has an immense number of these runners, receives dispatches with news from places ten days' journey off in one day and night; or, if need be, news from 100 days off in ten days and nights; and that is no small matter! ... The emperor exempts these men from all tribute, and pays them besides.

Moreover, there are also at those stations other men equipped similarly with girdles hung with bells, who are employed for expresses when there is a call for great haste in sending dispatches to any governor of a province, or to give news when any baron has revolted, or in other such emergencies; and these men travel a good 200 or 250 miles in the day, and as much in the night…. They take a horse from those at the station which are standing ready saddled, all fresh and in wind, and mount and go at full speed, as hard as they can ride in fact. And when those at the next post hear the bells they get ready another horse and a man equipped in the same way, and he takes over the letter or whatever it be, and is off full-speed to the third station, where again a fresh horse is found all ready, and so the dispatch speeds along from post to post, always at full gallop, with regular change of horses. And the speed at which they go is marvellous. (By night, however, they cannot go so fast as by day, because they have to be accompanied by footmen with torches, who could not keep up with them at full speed.)[54]

… Now all these numbers of post-horses cost the emperor nothing at all; and I will tell you the how and the why. Every city, or village, or hamlet, that stands near one of those post-stations, has a fixed demand made on it for as many horses as it can supply, and these it must furnish to the post. And in this way are provided all the posts of the cities, as well as the towns and villages round about them; only in uninhabited tracts the horses are furnished at the expense of the emperor himself….

And now I will tell you of the great bounty exercised by the emperor toward his people twice a year.

CHAPTER 27

HOW *the* EMPEROR BESTOWS HELP *on* *his* PEOPLE, WHEN *they are* AFFLICTED *with* DEARTH *or* MURRAIN

NOW YOU MUST know that the emperor sends his messengers over all his lands and kingdoms and provinces, to ascertain from his officers if the people are afflicted by any dearth through unfavourable seasons, or storms or locusts, or other like calamity; and from those who have suffered in this way no taxes are exacted for that year; nay more, he causes them to be supplied with corn of his own for food and seed. Now this is undoubtedly a great bounty on his part. And when winter comes, he causes inquiry to be made as to those who have lost their cattle, whether by murrain or other mishap, and such persons not only go scot free, but get presents of cattle. And thus, as I tell you, the Lord every year helps and fosters the people subject to him.

CHAPTER 28

HOW *the* GREAT KHAN CAUSES TREES
to be PLANTED *by the* HIGHWAYS

THE EMPEROR MOREOVER has taken order that all the highways travelled by his messengers and the people generally should be planted with rows of great trees a few paces apart; and thus these trees are visible a long way off, and no one can miss the way by day

or night. Even the roads through uninhabited tracts are thus planted, and it is the greatest possible solace to travellers. And this is done on all the ways, where it can be of service.[55] (The Great Khan plants these trees all the more readily because his astrologers and diviners tell him that he who plants trees lives long. But where the ground is so sandy and desert that trees will not grow, he causes other landmarks, pillars or stones, to be set up to show the way).

CHAPTER 29

CONCERNING *the* RICE-WINE DRUNK
by the PEOPLE *of* CATHAY

MOST OF THE people of Cathay drink wine of the kind that I shall now describe. It is a liquor which they brew of rice with a quantity of excellent spice, in such fashion that it makes a better drink than any other kind of wine; it is not only good, but clear and pleasing to the eye.[56] And being very hot stuff, it makes one drunk sooner than any other wine.

CHAPTER 30

CONCERNING *the* BLACK STONES *that are* DUG *in* CATHAY, *and are* BURNT *for* FUEL

IT IS A fact that all over the country of Cathay there is a kind of black stones existing in beds in the mountains, which they dig out and burn like firewood. If you supply the fire with them at night, and see that they are well kindled, you will find them still alight in the morning; and they make such capital fuel that no other is used throughout the country. It is true that they have plenty of wood also, but they do not burn it, because those stones burn better and cost less.[57]

(Moreover with that vast number of people, and the number of hot baths that they maintain – for everyone has such a bath at least three times a week, and in winter if possible every day, whilst every nobleman and man of wealth has a private bath for his own use – the wood would not suffice for the purpose.)

CHAPTER 31

HOW *the* GREAT KHAN CAUSED STORES *of* CORN *to be* MADE, *to* HELP *his* PEOPLE WITHAL IN TIME *of* DEARTH

YOU MUST KNOW that when the emperor sees that corn is cheap and abundant, he buys up large quantities, and has it stored in all his provinces in great granaries, where it is so well looked after that it will keep for three or four years.

And this applies, let me tell you, to all kinds of corn, whether wheat, barley, millet, rice, panic, or what not, and when there is any scarcity of a particular kind of corn, he causes that to be issued. And if the price of the corn is at one bezant the measure, he lets them have it at a bezant for four measures, or at whatever price will

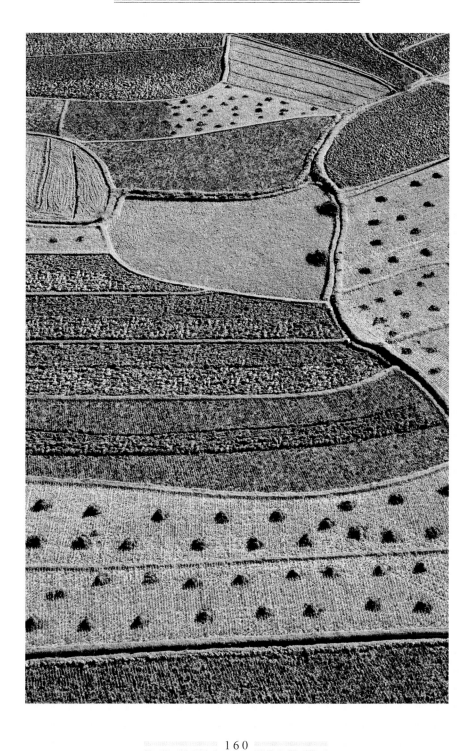

produce general cheapness; and every one can have food in this way. And by this providence of the emperor's, his people can never suffer from dearth. He does the same over his whole empire; causing these supplies to be stored everywhere, according to a calculation of the wants and necessities of the people.

CHAPTER 32

Of the CHARITY of the EMPEROR to the POOR

I HAVE TOLD you how the Great Khan provides for the distribution of necessaries to his people in time of dearth, by making store in time of cheapness. Now I will tell you of his alms and great charity to the poor of his city of Cambaluc.

You see he causes selection to be made of a number of families in the city which are in a state of indigence, and of such families some may consist of six in the house, some of eight, some of ten, more or fewer in each as it may happen to be, but the whole number being very great. And each family he causes annually to be supplied with wheat and other corn sufficient for the whole year. And this he never fails to do every year. Moreover, all those who choose to go to the daily dole at the court receive a great loaf apiece, hot from the baking, and nobody is denied; for so the lord has ordered. And so some 30,000 people go for it every day from year's end to year's end. Now this is a great goodness in the emperor to take pity of his poor people thus! And they benefit so much by it that they worship him as if he were God.

He also provides the poor with clothes. For he lays a tithe upon all wool, silk, hemp and the like, from which clothing can be made; and he has these woven and laid up in a building set apart for the purpose …. You should know that the Tartars, before they were converted to the religion of the idolaters, never practised almsgiving. Indeed, when any poor man begged of them they would tell him, "Go with God's curse, for if He loved you as He loves me, He would have provided for you". But the sages of the idolaters, and especially the *bacsis* mentioned before, told the Great Khan that it was a good work to provide for the poor, and that his idols would be greatly pleased if he did so. And since then he has taken to do for the poor so much as you have heard.

CHAPTER 33

CONCERNING *the* ASTROLOGERS
in the CITY *of* CAMBALUC

THERE ARE IN the city of Cambaluc, what with Christians, Muslims and Cathayans, some 5,000 astrologers and soothsayers, whom the Great Khan provides with annual maintenance and clothing, just as he provides the poor ..., and they are constantly exercising their art in this city.

They have a kind of astrolabe on which are inscribed the planetary signs, the hours and critical points of the whole year. And every year these Christian, Muslim and Cathayan astrologers ... investigate by means of this ... the course and character of the whole year, according to the indications of each of its moons, in order to discover by the natural course and disposition of the planets, and the other circumstances of the heavens, what shall be the ... weather, and what peculiarities shall be produced by each moon of the year; as, for example, under which moon there shall be ... tempests, under which there shall be disease ... treasons, and so on, according to the indications of each; but always adding that it lies with God to do less or more according to His pleasure. And they write down the results of their examination in certain little pamphlets for the year, which are called *tacuin*, and these are sold for a groat to all who desire to know what is coming....[58]

And if anyone having some great matter in hand, or proposing to make a long journey ..., desires to know what will be the upshot, he goes to one of these astrologers and says: "... see what is the present aspect of the heavens, for I am going away on such and such a business." Then the astrologer will reply that the applicant must also tell the year, month and hour of his birth; and when he has got that information he will see how the horoscope of his nativity combines with the indications of the time when the question is put, and then he predicts the result … according to the aspect of the heavens.

You must know, too, that the Tartars reckon their years by twelves; the sign of the first year being the Lion, of the second the Ox, of the third the Dragon, of the fourth the Dog, and so forth up to the twelfth;[59] so that when one is asked the year of his birth he answers that it was in the Year of the Lion (let us say), on such a day or night, at such an hour, and such a moment. And the father of a child always takes care to write these particulars down in a book. When the twelve yearly symbols have been gone through, then they come back to the first, and go through with them again in the same succession.

CHAPTER 34

CONCERNING *the* RELIGION *of the* CATHAYANS;[60]
THEIR VIEWS *as to the* SOUL;
and their CUSTOMS

AS WE HAVE said before, these people are idolaters, and as regards their gods, each has a tablet fixed … on the wall of his chamber, on which is inscribed a name which represents the heavenly god; and before this they pay daily worship, offering incense, raising their hands aloft, praying to Him to grant them health of mind and body; but of Him they ask nothing else. And below on the ground there is … Natagai, the god of things terrestrial. To him they give a wife and children, and they worship him in the same manner, with incense, and lifting up of hands; and of him they ask seasonable weather, and the fruits of the earth, children, and so forth.

They believe that as soon as a man dies, his soul enters into another body, going from a good to a better, or from a bad to a worse, according to whether he has conducted himself well or ill. That is to say, a poor man, if he has passed through life good and sober, shall be born again of a gentlewoman, and shall be a gentleman; and on a second occasion shall be born of a princess and shall be a prince, and so on, always rising, until he be absorbed into the deity. But if he has borne himself ill, he who was the son of a gentleman shall be reborn as the son of a boor, and from a boor shall become a dog, always going down lower and lower.

The people have an ornate style of speech; they salute each other with a cheerful countenance, and with great politeness; they behave like gentlemen, and eat with great propriety. They show great respect to their parents; and should there be any son who offends his parents, or fails to minister to their necessities, there is a public office which has no other charge but that of punishing unnatural children, who are proved to have acted with ingratitude toward their parents.[61] Criminals of sundry kinds who have been imprisoned, are released at a time fixed by the Great Khan (which occurs every three years), but on leaving prison they are branded on one cheek so that they may be recognized.

… I must not omit to tell you of the orderly way in which the *khan*'s barons and others conduct themselves when coming into his presence. In the first place, within a half mile of the place where he is, out of reverence for his exalted majesty, everybody preserves a mood of the greatest meekness and quiet, so that no noise of shrill voices or loud talk shall be heard.… Also, they all have certain handsome buskins[62] of white leather, which they carry with them, and, when summoned by the sovereign, on arriving at the entrance to the hall, they put on these white buskins so that they do not foul the fine carpets of silk and gold and divers colours.

JOURNEY

TO THE WEST AND

SOUTHWEST

OF

CATHAY

CHAPTER 35

HERE BEGINS *the* DESCRIPTION *of*
the INTERIOR *of* CATHAY; *and* FIRST
of the RIVER PULISANGHIN

NOW YOU MUST know that the emperor sent the aforesaid Messer Marco Polo, who is the author of this whole story, on business of his into the western provinces. On that occasion he travelled from Cambaluc a good four months' journey toward the west.[1] And so now I will tell you all that he saw on his travels as he went and returned.

When you leave the city of Cambaluc and have ridden 10 miles, you come to a very large river which is called Pulisanghin, and flows into the ocean, so that merchants with their merchandise ascend it from the sea. Over this river there is a very fine stone bridge, so fine indeed that it has very few equals. The fashion of it is this: it is 300 paces in length, and it must have a good eight paces of width, for ten mounted men can ride across it abreast. It has twenty-four arches and as many watermills, and 'tis all of very fine marble, well built and firmly founded. Along the top of the bridge there is on either side a parapet of marble slabs and columns, made in this way. At the beginning of the bridge there is a marble column, and under it a marble lion, so that the column stands upon the lion's loins, whilst on the top of the column there is a second marble lion, both being of great size and beautifully executed sculpture. At the distance of a pace from this column there is another precisely the same, also with its two lions, and the space between them is closed with slabs of grey marble to prevent people from falling over into the water....[2]

CHAPTER 36

ACCOUNT of the CITY of JUJU

WHEN YOU LEAVE the bridge, and ride toward the west, finding all the way excellent hostelries for travellers, with fine vineyards, fields, and gardens, and springs of water, you come after 30 miles to a fine large city called Juju, where there are many abbeys of idolaters, and the people live by trade and manufactures. They weave cloths of silk and gold, and very fine taffetas. Here too there are many hostelries for travellers.[3]

After riding a mile beyond this city you find two roads, one of which goes west and the other southeast. The westerly road is that through Cathay, and the southeasterly one goes toward the province of Manzi.[4] Taking the westerly one through Cathay, and travelling by it for ten days, you find a constant succession of cities and boroughs, with numerous thriving villages, all abounding with trade and manufactures, besides the fine fields and vineyards and dwellings of civilized people; but nothing occurs worthy of special mention; and so I will only speak of a kingdom called Taianfu.

CHAPTER 37

The KINGDOM of TAIANFU

AFTER RIDING THEN those ten days from the city of Juju, you find yourself in a kingdom called Taianfu, and the city at which you arrive, which is the capital, is also called Taianfu, a very great and fine city. (But at the end of five days' journey out of those ten, they say there is a city unusually large and handsome called Acbaluc, whereat terminate in this direction the hunting preserves of the emperor, within which no one dares to sport except the emperor and his family, and those who are on the books of the grand falconer. Beyond this limit anyone is at liberty to sport, if he be a gentleman. The Great Khan, however, scarcely ever went hunting in this direction, and hence the game, particularly the hares, had increased and multiplied to such an extent that all the crops of the province were destroyed. The Great Khan being informed of this, proceeded thither with all his court and the game that was taken was past counting.[5])

Taianfu[6] is a place of great trade and great industry, for here they manufacture a large quantity of the … equipment for the army of the emperor. There grow here many excellent vines, supplying plenty of wine; and in all Cathay this is the only place where wine is produced. It is carried hence all over the country. There is also a great deal of silk here, for the people have great quantities of mulberry trees and silkworms.

From this city of Taianfu you ride westward again for seven days, through fine districts with plenty of towns and boroughs, all enjoying much trade and practising various kinds of industry. Out of these districts go forth not a few great merchants, who travel to India and other foreign regions, buying and selling and getting gain. After those seven days' journey you arrive at a city called Pianfu, a large

and important place, with a number of traders living by commerce and industry. It is a place too where silk is largely produced.[7]

So we will leave it and tell you of a great city called Cachanfu. But stay – first let us tell you about the noble castle called Caichu.

CHAPTER 38

CONCERNING *the* CASTLE *of* CAICHU, *the* GOLDEN KING *and* PRESTER JOHN

ON LEAVING PIANFU you ride two days westward, and come to the noble castle of Caichu, which was built in time past by a king ... whom they used to call the Golden King, and who had there a ... beautiful palace. There is a great hall of this palace, in which are portrayed all the ancient kings of the country, done in gold and other beautiful colours, and a very fine sight they make. Each king in succession as he reigned added to those pictures.[8]

This Golden King was a great and potent prince, and during his stay at this place there used to be in his service none but beautiful girls, of whom he had a great number in his court ... in attendance on the king for everything pertaining to his convenience or pleasure.[9]

Now I will tell you a pretty passage that befell between the Golden King and Prester John, as it was related by the people of the castle. It came to pass, as they told the tale, that this Golden King was at war with Prester John. And the king held a position so strong that Prester John was not able to get at him; wherefore he was in great wrath. So seventeen gallants belonging to Prester John's court came to him in a body, and said that they were ready to bring him the Golden King alive. His answer was, that he desired nothing better, and would be much bounden to them if they would do so.

So when they had taken leave of their lord and master Prester John, they set off together, this goodly company ..., and went to the Golden King ... saying that they had come from foreign parts to enter his service. And he answered by telling them that ... he was glad to have their service, never imagining that they had any ill intent. And so these mischievous squires ... served him so well that he grew to love them dearly. And when they had abode with that king nearly two years ... they one day accompanied the king on a pleasure party when he had very few else along with him: for in those gallants the king had perfect trust, and thus kept them immediately about his person. So after they had crossed a certain river that is about a mile from the castle, and saw that they were alone with the king, they said one to another that now was the time to achieve that they had come for. Then they all incontinently drew, and told the king that he must go with them and make no resistance, or they would slay him. The king at this was in alarm and great astonishment, and said: "... and whither would you have me go?" They answered, and said: "You shall come with us, to Prester John our Lord."

CHAPTER 39

How PRESTER JOHN TREATED *the* GOLDEN KING *his* PRISONER

AND ON THIS the Golden King was so sorely grieved that he was like to die. And he said to them: "... for God's sake have pity and compassion upon me. You know well what kindly entertainment you have had in my house; and now you would deliver me into the hands of my enemy! If you do what you say, you will do a ... right villainous, deed." But they answered only that so it must be, and away they had him to ... their lord.

And when Prester John beheld the king he was right glad, and greeted him with something like a curse. The king answered not a word. So Prester John ordered him to be ... put to look after cattle, but to be well looked after himself.... This did Prester John of the grudge he bore the king, to heap insult on him, and to show what a nothing he was ....

And when the king had thus kept cattle for two years, Prester John sent for him, and treated him with honour, and clothed him in rich robes, and said to him: "Now sir king, art thou satisfied that thou were in no way a man to stand against me?" "Truly, my good lord, I ... always did know that I was in no way a man to stand against thee." And when he had said this Prester John replied: "I ask no more but henceforth thou shalt be waited on and honourably treated." So he caused horses and harness of war to be given him, with a goodly train, and sent him back to his own country. And after that he remained ever friendly to Prester John, and held fast by him. So now I will say no more of this adventure ... but I will proceed with our subject.

CHAPTER 40

CONCERNING *the* GREAT RIVER CARAMORAN *and the* CITY *of* CACHANFU

WHEN YOU LEAVE the castle, and travel about 20 miles westward, you come to a river called Caramoran,[10] so big that no bridge can

be thrown across it; for it is of immense width and depth, and reaches to the Great Ocean that encircles the universe – I mean the whole earth. On this river there are many cities and walled towns, and many merchants too therein, for much traffic takes place upon the river, there being a great deal of ginger and a great deal of silk produced in the country.[11]

... (On the lands adjoining this river there grow vast quantities of great canes, some of which are a foot or a foot and a half in girth, and these the natives employ for many useful purposes.[12])

After passing the river and travelling two days westward you come to the noble city of Cachanfu, which we have already named. The inhabitants are all idolaters. And I may as well remind you again that all the people of Cathay are idolaters. It is a city of great trade and of work in gold-tissues of many sorts, as well as other kinds of industry....

CHAPTER 41

CONCERNING *the* CITY *of* KENJANFU

AND WHEN YOU leave the city of Cachanfu of which I have spoken, and travel eight days westward, you meet with cities and boroughs abounding in trade and industry, and quantities of beautiful trees, and gardens, and fine plains planted with mulberries, which are the trees on the leaves of which the silkworms do feed.[13] The people are all idolaters. There is also plenty of game of all sorts, both of beasts and birds.

And when you have travelled those eight days' journey, you come to that great city ... called Kenjanfu.[14] A very ... fine city it is, and the capital of the kingdom of Kenjanfu, which in old times was a noble, rich and powerful realm, and had many great and wealthy and able kings.[15] But now the king thereof is a prince called Mangalai, the son of the Great Khan, who has given him this realm, and crowned him king thereof.[16] It is a city of great trade and industry. They have a great abundance of silk, from which they weave cloths of silk and gold of divers kinds, and they also manufacture all sorts of equipments for an army. They have every necessary of man's life very cheap. The city lies toward the west; the people are idolaters; and outside the city is the palace of Prince Mangalai, crowned king, and son of the Great Khan, as I told you before.

This is a fine palace. It stands in a great plain abounding in lakes and streams and springs of water. Round about it is a massive and lofty wall, five miles in compass, well built, and all garnished with battlements. And within this wall is the king's palace, so great ... that no one could imagine a finer one. There are in it many ... splendid halls, and many chambers, all painted and embellished with work in beaten gold. This Mangalai rules his realm with justice and equity, and is much beloved by his people....

So now let us quit this kingdom, and I will tell you of a very mountainous province called Cuncun, which you reach by a road right wearisome to travel.

CHAPTER 42

Concerning the PROVINCE *of* CUNCUN, *which is* RIGHT WEARISOME *to* TRAVEL THROUGH

ON LEAVING THE Palace of Mangalai, you travel westward for three days, finding a succession of cities and boroughs and beautiful plains, inhabited by people who live by trade and industry, and have plenty of silk. At the end of those three days, you reach the great mountains and valleys which belong to the province of Cuncun.[17] There are towns and villages in the land, and the people live by tilling the earth, and by hunting in the great woods; for the region abounds in forests, wherein are many wild beasts, such as lions, bears, lynxes, bucks and roes, and sundry other kinds, so that many are taken by the people of the country, who make a great profit thereof. So this way we travel over mountains and valleys, finding a succession of towns and villages, and many great hostelries for the entertainment of travellers, interspersed among extensive forests.

CHAPTER 43

Concerning the PROVINCE of ACBALEC MANZI

AFTER YOU HAVE travelled those twenty days through the mountains of Cuncun that I have mentioned, then you come to a province called Acbalec Manzi, which is all level country, with plenty of towns and villages, and belongs to the Great Khan. The people are idolaters, and live by trade and industry. I may tell you that in this province, there grows such a great quantity of ginger, that it is carried all over the region of Cathay, and it affords a maintenance to all the people of the province, who get great gain thereby. They have also wheat and rice, and other kinds of corn, in great plenty and cheapness; in fact the country abounds in all useful products. The capital city is called Acbalec Manzi (which signifies "the White City of the Manzi Frontier").[18]

This plain extends for two days' journey, throughout which it is as fine as I have told you, with towns and villages as numerous. After those two days, you again come to great mountains and valleys, and extensive forests, and you continue to travel westward through this kind of country for twenty days, finding ... numerous towns and villages. The people are idolaters, and live by agriculture, by cattle-keeping, and by the chase, for there is much game. And among other kinds, there are the animals that produce the musk, in great numbers.

CHAPTER 44

CONCERNING the PROVINCE of SINDAFU

WHEN YOU HAVE travelled those twenty days westward through the mountains, as I have told you, then you arrive at a plain belonging to a province called Sindafu, which still is on the confines of Manzi, and the capital city of which is (also) called Sindafu. This city was in former days a rich and noble one, and the kings who reigned there

were very great and wealthy. It is a good 20 miles in compass, but it is divided in the way that I shall tell you.

You see the king of this province ... when he found himself drawing near to death ... commanded that the city should be divided into three parts, and that each of his three sons should have one. So each of these three parts is separately walled about, though all three are surrounded by the common wall of the city. Each of the three sons was king, having his own part of the city, and his own share of the kingdom, and each of them in fact was a great and wealthy king. But the Great Khan conquered the kingdom of these three kings, and stripped them of their inheritance.[19]

Through the midst of this great city runs a large river ... a good half mile wide, and very deep withal, and so long that it reaches all the way to the Ocean Sea ... equal to eighty or 100 days' journey. And the name of the river is Kian-suy. The multitude of vessels that navigate this river is so vast, that no one who should read or hear the tale would believe it. The quantities of merchandise also which merchants carry up and down this river are past all belief. In fact, it is so big that it seems to be a sea rather than a river![20]

Let us now speak of a great bridge which crosses this river within the city. This bridge is of stone; it is seven paces in width and half a mile in length (the river being that much in width as I told you); and all along its length on either side there are columns of marble to bear the roof, for the bridge is roofed over from end to end with timber, and that all richly painted. And on this bridge there are houses in which a great deal of trade and industry is carried on. But these houses are all of wood merely, and they are put up in the morning and taken down in the evening. Also there stands upon the bridge the Great Khan's custom-house, where his toll and tax are levied. And I can tell you that the dues taken on this bridge bring to the lord 1,000 pieces of fine gold every day and more. The people are all idolaters.

When you leave this city you travel for five days across a country of plains and valleys, finding plenty of villages and hamlets, and the people of which live by husbandry. There are numbers of wild beasts, lions, and bears, and such like.

I should have mentioned that the people of Sindu[21] itself live by manufactures ...

After travelling those five days' march, you reach a province called Tibet,[22] which has been sadly laid waste; we will now say something of it.

CONCERNING *the* PROVINCE *of* TIBET

AFTER THOSE FIVE days' march that I spoke of, you enter a province which has been sorely ravaged; and this was done in the wars of Mangku Khan.[23] There are indeed towns and villages and hamlets, but all harried and destroyed.[24]

In this region you find quantities of canes, fully three palms in girth and fifteen paces in length, with some three palms' interval between the joints. And let me tell you that merchants and other travellers through that country are wont at nightfall to gather these canes and make fires of them; for as they burn they make such loud reports that the lions and bears and other wild beasts are greatly frightened, and make off as fast as possible; in fact nothing will induce them to come nigh a fire of that sort.[25] So you see the travellers make those fires to protect themselves and their cattle from the wild beasts which have so ... multiplied since the devastation of the country....

You ride for twenty days without finding any inhabited spot, so that travellers are obliged to carry all their provisions with them, and are constantly falling in with those wild beasts which are so numerous and so dangerous. After that you come at length to a tract where there are towns and villages in considerable numbers. The people of those towns have a strange custom in regard to marriage which I will now relate.

No man of that country would on any consideration take as his wife a girl who was a maid; for they say a wife is worth nothing unless she has been used to consort with men. And their custom is this, that when travellers come that way, the old women ... take their unmarried daughters, or other girls related to them, and go to the strangers who are passing, and make over the young women to whomsoever will accept them; and the travellers take them accordingly and do their pleasure; after which the girls are restored to the old women who brought them, for they are not allowed to follow the strangers away from their home. In this manner people travelling that way, when they reach a village or hamlet or other inhabited place, shall find perhaps twenty or thirty girls at their disposal. And if the travellers lodge with those people they shall have as many young women as they could wish coming to court them! You must know too that the traveller is expected to give the girl who has been with him a ring or some other trifle, something in fact that she can show as a lover's token when she comes to be married. And it is for this in truth and for this alone that they follow that custom; for every girl is expected to obtain at least twenty such tokens in the way I have described before she can be married. And those who have most tokens, and so can show they have been most run after, are in

the highest esteem, and most sought in marriage, because they say the charms of such a one are greatest. But after marriage these people hold their wives very dear, and would consider it a great villainy for a man to meddle with another's wife .... Now I have related to you this marriage custom as a good story to tell, and to show what a fine country that is for young fellows to go to!

The people are idolaters and an evil generation, holding it no sin to rob and maltreat: in fact, they are the greatest brigands on earth. They live by the chase, as well as on their cattle and the fruits of the earth.

I should tell you also that in this country there are many of the animals that produce musk, which are called in the Tartar language *gudderi*. Those rascals have great numbers of large and fine dogs, which are of great service in catching the musk-beasts, and so they procure a great abundance of musk. They have none of the Great Khan's paper money, but use salt instead of money. They are very poorly clad, for their clothes are only of the skins of beasts, and of canvas, and of buckram. They have a language of their own, and they are called Tibet. And this country of Tibet forms a very great province, of which I will give you a brief account.

CHAPTER 46

FURTHER DISCOURSE CONCERNING TIBET

THIS PROVINCE, CALLED Tibet, is of very great extent. The people, as I have told you, have a language of their own, and they are idolaters, and they border on Manzi and sundry other regions. Moreover, they are very great thieves.

The country is, in fact, so great that it embraces eight kingdoms, and a vast number of cities and villages. It contains in several quarters rivers and lakes, in which gold-dust is found in great abundance. Cinnamon also grows there in great plenty. Coral is in great demand in this country and fetches a high price, for they delight to hang it round the necks of their women and of their idols. They have also in this country plenty of fine woollens and other stuffs, and many kinds of spices are produced there which are never seen in our country.

Among this people, too, you find the best enchanters and astrologers that exist in all that quarter of the world; they perform such extraordinary marvels and sorceries by diabolic art that it astounds one to see or even hear of them. So I will relate none of them in this book ... people would be amazed if they heard them, but it would serve no good purpose.

These people of Tibet are an ill-conditioned race. They have mastiff dogs as big as donkeys, which are capital at seizing wild beasts (and in particular the wild oxen which are called *beyamini*, very great and fierce animals).[26] They have also sundry other kinds of sporting

dogs, and excellent lanner falcons (and sakers), swift in flight and well-trained, which are got in the mountains ....

Now I have told you in brief all that is to be said about Tibet, and so we will leave it, and tell you about another province that is called Caindu.

As regards Tibet, however, you should understand that it is subject to the Great Khan. So, likewise, all the other kingdoms, regions and provinces which are described in this book are subject to the Great Khan; nay, even those other kingdoms, regions, and provinces of which I had occasion to speak at the beginning of the book as belonging to the son of Arghun, the lord of the Levant, are also subject to the emperor; for the former holds his dominion of the *khan*, and is his liegeman and kinsman of the blood imperial. So you must know that from this province forward all the provinces mentioned in our book are subject to the Great Khan; and even if this be not specially mentioned, you must understand that it is so.

CHAPTER 47

CONCERNING *the* PROVINCE *of* CAINDU

CAINDU IS A province lying toward the west and there is only one king in it. The people are idolaters, subject to the Great Khan, and they have plenty of towns and villages. (The chief city is also called Caindu, and stands at the upper end of the province.) There is a lake here in which are found pearls. But the Great Khan will not allow them to be fished, for if people were to take as many as they could find there, the supply would be so vast that pearls would lose their value, and come to be worth nothing. Only when it is his pleasure they take from the lake so many as he may desire; but anyone attempting to take them on his own account would be ... put to death.

There is also a mountain in this country wherein they find a kind of stone called turquoise, in great abundance; and it is a very beautiful stone. These also the emperor does not allow to be extracted without his special order.

I must tell you of a custom that they have in this country regarding their women. No man considers himself wronged if a foreigner, or any other man, dishonour his wife, or daughter, or sister, or any woman of his family, but on the contrary he deems such intercourse a piece of good fortune. And they say that it brings the favour of their gods and idols, and great increase of temporal prosperity. For this reason they bestow their wives on foreigners and other people .... And such is the custom over all that province.[27]

The money matters of the people are conducted in this way. They have gold in rods which they weigh, and they reckon its value by its weight in *saggi*, but they have no coined money. Their small change again is made in this way. They have salt which they boil and set in a mould (flat below and round above),[28] and every piece from the mould weighs about half a pound. Now, eighty moulds of this salt are worth one *saggio* of fine gold, which is a weight so called. So this salt serves them for small change.

The musk animals are very abundant in that country, and thus of musk also they have great store. They have likewise plenty of fish which they catch in the lake in which the pearls are produced. Wild animals, such as lions, bears, wolves, stags, bucks and roes, exist in great numbers; and there are also vast quantities of fowl of every kind. Wine of the vine they have none, but they make a wine of wheat and rice and sundry good spices, and very good drink it is.[29] There grows also in this country a quantity of clove. The tree that bears it is a small one, with leaves like laurel but longer and narrower, and with a small white flower like the clove.[30] They have also ginger and cinnamon in great plenty, besides other spices which never reach our countries, so we need say nothing about them.

Now we may leave this province, as we have told you all about it. But let me tell you first of this same country of Caindu that you ride through it ten days, constantly meeting with towns and villages, with people of the same description that I have mentioned. After riding those ten days you come to a river called Brius,[31] which terminates the province of Caindu. In this river is found much gold-dust, and there is also much cinnamon on its banks. It flows to the Ocean Sea.

CHAPTER 48

CONCERNING *the* PROVINCE *of* CARAJAN

WHEN YOU HAVE passed that river you enter on the province of Carajan, which is so large that it includes seven kingdoms. It lies toward the west; the people are idolaters, and they are subject to the Great Khan. A son of his, however, is there as king of the country, by name Essentimur; a very great and rich and powerful prince; and he well and justly rules his dominion, for he is a wise man, and a valiant.

After leaving the river that I spoke of, you go five days' journey toward the west, meeting with numerous towns and villages. The country is one in which excellent horses are bred, and the people live by cattle and agriculture. They have a language of their own which is hard to understand. At the end of those five days' journey you come to the capital, which is called Yachi, a very great and noble city, in which are numerous merchants and craftsmen.[32]

The people are of sundry kinds, for there are not only Muslims and idolaters, but also a few Nestorian Christians.[33] They have wheat and rice in plenty. Howbeit they never eat wheaten bread, because in that country it is unwholesome. Rice they eat, and make of it sundry messes, besides a kind of drink which ... makes a man drunk just as wine does.

Their money is such as I will tell you. They use for the purpose certain white porcelain shells that are found in the sea, such as are sometimes put on dogs' collars; and eighty of these porcelain shells pass for a single weight of silver, equivalent to two Venice groats – that is, twenty-four *piccoli*. Also eight such weights of silver count equal to one such weight of gold.[34]

They have brine-wells in this country from which they make salt, and all the people of those parts make a living by this salt. The king, too, I can assure you, gets a great revenue from this salt.

There is a lake in this country of a good 100 miles in compass, in which are found great quantities of the best fish in the world; fish of great size, and of all sorts.

They reckon it no matter for a man to have intimacy with another's wife, provided the woman be willing.

Let me tell you also that the people of that country eat their meat raw, whether it be of mutton, beef, buffalo, poultry, or any other kind. Thus the poor people will go to the shambles,[35] and take the raw liver as it comes from the carcase and cut it small, and put it in a sauce of garlic and spices, and so eat it; and other meat in like manner, raw, just as we eat meat that is dressed.

CHAPTER 49

CONCERNING *a* FURTHER PART
of the PROVINCE *of* CARAJAN

AFTER LEAVING THAT city of Yachi ... and travelling ten days toward the west, you come to another capital city which is still in the province of Carajan, and is itself called Carajan.[36] The people are idolaters and subject to the Great Khan; and the king is Cogachin, who is a son of the Great Khan.

In this country gold-dust is found in great quantities; that is to say in the rivers and lakes, whilst in the mountains gold is also found in pieces of larger size. Gold is indeed so abundant that they give one *saggio* of gold for only six of the same weight in silver. And for small change they use porcelain shells as I mentioned before. These are not found in the country, however, but are brought from India.

In this province are found serpents of such vast size as to strike fear into those who see them, and so hideous that the very account of them must excite the wonder of those to hear it. I will tell you how long and big they are.

You may be assured that some of them are ten paces in length; some are more and some less. And in bulk they are equal to a great cask, for the bigger ones are about ten palms in girth. They have

two forelegs near the head, but for a foot nothing but a claw like the claw of a hawk or that of a lion. The head is very big, and the eyes are bigger than a great loaf of bread. The mouth is large enough to swallow a man whole, and is garnished with great (pointed) teeth. And in short they are so fierce-looking and so hideously ugly, that every man and beast must stand in fear and trembling of them. There are also smaller ones, such as of eight paces long, and of five, and of one pace only.

The way in which they are caught is this. You must know that by day they live underground because of the great heat, and in the night they go out to feed, and devour every animal they can catch. They go also to drink at the rivers and lakes and springs. And their weight is so great that when they travel in search of food or drink, as they do by night, the tail makes a great furrow in the soil as if a full ton of liquor had been dragged along. Now the huntsmen who go after them take them by a certain gyn[37] which they set in the track over which the serpent has past, knowing that the beast will come back the same way. They plant a stake deep in the ground and fix on the head of this a sharp blade of steel made like a razor or a lance-point, and then they cover the whole with sand so that the serpent cannot see it.... On coming to the spot the beast strikes against the iron blade with such force that it enters his breast and ... he dies on the spot (and the crows on seeing the brute dead begin to caw, and then the huntsmen ... come in search of him).

This then is the way these beasts are taken. Those who take them proceed to extract the gall from the inside, and this sells at a great price; for you must know it furnishes the material for a most precious medicine....

They also sell the flesh of this serpent, for it is excellent eating, and the people are very fond of it. And when these serpents are very hungry, sometimes they will seek out the lairs of lions or bears or other large wild beasts, and devour their cubs, without the sire and dam being able to prevent it. Indeed if they catch the big ones themselves they devour them too; they can make no resistance.[38]

In this province also are bred large and excellent horses which are taken to India for sale. And you must know that the people dock

two or three joints of the tail from their horses, to prevent them from
flipping their riders, a thing which they consider very unseemly.
They ride long like Frenchmen, and wear armour of boiled leather,
and carry spears and shields and arblasts ....

   I will tell you of a wicked thing they used to do before the Great
Khan conquered them. If it chanced that a man of fine person or
noble birth, or some other quality that recommended him, came to
lodge with those people, then they would murder him by poison,
or otherwise. And this they did, not for the sake of plunder, but
because they believed that in this way the goodly favour and wisdom
and repute of the murdered man would cleave to the house where
he was slain. And in this manner many were murdered before the
country was conquered by the Great Khan. But since his conquest,
some thirty-five years ago, these crimes and this evil practice have
prevailed no more; and this through dread of the Great Khan who
will not permit such things.

CHAPTER 50

CONCERNING *the* PROVINCE *of* ZARDANDAN

WHEN YOU HAVE left Carajan and have travelled five days
westward, you find a province called Zardandan. The people are
idolaters and subject to the Great Khan. The capital city is called
Vochan.[39]

   The people of this country all have their teeth gilt; or rather
every man covers his teeth with a sort of golden case made to fit
them, both the upper teeth and the lower. The men do this, but not
the women.[40] (The men also are wont to gird their arms and legs with
bands or fillets pricked in black, and it is done thus; they take five
needles joined together, and with these they prick the flesh till the
blood comes, and then they rub in a certain black colouring stuff,
and this is perfectly indelible. It is considered a piece of elegance
and the sign of gentility to have this black band.) The men are all
gentlemen in their fashion, and do nothing but go to the wars, or go

hunting and hawking. The ladies do all the business, aided by the slaves who have been taken in war.

And when one of their wives has been delivered of a child, the infant is washed and swathed, and then the woman gets up and goes about her household affairs, whilst the husband takes to bed with the child by his side, and so keeps his bed for forty days; and all the kith and kin come to visit him and keep up a great festivity. They do this because, say they, the woman has had a hard bout of it, and 'tis but fair the man should have his share of suffering.

They eat all kinds of meat, both raw and cooked, and they eat rice with their cooked meat as their fashion is. Their drink is wine made of rice and spices, and excellent it is. Their money is gold, and for small change they use pig-shells. And I can tell you they give one weight of gold for only five of silver; for there is no silver-mine within five months' journey. And this induces merchants to go thither carrying a large supply of silver to change among that people. And as they have only five weights of silver to give for one

of fine gold, they make immense profits by their exchange business in that country.

These people have neither idols nor churches, but worship the progenitor of their family .... They have no letters or writing; and 'tis no wonder, for the country is wild and hard of access, full of great woods and mountains which 'tis impossible to pass, the air in summer is so impure and bad; and any foreigners attempting it would die for certain. When these people have any business transactions with one another, they take a piece of stick, round or square, and split it, each taking half. And on either half they cut two or three notches. And when the account is settled the debtor receives back the other half of the stick from the creditor.

And let me tell you that in all those three provinces that I have been speaking of, to wit Carajan, Vochan and Yachi, there is never a leech. But when anyone is ill they send for their magicians, that is to say the devil-conjurors and those who are the keepers of the idols. When these are come the sick man tells what ails him, and then the conjurors incontinently begin playing on their instruments and singing and dancing; and the conjurors dance to such a pitch that at last one of them shall fall to the ground lifeless, like a dead man. And then the devil entereth into his body. And when his comrades see him in this plight they begin to put questions to him about the sick man's ailment. And he will reply: "Such or such a spirit has been meddling with the man,[41] for that he has angered the spirit ..." Then they say: "We pray thee to pardon him, and to take of his blood or of his goods what thou wilt in consideration of thus restoring him to health." And when they have so prayed, the malignant spirit that is in the body of the prostrate man will (mayhap) answer ... And then the kinsfolk of the sick man go and procure all that has been commanded, and do as has been bidden, and the conjuror who had uttered all that gets on his legs again.

... And when all that the spirit has commanded has been done with great ceremony, then it shall be announced that the man is pardoned and shall be speedily cured. So when they at length receive such a reply, they announce that it is all made up with the spirit, and that he is propitiated, and they fall to eating and drinking with great joy and mirth, and he who had been lying lifeless on the ground gets up and takes his share. So when they have all eaten and drunken, every man departs home. And presently the sick man gets sound and well.

Now that I have told you of the customs and naughty ways of that people, we will have done talking of them and their province, and I will tell you about others, all in regular order and succession.

CHAPTER 51

WHEREIN *is* RELATED *how the* KING *of* MIEN *and* BANGALA VOWED VENGEANCE *against the* GREAT KHAN

BUT I WAS forgetting to tell you of a famous battle that was fought in the kingdom of Vochan in the province of Zardandan, and that ought not to be omitted from our book. So we will relate all the particulars.

You see, in the year of Christ 1272[42] the Great Khan sent a large force into the kingdoms of Carajan and Vochan, to protect them from the ravages of ill-disposed people; and this was before he had sent any of his sons to rule the country, as he did afterwards when he made Essentimur king there, the son of a son of his who was deceased.

Now there was a certain king called the king of Mien and of Bangala, who was a very powerful prince, with much territory and treasure and people; and he was not as yet subject to the Great Khan, though it was not long after that the latter conquered him and took from him both the kingdoms that I have named.[43] And it came to pass that when this king heard that the host of the Great Khan was at Vochan, he said to himself that it behoved him to go against them with so great a force as should insure his cutting off the whole of them, insomuch that the Great Khan would be very sorry ever to send an army again thither ....

So this king prepared a great force and munitions of war; and he had, let me tell you, 2,000 great elephants, on each of which was set a tower of timber, well framed and strong, and carrying from twelve to sixteen well-armed fighting men.[44] And besides these, he had of horsemen and of footmen a good 60,000 men. In short, he equipped a fine force ... a host capable of doing great things.

And what shall I tell you ? When the king had completed these great preparations to fight the Tartars, he tarried not, but straightaway marched against them. And after advancing without meeting with anything worth mentioning, they arrived within three days of the Great Khan's host, which was then at Vochan in the territory of Zardandan, of which I have already spoken. So there the king pitched his camp, and halted to refresh his army.

CHAPTER 52

OF *the* BATTLE *that was* FOUGHT *by the* GREAT KHAN'S HOST *and his* SENESCHAL *against the* KING *of* MIEN

AND WHEN THE captain of the Tartar host had certain news that the king aforesaid was coming against him with so great a force, he waxed uneasy, seeing that he had with him but 12,000 horsemen. Nonetheless he was a most valiant and able soldier, of great experience in arms and an excellent captain; and his name was Nescradin. His troops too were very good, and he gave them very particular orders how to act, and took every measure for his own defence and that of his army. And why should I make a long story of it? The whole force of the Tartars, consisting of 12,000 well-mounted horsemen, advanced to receive the enemy in the plain of Vochan, and there they waited to give them battle. And this they did through the good judgment of the excellent captain who led them; for hard by that plain was a great wood, thick with trees. ...

After the king of Mien had halted long enough to refresh his troops, he resumed his march, and came to the plain of Vochan, where the Tartars were already in order of battle. And when the king's army ... was within a mile of the enemy, he caused all the castles that were on the elephants to be ordered for battle, and the fighting-men to take up their posts on them, and he arrayed his horse and his foot with all skill, like a wise king as he was. And when he had completed all his arrangements he began to advance .... The Tartars ... came on likewise with good order and discipline to meet them. And when they were near ... the horses of the Tartars took such fright at the sight of the elephants that they could not be got to face the foe, but always swerved and turned back; whilst all the time the king and his forces, and all his elephants, continued to advance upon them.

And when the Tartars perceived how the case stood, they were in great wrath ... for well enough they saw that unless they could get their horses to advance, all would be lost. But their captain acted

like a wise leader who had considered everything beforehand. He ...
gave orders that every man should dismount and tie his horse to the
trees of the forest that stood hard by, and that then they should take
to their bows .... They did as he bade them, and plied their bows
stoutly, shooting so many shafts at the advancing elephants that in a
short space they had wounded or slain the greater part of them ....
The enemy also shot at the Tartars, but the Tartars had the better
weapons, and were the better archers to boot.

And what shall I tell you? Understand that when the elephants
felt the smart of those arrows that pelted them like rain, they turned
tail and fled, and nothing on earth would have induced them to turn
and face the Tartars. So off they sped with such a noise and uproar
that you would have thought the world was coming to an end! And
then too they plunged into the wood and rushed this way and that,
dashing their castles against the trees, bursting their harness and
smashing and destroying everything that was on them.

So when the Tartars saw that the elephants had turned tail ...
they got to horse at once and charged the enemy. And then the battle
began to rage furiously with sword and mace. ... The king's troops
were far more in number than the Tartars, but they were not of such
metal, nor so inured to war; otherwise the Tartars who were so few
in number could never have stood against them. ... Great was the
medley, and dire and parlous was the fight that was fought on both
sides; but the Tartars had the best of it.[45]

In an ill hour indeed, for the king and his people, was that battle
begun, so many of them were slain therein. And when they had
continued fighting till midday the king's troops could stand against
the Tartars no longer; but felt that they were defeated, and turned
and fled. And when the Tartars saw them routed they gave chase,
and hacked and slew so mercilessly that it was a piteous sight to see.
But after pursuing a while they gave up, and returned to the wood to
catch the elephants that had run away, and to manage this they had
to cut down great trees to bar their passage. Even then they would
not have been able to take them without the help of the king's own
men who had been taken, and who knew better how to deal with the
beasts than the Tartars did. The elephant is an animal that has more

wit than any other; but in this way at last they were caught, more than 200 of them. And it was from this time forth that the Great Khan began to keep numbers of elephants.

So thus it was that the king aforesaid was defeated by the sagacity and superior skill of the Tartars as you have heard.

CHAPTER 53

Of the GREAT DESCENT that LEADS TOWARD the KINGDOM of MIEN

AFTER LEAVING THE province of which I have been speaking you come to a great descent. In fact you ride for two days and a half continually downhill. On all this descent there is nothing worthy of mention except only that there is a large place there where ... all the people of the country round come thither on fixed days, three times a week, and hold a market there. ...

After you have ridden those two days and a half downhill, you find yourself in a province toward the south which is pretty near to India, and this province is called Amien [Mien]. You travel therein for fifteen days through a very unfrequented country, and through great woods abounding in elephants and unicorns and numbers of other wild beasts. There are no dwellings and no people, so we need say no more of this wild country, for in sooth there is nothing to tell. But I have a story to relate which you shall now hear.[46]

CHAPTER 54

CONCERNING the CITY of MIEN, and the TWO TOWERS that are THEREIN, ONE of GOLD, and the OTHER of SILVER

AND WHEN YOU have travelled those fifteen days through such a difficult country as I have described, in which travellers have to carry provisions for the road because there are no inhabitants, then you arrive at the capital ... of this province of Mien, and it also is called Amien, and is a ... great and noble city. The people are idolaters and have a peculiar language, and are subject to the Great Khan.

And in this city there is a thing so rich and rare that I must tell you about it. You see there was in former days a rich and powerful king in this city, and when he was about to die he commanded that by his tomb they should erect two towers ..., one of gold and the other of silver, in such fashion as I shall tell you. The towers are built of fine stone; and then one of them has been covered with gold a good finger in thickness, so that the tower looks as if it were all of solid gold; and the other is covered with silver in like manner so that it seems to be all of solid silver. Each tower is a good ten paces in height and of breadth in proportion. The upper part of these towers is round, and girt all about with bells.... The king caused these towers to be erected to commemorate his magnificence and for the good of his soul; and really they do form one of the finest sights in the world; so exquisitely finished are they, so splendid and costly. And when they are lighted up by the sun they shine most brilliantly and are visible from a vast distance.

Now you must know that the Great Khan conquered the country in this fashion.

You see at the court of the Great Khan there was a great number of gleemen and jugglers; and he said to them one day that he wanted them to go and conquer the aforesaid province of Mien, and that he would give them a good captain to lead them and ... a body of men-at-arms to help them; and so they set out, and marched until they came to the country and province of Mien. And they did conquer the whole of it! And when they found in the city the two towers of gold and silver ... they ... sent word thereof to the Great Khan, asking what he would have them do with the two towers, seeing what a great quantity of wealth there was upon them. And the Great Khan, being well aware that the king had caused these towers to be made for the good of his soul, and to preserve his memory after his death, said that he would not have them injured, but would have them left precisely as they were. And that was no wonder either, for you must know that no Tartar in the world will ever, if he can help it, lay hand on anything appertaining to the dead.[47]

... Now having told you about the province of Mien, I will tell you about another province which is called Bangala, as you shall hear presently.

CHAPTER 55

CONCERNING *the* PROVINCE *of* BANGALA

BANGALA IS A province toward the south, which up to the year 1290, when the aforesaid Messer Marco Polo was still at the court

of the Great Khan, had not yet been conquered; but his armies had gone thither to make the conquest. You must know that this province has a peculiar language, and that the people are wretched idolaters. They are tolerably close to India. There are numbers of eunuchs there, insomuch that all the barons who keep them get them from that province.[48]

The people have oxen as tall as elephants, but not so big.[49] They live on flesh and milk and rice. They grow cotton, in which they drive a great trade, and also spices such as spikenard, galingale, ginger, sugar, and many other sorts.

And the people of India also come thither in search of the eunuchs that I mentioned, and of slaves, male and female, of which there are great numbers, taken from other provinces with which those of the country are at war; and these eunuchs and slaves are sold to the Indian and other merchants who carry them thence for sale about the world.

There is nothing more to mention about this country, so we will quit it, and I will tell you of another province called Caugigu.

C H A P T E R   5 6

DISCOURSES *on the* PROVINCE *of* CAUGIGU

CAUGIGU IS A province toward the east, which has a king.[50] The people are idolaters, and have a language of their own. They have made their submission to the Great Khan, and send him tribute every year. And let me tell you their king is so given to luxury that he has at least 300 wives ....

They find in this country a good deal of gold, and they also have an abundance of spices. But they are such a long way from the sea that the products are of little value, and thus their price is low. They have elephants in great numbers, and other cattle of sundry kinds, and plenty of game. They live on flesh and milk and rice, and have wine made of rice and good spices. The whole of the people, or nearly so, have their skin marked with the needle in patterns representing lions, dragons, birds, and what not, done in such a way that it can never be obliterated. This work they cause to be wrought over face and neck and chest, arms and hands, and belly, and, in short, the whole body; and they look on it as a token of elegance, so that those who have the largest amount of this embroidery are regarded with the greatest admiration.

C H A P T E R   5 7

CONCERNING *the* PROVINCE *of* ANIN

ANIN IS A province toward the east, the people of which are subject to the Great Khan, and are idolaters. They live by cattle and tillage, and have a peculiar language. The women wear on the legs and arms bracelets of gold and silver .... They have plenty of horses which they sell in great numbers to the Indians .... And they have vast herds of buffaloes and oxen, having excellent pastures for these. They have likewise all the necessaries of life in abundance.[51]

Now you must know that between Anin and Caugigu, which we have left behind us, there is a distance of twenty-five days' journey;[52] and from Caugigu to Bangala, the third province in our rear, is thirty days' journey. We shall now leave Anin and proceed to another province which is eight days' journey further, always going eastward.

CHAPTER 58

CONCERNING *the* PROVINCE *of* COLOMAN

COLOMAN IS A province toward the east, the people of which are idolaters and have a peculiar language, and are subject to the Great Khan. They are a (tall and) very handsome people, though in complexion brown rather than white, and are good soldiers.[53] They have a good many towns, and a vast number of villages, among great mountains, and in strong positions.

When any of them die, the bodies are burnt, and then they take the bones and put them in little chests. These are carried high up the mountains, and placed in great caverns, where they are hung up in such wise that neither man nor beast can come at them.

A good deal of gold is found in the country, and for petty traffic they use porcelain shells such as I have told you of before. All these provinces that I have been speaking of, to wit Bangala and Caugigu and Anin, employ for currency porcelain shells and gold. There are merchants in this country who are very rich and dispose of large quantities of goods. The people live on flesh and rice and milk, and brew their wine from rice and excellent spices.

CHAPTER 59

CONCERNING *the* PROVINCE *of* CUIJU

CUIJU IS A province toward the east.[54] After leaving Coloman you travel along a river for twelve days, meeting with a good number of towns and villages, but nothing worthy of particular mention. After you have travelled those twelve days along the river you come to a great and noble city which is called Fungul.

The people are idolaters and subject to the Great Khan, and live by trade and handicrafts. You must know they manufacture stuffs of the bark of certain trees which form very fine summer clothing.[55] They are good soldiers, and have paper-money. For you must understand that henceforward we are in the countries where the Great Khan's paper-money is current.

The country swarms with lions to that degree that no man can venture to sleep outside his house at night.[56] Moreover, when you travel on that river, and come to a halt at night, unless you keep a good way from the bank the lions will spring on the boat and snatch one of the crew and make off with him and devour him. And but for a certain help that the inhabitants enjoy, no one could venture to travel in that province, because of the multitude of those lions, and because of their strength and ferocity.

But you see they have in this province a large breed of dogs, so fierce and bold that two of them together will attack a lion. So every man who goes on a journey takes with him a couple of those dogs, and when a lion appears they have at him with the greatest

boldness, and the lion turns on them, but can't touch them for they are very deft at eschewing his blows. So they follow him … watching their chance to give him a bite in the rump or in the thigh, or wherever they may. The lion makes no reprisal except now and then to turn fiercely on them, and then indeed were he to catch the dogs it would be all over with them, but they take good care that he shall not. So, to escape the dogs' din, the lion makes off, and gets into the wood, where mayhap he stands at bay against a tree to have his rear protected from their annoyance. And when the travellers see the lion in this plight they take to their bows, for they are capital archers, and shoot their arrows at him till he falls

dead. And 'tis thus that travellers in those parts do deliver themselves from those lions.

They have a good deal of silk and other products which are carried up and down, by the river of which we spoke, into various quarters.[57]

You travel along the river for twelve days more, finding a good many towns all along, and the people always idolaters, and subject to the Great Khan, with paper-money current, and living by trade and handicrafts. There are also plenty of fighting men. And after travelling those twelve days you arrive at the city of Sindafu of which we spoke in this book some time ago.[58]

From Sindafu you set out again and travel some seventy days through the provinces and cities and towns which we have already visited, and all which have been already particularly spoken of in our book. At the end of those seventy days you come to Juju where we were before.[59]

From Juju you set out again and travel four days toward the south, finding many towns and villages. The people are great traders and craftsmen, are all idolaters, and use the paper-money of the Great Khan their sovereign. At the end of those four days you come to the city of Cacanfu belonging to the province of Cathay, and of it I shall now speak.

JOURNEY SOUTHWARD

THROUGH THE

EASTERN PROVINCES

of CATHAY and MANZI

CHAPTER 60

CONCERNING *the* CITIES *of*
CACANFU *and* CHANGLU

CACANFU IS A noble city. The people are idolaters and burn their dead; they have paper-money, and live by trade and handicrafts. For they have plenty of silk from which they weave stuffs of silk and gold. (There are also certain Christians, who have a church.) And the city is at the head of an important territory containing numerous towns and villages. A great river passes through it, on which much merchandise is carried to the city of Cambaluc, for by many channels and canals it is connected therewith.[1]

We will now set forth again, and travel three days toward the south, and then we come to … Changlu. This is another great city belonging to the Great Khan, and to the province of Cathay. The people have paper-money, are idolaters and burn their dead.[2] And you must know they make salt in great quantities at this place; I will tell you how 'tis done.

A kind of earth is found there which is exceedingly salt. This they dig up and pile in great heaps. Upon these heaps they pour water in quantities until it runs out at the bottom; and then they take up this water and boil it well in great iron cauldrons, and as it cools it deposits a fine white salt in very small grains. This salt they then carry about for sale to many neighbouring districts, and get great profit thereby.

There is nothing else worth mentioning, so let us go forward five days' journey, and we shall come to … Chinangli.

CHAPTER 61

CONCERNING *the* CITY *of* CHINANGLI, *and*
that of TADINFU, *and the* REBELLION *of* LIYTAN

CHINANGLI IS A city of Cathay as you go south, and it belongs to the Great Khan; the people are idolaters [and so forth]. There runs through the city a great and wide river, on which a large traffic in silk goods and spices and other costly merchandise passes up and down.

When you travel south from Chinangli for five days, you meet everywhere with fine towns and villages …. But there is nothing particular to mention on the way until you come, at the end of those five days, to Tadinfu.[3]

This, you must know, is a very great city, and in old times was the seat of a great kingdom; but the Great Khan conquered it by force of arms. Nevertheless it is still the noblest city in all those provinces. There are very great merchants here, who trade on a great scale, and the abundance of silk is something marvellous. They have, moreover, most charming gardens abounding with fruit of large size. The city of Tadinfu has also under its rule eleven imperial cities of great importance, all of which enjoy a large and profitable trade, owing to that immense produce of silk.

Now, you must know, that in the year of Christ 1273 the Great Khan had sent a ... baron called Liytan Sangon, with some 80,000 horse, to this province and city, to garrison them. And after the said captain had tarried there a while, he formed a disloyal and traitorous plot ... against the Great Khan. ...[4]

When the Great Khan heard he straightaway dispatched two of his barons, one of whom was called Aguil and the other Mongotay; giving them 100,000 horse and a great force of infantry. But the affair was a serious one, for the barons were met by the rebel Liytan with all those whom he had collected from the province, mustering more than 100,000 horse and a large force of foot. Nevertheless in the battle Liytan and his party were utterly routed, and the two barons whom the emperor had sent won the victory. When the news came to the Great Khan he was well pleased, and ordered that all the chiefs who had rebelled, or excited others to rebel, should be put to a cruel death, but that those of lower rank should receive a pardon. And so it was done. The two barons had all the leaders of the enterprise put to a cruel death, and all those of lower rank were pardoned. And thenceforward they conducted themselves with loyalty toward their lord. Now having told you all about this affair, let us have done with it, and I will tell you of another place that you come to in going south, which is called Sinjumatu.

CHAPTER 62

CONCERNING *the* NOBLE CITY *of* SINJUMATU

ON LEAVING TADINFU you travel three days toward the south, always finding ... noble and populous towns and villages flourishing with trade and manufactures. There is ... everything in profusion.

When you have travelled those three days you come to the noble city of Sinjumatu, a rich and fine place, with great trade and manufactures. The people are idolaters [and so forth], and they have a river which I can assure you brings them great gain, and I will tell you about it.

You see the river in question flows from the south to this city of Sinjumatu. And the people of the city have divided this larger river in two, making one half of it flow east and the other half flow west; that is to say, the one branch flows toward Manzi and the other toward Cathay. And it is a fact that the number of vessels at this city is what no one would believe without seeing them. The quantity of merchandise also which these vessels transport to Manzi and Cathay is something marvellous; and then they return loaded with other merchandise, so that the amount of goods borne to and fro on those two rivers is quite astonishing.[5]

CHAPTER 63

CONCERNING *the* CITIES *of* LINJU *and* PIJU

ON LEAVING THE city of Sinjumatu you travel for eight days toward the south, always coming to great and rich towns and villages flourishing with trade and manufactures. The people are all subjects of the Great Khan [and so forth]. At the end of those eight days you come to the city of Linju, in the province of the same name of which it is the capital. It is a rich and noble city, and the men are good soldiers, though they carry on great trade and manufactures. There is a great abundance of game in both beasts and birds, and all the necessaries of life are in profusion. The place stands on the river of which I told you above. And they have here great numbers of vessels, even greater than those of which I spoke before, and these transport a great amount of costly merchandise.

So, quitting this province and city of Linju, you travel three days more toward the south, constantly finding numbers of rich towns and villages. ...

At the end of those three days you find the city of Piju,[6] a great, rich and noble city, with large trade and manufactures, and a great production of silk. This city stands at the entrance to the province of Manzi, and there reside at it a large number of merchants who dispatch carts from this place loaded with immense quantities of goods to the different towns of Manzi. The city brings in a great revenue to the Great Khan.

CHAPTER 64

CONCERNING *the* CITY *of* SIJU, *and the* GREAT RIVER CARAMORAN

WHEN YOU LEAVE Piju you travel toward the south for two days, through beautiful districts abounding in everything, and in which you find quantities of all kinds of game. At the end of those two days you reach the city of Siju,[7] a great, rich and noble city, flourishing with trade and manufactures. The people are idolaters [and so forth]. They possess extensive and fertile plains producing an abundance of … grain. But there is nothing else to mention, so let us proceed ….

On leaving Siju you ride south for three days, constantly falling in with fine towns and villages and hamlets and farms, with their cultivated lands. There is plenty of wheat and other corn, and of game also …. At the end of those three days you reach the River Caramoran,[8] which flows hither from Prester John's country. It is a great river, and more than a mile in width, and so deep that great ships can navigate it. It abounds in fish, and very big ones too. You must know that in this river there are some 15,000 vessels, all belonging to the Great Khan, and kept to transport his troops to the Indian Isles whenever there may be occasion; for the sea is only one day distant from the place we are speaking of. …

Hither and thither, on either bank of the river, stands a town; the one facing the other. The one is called Coiganju and the other Caiju; the former is a large place, and the latter a little one. And when you pass this river you enter the great province of Manzi.[9]

CHAPTER 65

How the GREAT KHAN CONQUERED *the* PROVINCE *of* MANZI

YOU MUST KNOW that there was a king and sovereign lord of the ... territory of Manzi who was styled Facfur,[10] so great and powerful ... that for ... wealth and number of subjects and extent of dominion, there was hardly a greater in all the earth except the Great Khan himself. But the people of his land were anything rather than warriors; all their delight was in women ... and so it was above all with the king himself, for he thought of nothing else ..., unless it were of charity to the poor.

In all his dominion there were no horses; nor were the people ever inured to battle or arms, or military service of any kind. Yet the province of Manzi is very strong by nature, and all the cities are encompassed by sheets of water of great depth, and more than an arblast-shot in width; so that the country never would have been lost, had the people but been soldiers. But that is just what they were not; so lost it was.[11]

Now it came to pass, in the year of Christ's incarnation 1268 that the Great Khan, the same that now reigneth, dispatched thither a baron of his whose name was Bayan Chincsan, which is as much as to say "Bayan 100-Eyes". And you must know that the king of Manzi had found in his horoscope that he never should lose his kingdom except through a man that had 100 eyes; so he held himself assured in his position, for he could not believe that any man in existence could have 100 eyes. There, however, he deluded himself, in his ignorance of the name of Bayan.[12]

This Bayan had an immense force of horse and foot entrusted to him by the Great Khan, and with these he entered Manzi, and he had also a great number of boats to carry both horse and food when needed. And when he, with all his host, entered the territory of Manzi and arrived at ... Coiganju – whither we now are got, and of which we shall speak presently – he summoned the people thereof to surrender to the Great Khan; but this they flatly refused to do. On this Bayan went on to another city, with the same result, and then still went forward; acting thus because he was aware that the Great Khan was dispatching another great host to follow him up.

What shall I say then? He advanced to five cities in succession, but got possession of none of them; for he did not wish to engage in besieging them and they would not give themselves up. But when he came to the sixth city he took that by storm, and so with a second, and a third, and a fourth, until he had taken twelve cities in succession. And when he had taken all these he advanced straight against the capital city of the kingdom, which was called Kinsay, and which was the residence of the king and queen.

And when the king beheld Bayan coming with all his host, he was in great dismay, as one unused to seeing such sights. So he and a great company of his people got on board 1,000 ships and fled to the islands of the Ocean Sea, whilst the queen who remained behind in the city took all measures in her power for its defence, like a valiant lady.

Now it came to pass that the queen asked what was the name of the captain of the host, and they told her that it was Bayan 100-Eyes. So when she knew that he was styled 100-Eyes, she called to mind how their astrologers had foretold that a man of 100 eyes should strip them of the kingdom. Wherefore she gave herself up to Bayan, and surrendered to him the whole kingdom and all the other cities and fortresses, so that no resistance was made. And this was a goodly conquest, for there was no realm on earth half so wealthy.[13] The amount that the king used to expend was perfectly marvellous; and as an example I will tell you somewhat of his liberal acts.

In those provinces they are wont to expose their new-born babes; I speak of the poor, who have not the means of bringing them up. But the king used to have all those foundlings taken charge of, and had note made of the signs and planets under which each was born, and then put them out to nurse about the country. And when any rich man was childless he would go to the king and obtain from him as many of these children as he desired. … I will tell you another thing this king used to do. If he was taking a ride through the city and chanced to see a house that was very small and poor standing among other houses that were fine and large, he would ask why it was so, and they would tell him it belonged to a poor man who had not the means to enlarge it. Then the king would himself supply the means. ...

... No one could do justice in the telling to the great riches of that country, and to the good disposition of the people. Now that I have told you about the kingdom, I will go back to the queen. You must know that she was conducted to the Great Khan, who gave her an honourable reception, and caused her to be served with all state, like a great lady as she was. But as for the king her husband, he never more did quit the isles of the sea to which he had fled, but died there. So leave we him and his wife and all their concerns, and let us return to our story, and go on regularly with our account of the great province of Manzi and of the manners and customs of its people. And, to begin at the beginning, we must go back to the city of Coiganju, from which we digressed ....

CHAPTER 66

CONCERNING *the* CITY *of* COIGANJU

COIGANJU IS, AS I have told you already, a very large city standing at the entrance to Manzi. ... Owing to its being on the river, many cities send their produce thither to be again thence distributed in every direction. A great amount of salt also is made here, furnishing some forty other cities with that article, and bringing in a large revenue to the Great Khan.

CHAPTER 67

Of the CITIES *of* PAUKIN *and* CAYU

WHEN YOU LEAVE Coiganju you ride southeast for a day along a causeway laid with fine stone .... At the end of the journey you reach the fine city of Paukin.[14] The people are idolaters [and so on]. They live by trade and manufactures and have a great abundance of silk, whereof they weave a great variety of fine stuffs of silk and gold. ...

When you leave Paukin you ride another day to the southeast, and then you arrive at ... Cayu. The people are idolaters [and so forth]. They live by trade and manufactures and have great store of all necessaries, including fish in great abundance. There is also much game, both beast and bird, insomuch that for a Venice groat you can have three good pheasants.

CHAPTER 68

Of the CITIES *of* TIJU, TINJU *and* YANJU

WHEN YOU LEAVE Cayu, you ride another day to the southeast through a constant succession of villages and fields and fine farms until you come to Tiju, which is a city of no great size but abounding in everything. The people are idolaters [and so forth]. There is a great amount of trade, and they have many vessels. And you must know that on your left hand, that is toward the east, and three days' journey distant, is the Ocean Sea. At every place between the sea and the city salt is made in great quantities. And there is a rich and noble city called Tinju, at which there is produced salt enough to supply the whole province, and I can tell you it brings the Great Khan an incredible revenue. ... Let us quit this, however, and go back to Tiju.[15]

Again, leaving Tiju, you ride another day toward the southeast, and at the end of your journey you arrive at the very great and noble city of Yanju, which has twenty-seven other wealthy cities under its administration; so that this Yanju is, you see, a city of great importance.[16] It is the seat of one of the Great Khan's twelve barons, for it has been chosen to be one of the twelve *sings*. The people are idolaters [and so forth]. And Messer Marco Polo himself, of whom this book speaks, did govern this city for three full years, by the order of the Great Khan.[17] The people live by trade and manufactures, for a great amount of harness for knights and men-at-arms is made there.

And in this city and its neighbourhood a large number of troops are stationed by the *khan*'s orders.

There is no more to say about it. So now I will tell you about two great provinces of Manzi which lie toward the west.

CHAPTER 69

CONCERNING *the* CITY *of* NANGHIN

NANGHIN IS A very noble province toward the west.[18] The people are idolaters [and so forth] and live by trade and manufactures. They have silk in great abundance, and they weave many fine tissues of silk and gold. They have all sorts of corn and victuals very cheap, for

the province is a most productive one. Game also is abundant, and lions too are found there. The merchants are great and opulent, and the emperor draws a large revenue from them, in the shape of duties on the goods which they buy and sell.

And now I will tell you of the very noble city of Saianfu, which well deserves a place in our book, for there is a matter of great moment to tell about it.

CHAPTER 70

CONCERNING *the* VERY NOBLE CITY *of* SAIANFU, *and how its* CAPTURE *was* EFFECTED

SAIANFU IS A very great and noble city, and it rules over twelve other large and rich cities, and is itself a seat of great trade and manufacture. The people are idolaters [and so forth]. They have much silk, from which they weave fine silken stuffs; they have also a quantity of game, and in short the city abounds in all that it behoves a noble city to possess.

Now you must know that this city held out against the Great Khan for three years after the rest of Manzi had surrendered. The Great Khan's troops made incessant attempts to take it, but they could not succeed because of the great and deep waters that were round about it, so that they could approach from one side only, which was the north. And I tell you they never would have taken it, but for a circumstance that I am going to relate.

You must know that when the Great Khan's host had lain three years before the city without being able to take it, they were greatly chafed thereat. Then Messer Nicolo Polo and Messer Maffeo and Messer Marco said: "We could find you a way of forcing the city to surrender speedily." Whereupon those of the army replied that they would be right glad to know how that should be. All this talk took place in the presence of the Great Khan. For messengers had been dispatched from the camp to tell him that there was no taking the city by blockade, for it continually received supplies of victual from those sides which they were unable to invest; and the Great Khan had sent back word that take it they must, and find a way how. Then spoke up the two brothers and Messer Marco the son, and said: "Great prince, we have with us among our followers men who are able to construct mangonels which shall cast such great stones that the garrison will never be able to stand them, but will surrender incontinently, as soon as the mangonels or trebuchets shall have shot into the town."

The *khan* bade them with all his heart have such mangonels made as speedily as possible. Now Messer Nicolo and his brother and his son immediately caused timber to be brought .... And they had two men among their followers ... who were masters of that business, and these they directed to construct two or three mangonels capable of casting stones of 300lbs in weight. Accordingly they made three fine mangonels .... And when they were complete and ready for use, the emperor and the others were greatly pleased to see them, and caused several stones to be shot in their presence; whereat they marvelled greatly and ... praised the work. And the *khan* ordered that the engines should be carried to his army ... at Saianfu.[19]

And when the engines were got to the camp they were forthwith set up, to the great admiration of the Tartars. And what shall I tell you? When the engines were set up and put in gear, a stone was shot from each of them into the town. These took effect among the buildings, crashing and smashing through everything with huge din and commotion. And when the townspeople witnessed this new and strange visitation they were so astonished and dismayed that they knew not what to do or say. They took counsel together, but no counsel could be suggested how to escape from these engines, for the thing seemed to them to be done by sorcery. They declared that they were all dead men if they yielded not, so they determined to surrender on such conditions as they could get. Wherefore they straightaway sent word to the commander of the army that they were ready to surrender on the same terms as the other cities of the province had done ....

So the men of the city surrendered, and were received to terms; and this all came about through the exertions of Messer Nicolo, and Messer Maffeo, and Messer Marco; and it was no small matter. For this city and province is one of the best that the Great Khan possesses, and brings him in great revenues.[20]

CONCERNING *the* CITY *of* SINJU
and the GREAT RIVER KIAN

YOU MUST KNOW that when you leave the city of Yanju, after going 15 miles southeast, you come to a city called Sinju,[21] of no great size, but possessing a very great amount of shipping and trade. The people are idolaters [and so forth].

And you must know that this city stands on the greatest river in the world, the name of which is Kian.[22] It is in some places 10 miles wide, in others eight, in others six, and it is more than 100 days' journey in length from one end to the other. This it is that brings so

much trade to the city we are speaking of; for on the waters of that river merchandise is perpetually coming and going, from and to the various parts of the world ... and bringing a great revenue to the Great Khan.

And I assure you this river flows so far and traverses so many countries and cities that in good sooth there pass and re-pass on its waters a great number of vessels, and more wealth and merchandise than on all the rivers and all the seas of Christendom put together! It seems indeed more like a sea than a river. Messer Marco Polo said that he once beheld at that city 15,000 vessels at one time. And you may judge, if this city, of no great size, has such a number, how many must there be altogether, considering that on the banks of this river there are more than sixteen provinces and more than 200 great cities, besides towns and villages, all possessing vessels?

Messer Marco Polo aforesaid tells us that he heard from the officer employed to collect the Great Khan's duties on this river that there passed upstream 200,000 vessels in the year, without counting those that passed down! ...

The vessels which ply on this river are decked. They have but one mast, but ... I can assure you they carry (reckoning by our weight) from 4,000 up to 12,000 cantars each.[23]

Now we will quit this matter and I will tell you of another city called Caiju. But first I must mention a point I had forgotten. You must know that the vessels on this river, in going upstream have to be tracked, for the current is so strong that they could not make head in any other manner. Now the towline, which is some 300 paces in length, is made of nothing but cane. 'Tis in this way: they have those great canes of which I told you before that they are some fifteen paces in length; these they take and split from end to end (into many slender strips), and then they twist these strips together so as to make a rope of any length they please. And the ropes so made are stronger than if they were made of hemp.

There are at many places on this river, hills and rocky eminences on which the idol-monasteries and other edifices are built; and you find on its shores a constant succession of villages and inhabited places.

CHAPTER 72

CONCERNING *the* CITY *of* CAIJU

CAIJU IS A small city toward the southeast. ... It stands upon the river before mentioned.[24] At this place are collected great quantities of corn and rice to be transported to ... Cambaluc for the use of the *khan*'s court; for the grain for the court all comes from this part of the country. You must understand that the emperor has caused a water-communication to be made from this city to Cambaluc, in the shape of a wide and deep channel dug between stream and stream, between lake and lake, forming as it were a great river on which large vessels can ply. And thus there is a communication all the way from ... Caiju to Cambaluc ... so that great vessels with their loads can go the whole way. A land road also exists, for the earth dug from those channels has been thrown up so as to form an embanked road on either side.[25]

Just opposite ... Caiju ... there stands a rocky island on which there is an idol-monastery containing some 200 idolatrous friars, and a vast number of idols. And this abbey holds supremacy over a number of other idol-monasteries, just like an archbishop's see among Christians.

Now we will leave this and cross the river, and I will tell you of a city called Chinghianfu.[26]

CHAPTER 73

Of the CITY *of* CHINGHIANFU

CHINGHIANFU IS A city of Manzi. The people are idolaters [and so forth]. They have plenty of silk, from which they make sundry kinds of stuffs of silk and gold. There are great and wealthy merchants in the place; plenty of game is to be had, and of all kinds of victual. There are in this city two churches of Nestorian Christians, which were established in the year of our Lord 1278; and I will tell you how that happened. You see, in the year just named, the Great Khan sent a baron of his whose name was Mar Sarghis, a Nestorian Christian, to be governor of this city for three years. And during the three years that he abode there he caused these two Christian churches to be built, and since then there they are. But before his time there was no church, neither were there any Christians.

CHAPTER 74

Of the CITY of CHINGINJU and the SLAUGHTER of CERTAIN ALANS THERE

LEAVING THE CITY of Chinghianfu and travelling three days southeast through a constant succession of busy and thriving towns and villages, you arrive at the great and noble city of Chinginju. The people are idolaters [and so forth]. They live by trade and handicrafts, and they have plenty of silk. They have also abundance of game, and of all manner of victuals, for it is a most productive territory.[27] Now I must tell you of an evil deed that was done, once upon a time, by the people of this city, and how dearly they paid for it.

You see, at the time of the conquest of the great province of Manzi, when Bayan was in command, he sent a company of his troops, consisting of a people called Alans, who are Christians, to take this city.[28] They took it accordingly, and when they had made their way in, they lighted upon some good wine. Of this they drank until they were all drunk, and then they lay down and slept like so many swine. So when night fell, the townspeople, seeing that they were all dead-drunk, fell upon them and slew them all; not a man escaped.

And when Bayan heard that the townspeople had thus treacherously slain his men, he sent another admiral of his with a great force, and stormed the city, and put the whole of the inhabitants to the sword; not a man of them escaped death. And thus the whole population of that city was exterminated.

Now we will go on, and I will tell you of ... Suju.

CHAPTER 75

Of the NOBLE CITY *of* SUJU

SUJU IS A very great and noble city.[29] The people are idolaters [and so forth]. They possess silk in great quantities, from which they make gold brocade and other stuffs, and they live by their manufactures and trade.

The city ... has a circuit of some 60 miles; it has merchants of great wealth and an incalculable number of people. Indeed, if the men of this city and of the rest of Manzi had but the spirit of soldiers they would conquer the world; but they are no soldiers at all, only accomplished traders and most skilful craftsmen. There are also in this city many philosophers and leeches, diligent students of nature.

And you must know that in this city there are 6,000 bridges, all of stone, and so lofty that a galley, or even two galleys at once, could pass underneath one of them.[30]

In the mountains belonging to this city, rhubarb and ginger grow in great abundance; insomuch that you may get some 40lbs of excellent fresh ginger for a Venice groat. And the city has sixteen other great trading cities under its rule. In our tongue the name of the city, Suju, signifies "Earth", and that of another near it, of which we shall speak presently, called Kinsay, signifies "Heaven", and these names are given because of the great splendour of the two cities.[31]

Now let us quit Suju, and go on to another which is called Vuju, one day's journey distant; it is a great and fine city, rife with trade and manufactures. But as there is nothing more to say of it we shall go on and I will tell you of another great and noble city called Vughin. The people are idolaters [and so forth], and possess much silk and other merchandise, and they are expert traders and craftsmen. Let us now quit Vughin and tell you of another city called Changan, a great and rich place. The people are idolaters [and so forth] .... They make great quantities of sendal of different kinds, and they have much game in the neighbourhood. There is however nothing more to say about the place, so we shall now proceed.[32]

CHAPTER 76

DESCRIPTION *of the* GREAT CITY *of* KINSAY, *which is the* CAPITAL *of the* WHOLE COUNTRY *of* MANZI

WHEN YOU HAVE left the city of Changan and have travelled for three days through a splendid country, passing a number of towns and villages, you arrive at the most noble city of Kinsay, a name which is as much as to say in our tongue "The City of Heaven", as I told you before.[33]

And since we have got thither I will enter into particulars about its magnificence; and these are well worth the telling, for the city is beyond dispute the finest and the noblest in the world. In this we shall speak according to the written statement which the queen of this realm sent to Bayan, the conqueror of the country, for transmission to the Great Khan, in order that he might be aware of the surpassing grandeur of the city and might be moved to save it from destruction or injury. I will tell you all the truth as it was set down in that document. For truth it was, as the said Messer Marco Polo at a later date was able to witness with his own eyes. And now we shall rehearse those particulars.

First and foremost, then, the document stated the city of Kinsay to be so great that it has 100 miles of compass. And there are in it 12,000 bridges of stone, for the most part so lofty that a great fleet could pass beneath them. And let no man marvel that there are so many bridges, for you see the whole city stands as it were in the water and surrounded by water, so that a great many bridges are required to give free passage about it.[34]

The document aforesaid also went on to state that there were in this city twelve guilds ... and that each guild had 12,000 houses in the occupation of its workmen. Each of these houses contains at least twelve men, whilst some contain twenty and some forty, not that these are all masters, but inclusive of the journeymen who work under the masters. And yet all these craftsmen had full occupation, for many other cities of the kingdom are supplied from this city with what they require.

The document aforesaid also stated that the number and wealth of the merchants, and the amount of goods that passed through their hands, was so enormous that no man could form a just estimate thereof. ... Moreover it was an ordinance laid down by the king that every man should follow his father's business ... no matter if he possessed 100,000 bezants.[35]

Inside the city there is a lake[36] which has a compass of some 30 miles: and all round it are erected beautiful palaces and mansions ... belonging to the nobles of the city. There are also on its shores many abbeys and churches of the idolaters. In the middle of the lake are two islands, on each of which stands a rich, beautiful and spacious edifice, furnished in such style as to seem fit for ... an emperor. And when any one of the citizens desired to hold a marriage feast, or to give any other entertainment, it used to be done at one of these palaces. And everything would be found there ready to order, such as silver plate, trenchers and dishes ... and whatever else was needful. ... the place was open to everyone who desired to give an entertainment. ...

The houses of the city are provided with lofty towers of stone in which articles of value are stored for fear of fire; for most of the houses themselves are of timber, and fires are very frequent in the city.

The people are idolaters; and since they were conquered by the *khan* they use paper-money. ... And you must know they eat every kind of flesh, even that of dogs and other unclean beasts, which nothing would induce a Christian to eat.

Since the Great Khan occupied the city he has ordained that each of the 12,000 bridges[37] should be provided with a guard ... in case of any disturbance, or of any being so rash as to plot treason or insurrection against him. Each guard is provided with a ... timekeeper to enable them to know the hour of the day or night. And so when one hour of the night is past the sentry strikes one ... so that the whole quarter of the city is made aware that one hour of the night is gone. At the second hour he gives two strokes, and so on, keeping always wide awake and on the lookout. In the morning again, from the sunrise, they begin to count anew, and strike one hour as they did in the night, and so on hour after hour.

Part of the watch patrols the quarter, to see if any light or fire is burning after the lawful hours; if they find any they mark the door, and in the morning the owner is summoned before the magistrates, and unless he can plead a good excuse he is punished. Also if they find anyone going about the streets at unlawful hours they arrest him, and in the morning they bring him before the magistrates. Likewise if in the daytime they find any poor cripple unable to work for his livelihood, they take him to one of the hospitals, of which there are many, founded by the ancient kings, and endowed with great revenues. Or if he be capable of work they oblige him to take up some trade. If they see that any house has caught fire they ... give the alarm, and this brings together the watchmen from the other bridges to help to extinguish it, and to save the goods of the merchants or others, either by removing them to the towers above mentioned, or by putting them in boats and transporting them to the islands in the lake. ...

Moreover, within the city there is an eminence on which stands a tower, and at the top of the tower is hung a slab of wood. Whenever fire or any other alarm breaks out in the city a man who stands there with a mallet in his hand beats upon the slab, making a noise that is heard to a great distance. So ... everybody is aware that fire has broken out, or that there is some other cause of alarm.

The *khan* watches this city with especial diligence because it forms the head of all Manzi; and because he has an immense revenue from the duties levied on the transactions of trade therein, the amount of which is such that no one would credit it on mere hearsay.

All the streets of the city are paved with stone or brick, as indeed are all the highways throughout Manzi, so that you ride and travel in every direction without inconvenience. ... But as the Great Khan's couriers could not gallop their horses over the pavement, the side of the road is left unpaved for their convenience. The pavement of the main street of the city also is laid out in two parallel ways of ten paces in width on either side, leaving a space in the middle laid with fine gravel, under which are vaulted drains which convey the rainwater into the canals; and thus the road is kept ever dry.

You must know also that ... Kinsay has some 3,000 baths, the water of which is supplied by springs. They are hot baths, and the people take great delight in them, frequenting them several times a month .... They are ... large enough for 100 persons to bathe together.

And the Ocean Sea comes within 25 miles of the city at a place called Ganfu, where there is a town and an excellent haven, with a vast amount of shipping which is engaged in the traffic to and from India and other foreign parts, exporting and importing many kinds of wares .... And a great river flows from the city of Kinsay to that sea-haven, by which vessels can come up to the city itself. This river extends also to other places further inland.[38]

Know also that the Great Khan has ... constituted Manzi into nine kingdoms. To each of these kingdoms a king[39] is appointed who is subordinate to the Great Khan, and every year renders the accounts of his kingdom to the fiscal office at the capital. ... Kinsay is the seat of one of these kings, who rules over 140 great and wealthy cities. For in the whole of this vast country of Manzi there are more than 1,200 great and wealthy cities, without counting the towns and villages, which are in great numbers. ...

I repeat that everything appertaining to this city is on so vast a scale, and the Great Khan's yearly revenues ... are so immense, that it is not easy even to put it in writing, and it seems past belief to one who merely hears it told. But I *will* write it down for you.

First, however, I must mention another thing. The people of this country have a custom, that as soon as a child is born they write down the day and hour and the planet and sign under which [the birth] has taken place .... And when anyone intends a journey he goes to the astrologers and gives the particulars of his nativity in order to learn whether he shall have good luck. Sometimes they will say no, and in that case the journey is put off until such day as the astrologer may recommend. These astrologers are very skilful ... and often their words come to pass, so the people have great faith in them.

... when anyone dies the friends and relations make a great mourning for the deceased .... And when they come to the burning place, they take representations of things cut out of parchment, such as caparisoned horses, male and female slaves, camels ... and these things they put on the fire along with the corpse, so that they are all burnt with it. And they tell you that the dead man shall have all these slaves and animals of which the effigies are burnt, alive in flesh and blood ... at his disposal in the next world ....

Furthermore there exists in this city the palace of the king who fled, him who was emperor of Manzi, and that is the greatest palace in the world .... For you must know its demesne has a compass of 10 miles, all enclosed with lofty battlemented walls; and inside the walls are the ... most delectable gardens upon earth, and filled too with the finest fruits. There are numerous fountains ... and lakes full of fish. In the middle is the palace .... It contains twenty great and handsome halls .... And besides these halls the palace contains 1,000 large and handsome chambers, all painted in gold and divers colours.

Moreover, I must tell you that in this city there are 160 *tomans* of fires, or in other words 160 *tomans* of houses. ... the *toman* is 10,000, so that you can reckon the total as altogether 1,600,000 houses, among which are a great number of rich palaces. There is one church only, belonging to the Nestorian Christians.

There is another thing I must tell you. It is the custom for every ... description of person in the city to write over his door his own name, the name of his wife, and those of his children, his slaves, and all the inmates of his house, and also the number of animals that he keeps. And if anyone dies in the house then the name of that person is erased, and if any child is born its name is added. So in this way the sovereign is able to know exactly the population of the city. And this is the practice also throughout all Manzi and Cathay.

And I must tell you that every hosteler who keeps a hostel for travellers is bound to register their names and surnames, as well as the day and month of their arrival and departure. And thus the sovereign has the means of knowing, whenever it pleases him, who comes and goes throughout his dominions.

CHAPTER 77

FURTHER PARTICULARS CONCERNING
the GREAT CITY *of* KINSAY[40]

THE POSITION OF the city is such that it has on one side a lake of fresh and exquisitely clear water ... and on the other a very large river. The waters of the latter fill a number of canals of all sizes which run through the different quarters of the city, carry away all impurities, and then enter the lake; whence they issue again and flow to the ocean, thus producing a most excellent atmosphere. ...

At the opposite side the city is shut in by a channel, perhaps 40 miles in length, very wide, and full of water derived from the river .... This serves also as a defence ... and the earth dug from it has been thrown inwards, forming a kind of mound enclosing the city.

In this part are the ten principal markets ... frequented by 40,000 or 50,000 persons, who bring thither for sale every possible necessary of life, so that there is always an ample supply of every kind of meat and game ....

Those markets make a daily display of every kind of vegetables and fruit ... and all sorts of wares are on sale, including spices and jewels and pearls. ...

CHAPTER 78

TREATING *of the* YEARLY REVENUE
that the GREAT KHAN *has* FROM KINSAY

NOW I WILL tell you about the great revenue which the Great Khan draweth every year from the said city of Kinsay and its territory, forming a ninth part of the whole country of Manzi.

First there is the salt .... For it produces every year, in round numbers, fourscore *toman*s of gold; and the *toman* is worth 70,000 *saggi* of gold, so that the total value of the fourscore *toman*s will be 5,600,000 *saggi* of gold, each *saggio* being worth more than a gold florin or ducat; in sooth, a vast sum of money! ...

You must know that in this city and its dependencies they make great quantities of sugar, as indeed they do in the other eight divisions of this country; so that I believe the whole of the rest of the world together does not produce such a quantity ... and the sugar alone again produces an enormous revenue. However, I will not repeat the duties on every article separately, but tell you how they go in the lump. Well, all spicery pays 3⅓ percent, on the value; and all merchandise likewise pays 3⅓ percent. (But seaborne goods from India and other distant countries pay 10 percent.) The rice-wine also makes a great return, and coals, of which there is a great quantity; and so do the twelve guilds of craftsmen ... with their 12,000 stations apiece, for every article they make pays duty. And the silk, which is produced in such abundance, makes an immense return. But why should I make a long story of it? The silk, you must know, pays 10 percent, and many other articles also pay 10 percent.

And you must know that Messer Marco Polo, who relates all this, was several times sent by the Great Khan to inspect the amount of his customs and revenue from this ninth part of Manzi,[41] and he found it to be, exclusive of the salt revenue which we have mentioned already, 210 *toman*s of gold, equivalent to 14,700,000 *saggi* of gold; one of the most enormous revenues that ever was heard of. And if the sovereign has such a revenue from one-ninth part of the country, you may judge what he must have from the whole of it! However, to speak the truth, this part is the greatest and most productive; and because of the great revenue that the Great Khan derives from it, it is his favourite province, and he takes all the more care to watch it well, and to keep the people contented.

Now we will quit this city and speak of others.

CHAPTER 79

Of the CITY of TANPIJU and OTHERS

WHEN YOU LEAVE Kinsay and travel a day's journey to the southeast … passing a succession of dwellings and charming gardens, you reach … Tanpiju, a great, rich and fine city, under Kinsay. The people are subject to the Great Khan [and so forth]. They live by trade and manufactures and handicrafts, and have all necessaries in great plenty and cheapness.[42]

But there is no more to be said about it, so we proceed, and I will tell you of another city called Vuju at three days' distance from Tanpiju. The people are idolaters [and so forth], and the city is under Kinsay. They live by trade and manufactures.

Travelling through a succession of towns and villages that look like one continuous city, two days further on to the southeast you find the great and fine city of Ghiuju, which is under Kinsay. The people are idolaters [and so forth]. They have plenty of silk, and live by trade and handicrafts, and have all things necessary in abundance. At this city you find the largest and longest canes that are in all Manzi; they are full four palms in girth and fifteen paces in length.

When you have left Ghiuju you travel four days southeast through a beautiful country, in which towns and villages are very numerous. There is abundance of game both in beasts and birds; and there are very large and fierce lions. After those four days you come to the great and fine city of Chanshan. It is situated upon a hill which divides the river, so that the one portion flows up country and the other down. It is still under the government of Kinsay.

... When you leave Chanshan you travel three days through a very fine country with many towns and villages, traders and craftsmen, and abounding in game of all kinds, and arrive at the city of Cuju. The people are idolaters [and so forth], and live by trade and manufactures. It is a fine, noble and rich city, and is the last of the government of Kinsay in this direction.[43] The other kingdom which we now enter, called Fuju, is also one of the nine great divisions of Manzi as Kinsay is.

CHAPTER 80

CONCERNING *the* KINGDOM *of* FUJU

ON LEAVING CUJU, which is the last city of the kingdom of Kinsay, you enter the kingdom of Fuju,[44] and travel six days in a southeasterly direction through a country of mountains and valleys, in which are a number of towns and villages with great plenty of victuals and an abundance of game. Lions, great and strong, are also very numerous. The country produces ginger and galingale in immense quantities, insomuch that for a Venice groat you may buy fourscore pounds of good fine-flavoured ginger. They have also a kind of fruit resembling saffron, and which serves the purpose of saffron just as well.[45]

And you must know the people eat all manner of unclean things, even the flesh of a man, provided he has not died a natural death. So they look out for the bodies of those that have been put to death and eat their flesh, which they consider excellent.[46]

Those who go to war in those parts ... shave the hair off the forehead and cause it to be painted in blue like the blade of a glaive. They all go afoot except the chief; they carry spears and swords, and are the most savage people in the world, for they go about constantly killing people, whose blood they drink, and then devour the bodies.[47]

Now I will quit this and speak of other matters. You must know that after going three days out of the six ... you come to ... Kelinfu, a very great and noble city, belonging to the Great Khan. This city has three stone bridges, which are among the finest and best in the

world. They are a mile long and some nine paces in width, and they are all decorated with rich marble columns. Indeed they are such fine … works that to build any one of them must have cost a treasure.

The people live by trade and manufactures, and have great store of silk (which they weave into various stuffs), and of ginger and galingale.[48] (They also make cotton cloth …, which is sent all over Manzi.) Their women are particularly beautiful. …

In the other three days of the six … you continue to meet with many towns and villages, with traders, and goods for sale, and craftsmen. The people have much silk …. There is plenty of game of all kinds, and there are great and fierce lions which attack travellers.[49] In the last of those three days' journey, when you have gone 15 miles you find a city called Unken, where there is an immense quantity of sugar made. From this city the Great Khan gets all the sugar for the use of his court, a quantity worth a great amount of money.

There is no more to say … so now we shall speak of the splendour of Fuju. When you have gone 15 miles from the city of Unken, you come to this noble city which is the capital of the kingdom. …[50]

CHAPTER 81

CONCERNING *the* GREATNESS *of the* CITY *of* FUJU

NOW THIS CITY of Fuju is the key of the kingdom which is called Chonka, and which is one of the nine great divisions of Manzi.[51] The city is a seat of great trade and great manufactures. The people are idolaters [and so forth]. And a large garrison is maintained there by that prince to keep the kingdom in peace and subjection. For the city is one which is apt to revolt on very slight provocation.

There flows through the middle of this city a great river, which is about a mile in width, and many ships are built at the city which are launched upon this river. Enormous quantities of sugar are made there, and there is a great traffic in pearls and precious stones. For many ships of India come to these parts bringing many merchants who traffic about the Isles of the Indies. For this city is, as I must tell you, in the vicinity of the ocean port of Zayton, which is greatly frequented by the ships of India with their cargoes of various merchandise; and from Zayton ships come this way right up to the city of Fuju by the river I have told you of; and 'tis in this way that the precious wares of India come hither.[52]

The city is a ... fine one and kept in good order, and all necessaries of life are there to be had in great abundance and cheapness.

CHAPTER 82

Of the CITY and GREAT HAVEN of ZAYTON

NOW WHEN YOU quit Fuju and cross the river, you travel for five days southeast through a fine country, meeting with a constant succession of flourishing cities, towns and villages, rich in every product. You travel by mountains and valleys and plains, and in some places by great forests in which are many of the trees which give camphor.[53] There is plenty of game on the road, both of bird and beast. The people are all traders and craftsmen, subjects of the Great Khan, and under the government of Fuju. When you have accomplished those five days' journey you arrive at the very great and noble city of Zayton, which is also subject to Fuju.[54]

At this city you must know is the haven of Zayton, frequented by all the ships of India, which bring thither spicery and all other kinds of costly wares. It is the port also that is frequented by all the merchants of Manzi, for hither is imported the most astonishing quantity of goods and of precious stones and pearls, and from this they are distributed all over Manzi. And I assure you that for one shipload of pepper that goes to Alexandria or elsewhere, destined for Christendom, there come 100 such, aye and more too, to ... Zayton; for it is one of the two greatest havens in the world for commerce.[55]

The Great Khan derives a very large revenue from the duties paid in this city and haven; for you must know that on all the merchandise imported, including precious stones and pearls, he levies a duty of 10 percent, or in other words takes tithe of everything. Then again the ship's charge for freight on small wares is 30 percent, on pepper 44 percent, and on lignaloes, sandalwood and other bulky goods 40 percent, so that between freight and the *khan*'s duties the merchant has to pay a good half the value of his investment (though on the other half he makes such a profit that he is always glad to come back with a new supply of merchandise). But you may well believe from what I have said that the *khan* has a vast revenue from this city.

There is a great abundance here of all provision for every necessity of man's life. ... the people are very quiet, and fond of an easy life. Many come hither from Upper India to have their bodies painted with the needle in the way we have elsewhere described, there being many adepts at this craft in the city.[56]

Let me tell you also that in this province there is a town called Tyunju, where they make vessels of porcelain of all sizes, the finest that can be imagined. They make it nowhere but in that city, and thence it is exported all over the world. Here it is abundant and very cheap, insomuch that for a Venice groat you can buy three dishes so fine that you could not imagine better.

I should tell you that in ... Zayton ... they have a peculiar language. For you must know that throughout all Manzi they employ one speech and one kind of writing only, but yet there are local differences of dialect, as you might say of Genoese, Milanese, Florentines, and Neapolitans, who though they speak different dialects can understand one another.[57]

And I assure you that the Great Khan has as large customs and revenues from this kingdom of Chonka as from Kinsay, aye and more too.

We have now spoken of but three out of the nine kingdoms of Manzi, to wit Yanju and Kinsay and Fuju. We could tell you about the other six, but it would be too long a business; so we will say no more about them.

And now you have heard all the truth about Cathay and Manzi and many other countries, as has been set down in this book; the customs of the people and the various objects of commerce, the beasts and birds, the gold and silver and precious stones, and many other matters have been rehearsed to you. ...

CONCLUSION[58]

AND NOW YE have heard all that we can tell you about the Tartars ... and their customs, and likewise about the other countries of the world as far as our researches and information extend. Only we have said nothing whatever about the Greater Sea and the provinces that lie round it, although we know it thoroughly. But it seems to me a needless and useless task to speak about places which are visited by people every day. For there are so many who sail all about that sea constantly, Venetians, and Genoese, and Pisans, and many others, that everybody knows all about it, and that is the reason that I pass it over and say nothing of it.

Of the manner in which we took our departure from the court of the Great Khan you have heard at the beginning of the book, in that chapter where we told you of all the vexation and trouble that Messer Maffeo and Messer Nicolo and Messer Marco had about getting the Great Khan's leave to go; and in the same chapter is related the lucky chance that led to our departure. And you may be sure that but for that lucky chance, we should never have got away in spite of all our trouble, and never have got back to our country again. But I believe it was God's pleasure that we should get back in order that people might learn about the things that the world contains. For according to what has been said in the introduction at the beginning of the book, there never was a man, be he Christian or Muslim or Tartar or Heathen, who ever travelled over so much of the world as did that noble and illustrious citizen of the city of Venice, Messer Marco the son of Messer Nicolo Polo.

Thanks be to God! Amen! Amen!

Note: These notes are a mixture of material that appeared originally in the 1908 Marsden edition, the 1903 Yule edition (including many excerpts from the notes supplied by the French scholar Henri Cordier), and a number of up-to-date clarifications (especially of place names, where identified) for modern readers.

INTRODUCTION

1 Euxine is derived from Pontus Euxinus, the ancient name in Latin for the Black Sea.
2 "Bruce" may refer to William Speirs Bruce, a pioneer polar scientist and explorer from the 1890s to the early 1900s.
3 A reference to "The Earthly Paradise" by William Morris.

PROLOGUE

1 Marsden writes Rustgielo, Yule Rusticiano. Modern scholars identify Rustichello, a Pisan writer of Arthurian romances who had been captured in 1284 during the Battle of Meloria.
2 In 1299 a truce was signed between Genoa and Venice as a result of which both Marco Polo and Rustichello were probably released.
3 Marsden's edition has the date 1250, in accordance with all the chief texts, though a note questions the accuracy of the date and suggests it could not have been before 1255. Yule calculates this date from the fact that the brothers reached the Volga in 1261.
4 Baldwin II, the last Latin emperor of Constantinople, reigned 1228–1261.
5 Modern-day Sudak in Crimea (Ukraine).
6 Sarai (Sara/Saraa/Assara/Saraj/Saray – *srai* is Persian for "palace") was a large city in the medieval world, established by Barka's predecessor in the 1240s, but it was destroyed by Timur (or Tamerlane) in the 1390s. Bolgara, or Bolghar, was the capital

of Volga Bulgaria until the fifteenth century when it was absorbed by Russia.
7 Oukaka (Ucaca/Ukek) was on the right bank of the Volga, between Sarai and Bolgara.
8 This great river was probably the Sihun, also known as the Sirr or Syr Darya (to the Greeks it was the Jaxartes, marking the northern limit of Alexander's conquests).
9 The Karak Desert.
10 This vague designation must be understood as applying to Khatai. Also, the language used implies that the envoys were the Great Khan's own people returning to his court.
11 By the emperor of the Romans is meant the emperor, whether Greek or Roman, who reigned at Constantinople.
12 A reference to the degrees of a liberal education: Rhetoric, Logic, Grammar, Arithmetic, Astronomy, Music and Geometry.
13 We may reasonably suspect that the expressions here have been heightened by the zeal of Christian transcribers.
14 The Chinghizide princes were eminently liberal – or indifferent – in religion. They were rarely persecutors.
15 Lesser Armenia was also called Armenia Minor and during this period was the Armenian kingdom of Cilicia, distinct from the ancient kingdom of Armenia.
16 Laiassus is modern-day Ayas (Layas/Lajazzo/Aias/Ajazzo). It is on the northern side of Iskenderun Bay in the eastern Mediterranean. It was once a chief port for the shipment of Asiatic wares and was much frequented by vessels of the Italian republics.
17 Acre was taken from the Saracens (an ancient term that had become synonymous with Muslim) by the Crusaders in 1110 and was fought over periodically thereafter. In 1265, and again in 1269 (about the period at which our travellers arrived there), it was unsuccessfully attacked by the sultan of Egypt. In 1291 it was finally conquered by another Egyptian sultan.

18 Yule states Marco's age as fifteen and points out that nineteen (as used in Marsden, though with a footnote which includes the information about being aged fifteen) was an arbitrary correction to suit the mistaken date (1250) assigned for the departure of the father from Constantinople.

19 A vacancy existed for a period of nearly three years, until 1 September 1271. In order to prevent this in the future the institution of the Conclave was established.

20 Founded in 1216 in France, the Order of Preachers (*Ordo Praedicatorum*) became more commonly known later as the Dominican Order, or Dominicans.

21 As it may be presumed that our travellers commenced their journey about the time of the sailing of Pope Gregory X from Acre, the period is fixed to late 1271 or early 1272.

22 This was Bibars (Baibars/Baybars) Bunduqdari, the first Mameluke sultan of Egypt (which is meant by Babylonia – "Babylon" being Cairo), who had conquered the greater part of Syria, invaded Armenia and made himself master of Antioch. As a commander under the sultan, in 1260 Bibars had defeated the Mongols at the Battle of Ain Jalut. Yule points out that these events took place in the 1260s, before the Polo party reached the region – but the matters were ongoing and therefore they reflect the general sense of alarm at Bibars' advance.

23 Clemenfu, or Kaipingfu (meaning "city of peace"), was founded in 1256, four years before Kublai's accession, some distance to the north of the Chinese wall. It became his favourite summer residence, and from 1264 was styled Shangdu (or "upper court").

24 The city of Khorasan, then (with Persia) under the dominion of the second son of Alaü (also spelled Hulagu), who succeeded his brother Abaka, and took the name of Ahmed Khan when he embraced Islam.

25 Several ladies of this name have a place in Mongol–Persian history. This one, a woman of great beauty and ability, was known as the Great Khatun (or Lady) Bolgana, and was (according to Mongol custom) the wife successively of Abaka and of his son Arghun, Mongol sovereign of Persia.

26 Khatai or Kataia – or Cathay, as it was usually called by medieval writers – applies to the northern provinces of what we now call China, which were conquered by Genghis Khan and his son Ogodei, not from the Chinese government but a race of eastern Tartars called Niu-che and Kin.

27 Not India but islands in the eastern archipelago, perhaps the Philippines.

28 The mention of the king of England appears for the first time in Pauthier's text. The Mongol *khan*s of Persia (Abaka in 1277, Arghun in 1289 and 1291, Ghazan in 1302, and Oljailu in 1307) sent several embassies to the kings of England seeking cooperation in attacks on the Egyptian sultan.

29 The sailing of this expedition we may infer, from circumstances mentioned in different parts of the work, took place about the beginning of 1291, three years before the death of Kublai and four years before the arrival of the Polo family at Venice in 1295.

30 There are strong grounds for deducing the expedition ultimately arrived at Ormuz.

31 In March 1291.

32 The brother of Arghun, perhaps as regent or protector to his nephew, then a minor.

33 We may presume this place was Tabriz.

34 Kublai died in the beginning of 1294. It is not surprising that the news of an event so important to all the tribes of Mongols or Tartars should have found its way to Persia, and consequently to our travellers.

BOOK I

1 Lesser Armenia of the Middle Ages was distinct from Armenia Minor, a name the ancients applied to the western portion

of Armenia, west of the Euphrates, and immediately north of Cappadocia. Polo's contemporary, Marino Sanuto, compares the kingdom of the pope's faithful Armenians to one between the teeth of four fierce beasts, the Tartar lion, the Soldan panther, the Turkish wolf and the Corsair serpent.

2 Langlois spoke of the Cilician plain as a region once fair now covered by swamps, where fever decimates the population.

3 See Prologue note 16.

4 Turcomania, or Turkomania, was understood to be the Seljuk possessions in Asia Minor, from Cilicia and Iconium (Rum) to Sivas (Sebastea). From the Seljuks sprang the empire of the Ottomans.

5 Or Turki, esteemed for spirit and hardiness.

6 Conia is Iconium/Kogni/Kuniyah/Konya. Savast is Sivas/Sevasta. Casaria is ancient Caesarea of Cappadocia–Kaisariah/ Kaisareah/Kayseri. All were metropolitan sees under the Catholicos of Sis.

7 Arzingan/Arzengan/Arsengan/Arzenjan/ Arsinga are older variants for modern-day Erzincan in eastern Anatolia.

8 What is meant here by buckram is not the same as understood today (coarse linen or cotton). Marsden explains that it is a fine, soft cotton cloth. Yule explains that it was probably a kind of quilting.

9 Mount Ararat.

10 The quantities outlined here suggest that these are the Baku oilfields on the Caspian in the Caucasus, modern-day Azerbaijan.

11 Or David Melik. The name David or Davit was used frequently by kings of Georgia.

12 Tonsure is mentioned by other writers.

13 A pass between the foot of the Tabasaran Mountains (part of the Caucasus) and the Caspian Sea where the walled city of Derbent stands, in modern-day Dagestan, Russia. Arabs called it the Gate of Gates. In a lengthy note, Yule relates the mythical (the *Alexander Romance*) and biblical (Genesis and other books) resonances of the erection

of gates and walls to keep out unwanted races, such as, for example, the Caspian Gates which were thought to hold at bay the corrupted Gog and Magog who would be set loose by the Antichrist to wreak havoc. A theory that the Tartars were Gog and Magog led to the wall built by Alexander being confounded with the Great Wall of China (see chapter 59, note 164).

14 An important article of Genoese trade.

15 Yule failed to identify any convent of St Leonard's and claimed it as an unlikely name for an Armenian saint, suggesting instead that the saint was Nina or Helena, which is Elenovka in Russian – and there is just such a place on the shores of Lake Sevan, which is well-stocked with fish, especially trout. This "miracle" is believed to be due to a rise in the level of the lake caused by snowmelt that coincides with Lent. Marsden speculates that the place is Lake Van in Armenia.

16 To the Caspian Marco assigned the name "Mer de Gheluchelan" or "La Mer de Ghel ou de Ghelan", a name taken from the districts (called Gil/Gilan) of the ancient Gelae on the Caspian's southwestern shores.

17 The province of Gil/Gelan gave its name to the silk for which the area became famous.

18 The enormous quantity of fish found in the Caspian Sea is ascribed to the mass of food to be found in the shallower waters of the North and the mouth of the Volga.

19 Mausul is Mosul. According to Yule, calling it "a very great kingdom" can scarcely have been justified – a hyperbolic tendency of Polo's that Yule describes as "a bad habit".

20 Muslims do not, of course, worship Muhammad, so much as practise the tenets of their faith, Islam, according to which the most revered Prophet is Muhammad.

21 In the preceding centuries the Nestorian Church had diffused over Asia, with bishops from Jerusalem to Beijing. The Jacobites took their name from Jacob

Baradaeus, bishop of Edessa, who formed an independent church over a similar point of doctrine as the Nestorians.

22 It can be seen that *mosolin* – muslin – had a different meaning from what it has now.

23 Baudas (Baldach/Bagadet), is Baghdad. "Saracen" is used by both Yule and Marsden; today the preferred word would be "Muslim".

24 Meaning the Tigris and the Persian Gulf.

25 Kish in modern-day Iran is a small island on the eastern side of the gulf.

26 Modern-day Basra, still noted for its dates.

27 Some of these brocades were called *baldachini* – and from their use in canopies the architectural word *baldacchino* arose.

28 Alaü is Hulagu Khan (Ulaù in Marsden), who left Karakorum in May 1253 and arrived in Samarkand in September 1255. Historians agree that the fall of Baghdad (and thus the caliphate) to the Mongols occurred in February 1258. Alaü was one of four Mongol brothers who set out to create a global empire.

29 Henry Wadsworth Longfellow tells the tale in "Kambalu" in *Flower-de-luce* (1867).

30 Rasmusio has 1225, which Marsden uses.

31 Matthew 17: 14–21.

32 Yule admits he is uncertain what the English word should really be. Marsden uses "shoemaker" rather than "cobbler".

33 Some copies place this at Tauris. Only three years before Marco told this story the House of Loreto in Italy was said to have moved miraculously to its final resting place.

34 Yrac is Iraq. However, Tauris is actually Tabriz in Iranian Azerbaijan rather than Iraq. After Alaü destroyed Baghdad, Tabriz became the great commercial city of Asia. Armenia's destruction closed to Europeans the route of Tauris.

35 Cremesor is Ormuz/Hormuz at the entrance to the Persian Gulf.

36 Barsimaeus, one-time bishop of Edessa.

37 Marsden explains that *Kalah atish perestan* is, literally, "castle of the fire-worshippers".

38 Marsden translates this as "mortal man" rather than physician.

39 Marsden relates that the citizens go to the original well, which is never extinguished, should they need to re-light their fire.

40 The term "kingdoms" is used deliberately rather than "provinces", though Yule does not know why some are kingdoms rather than just "cities". He lists the eight as Kazvín, Kurdistan, Lúr, Shúlistán, Isfahan, Shíráz, Sháwankára and Tún-o-Kâin.

41 Marsden names them as Kasibin, Kurdistan (though wonders whether this should really be Khuristan/Khuzistan – there is a Khuzestan province in modern-day Iran), Lor (there is a Lorestan province in modern-day Iran), Suolistan (also written Sejestan/Siyestan), Spaan (Isfahan), Siras (Shiraz), Soncara (Korkan or Gurkan), and Timocain (the city of Damghan in Qumis province, now Semnan province).

42 Marsden uses Arbor Secco.

43 The *livre tournois* was minted between 1360 and 1641. The excellence of Persian horses was no doubt due to the mixture of the Arabian and Turki or Turkoman breeds.

44 Marsden states that the second of these cities is Hormuz, which would mean that Curmosa is Cremesor (see note 35).

45 Polo goes on to explain that the Muslims circumvent their prohibition on drinking wine by boiling it, "for it is then no longer called wine, the name being changed with the change of flavour".

46 Yasdi/Yazd is in eastern Fars and a famous historic centre of Zoroastrianism.

47 Yule has a lengthy note on *ondanique*, concluding that it refers to steel or "Indian steel", which was famed throughout the East. Marsden translates this as antimony, but acknowledges this may well be an error.

48 Kermán was said to be celebrated throughout Asia for its shawls, felts and suchlike. Carpet-weaving remains an important industry.

49 The city is nearly 6,000ft above sea level.

50 Marsden calls it Kamandu. The place appears no longer to exist.

51 Marsden translates this as "Adam's apple" (*pomum adami*), which is actually a type of citrus known as pear lemon (*citrus lumia*).

52 A breed of sheep (*ovis laticaudata*) native to parts of Asia and Africa.

53 Marsden presumes these to be the inhabitants of an area known as Makran that extends from the vicinity of the Indus toward the Persian Gulf, taking the name from the word *karána*, which signifies a "shore, coast or border".

54 The then Great Khan being Ogodei (Oktay/ Ogotai, and other variant spellings).

55 Soldan being Sultan. Asedin is variously rendered As-idin/Azz-eddin.

56 Marsden believes this was near Lahore.

57 The plain of Ormus/Hormuz in Marsden.

58 In Marsden the text reads "upon an island, at no great distance from the shore, stands a city named Ormus" (p.63). He explains that this island of Jerun was where a new city was founded after the old one was destroyed by the Seljuks; the mainland coastal city later moving to Gambrun.

59 Marsden spells it Rukmedin Achomak.

60 Ibn Batuta says the people of Hormuz had a saying, "Dates and fish make an emperor's dish". The tunny, or something like it, comes in search of the shoals of anchovies.

61 The fish-oil was whale oil. A trenail or trunnel is a wooden pin to fasten timbers.

62 The hot wind that we now know by the Italian word Sirocco.

63 The bread may have owed its bitterness to the use of acorns. The therapeutic hot springs near Dashtáb were sulphurous.

64 Rather than the direct road to Cobinan (Kúbenán/Kuh-Banán/Kobiam) Marco Polo probably took a circuitous route to the east of the mountains, via Kúhpáyeh and the desert to the north of Khabis.

65 The salt of these deserts may contain sulphate of magnesia, and the green may be due to a mixture of sulphate of iron.

66 Persia has many subterranean canals (*kanát* or *kárez*); this "stream" is probably one such.

67 Cobinan (Kúbenán/Kuh-Banán/Kobiam) is thought to mean "hill of the wild pistachios".

68 *Tutia* is an impure oxide of zinc, which provides a valuable eye-ointment.

69 Although Yule spells this place Tonocain, this seems likely to be the same place earlier spelled Tunocain in chapter 15. Tonocain/ Tunocain (Tunokain/Tún-o-Kâin) is eastern Kuhistan in Persia (Iran) but as extended here by Polo seems to include Khorasan too. Yule thinks this is Tún-o-Kâin in the vicinity of Tabas (Yazd province).

70 The oracular "tree of the sun" was prominent in the legendary history of Alexander. Here Marco Polo has mixed up this legend with a medieval Christian one about the "dry tree", often featured in mystic literary references to the Cross. The last battle between the two men was actually fought in Kurdistan, but fables about the Macedonian abound in this region.

71 "Old man of the mountain" is an injudicious translation of the Arabic *sheikh al jabal*, signifying "chief of the mountainous region". The title referred to the head of an Ismailite Shia Muslim sect within Kuhestan/Kohistan, which had strong fortresses at places such as Alamút. The name Mulehet refers to the "abode of heretics". Aloadin had been killed by about 1255, after a long reign. The *ashishin*, or *hashíshín*, were so called because they used hashish; their system of murder gave the world the word "assassin".

72 There is evidence of Ismaili assassins, loyal to Alamút, in Syria but none for a related sect in Kurdistan.

73 Both Yule and Marsden note the difficulties of chronology. Marsden dates this to 1262 but explains that it must actually have been in about 1256 or 1257. Sapurgan is Sheberghan, northern Afghanistan.

74 Balc (Balkh in Afghanistan) suffered mercilessly under Genghis Khan.

75 Dogana may be a people rather than a place. Yule was puzzled by the reference.

76 Taican is Taloqan in Afghanistan.

77 At the time of Polo's visit these Tajiks were probably in a state of transition to Islam.

78 Casem is Kishim in Badakhshan, in the Pamir (which means "roof of the world") area of Afghanistan.

79 The belief that the porcupine projected its quills at assailants was a persistent one.

80 Badashan is Badakhshan.

81 There was a Graeco–Bactrian kingdom long ago. Zulcarniain or *zul'-karnein* signifies "having horns" – Alexander appeared in this manner on Greek coins.

82 Syghinan is Sikinan in Marsden.

83 Marsden adds lapis lazuli and ultramarine.

84 A paragraph has been edited from here about the province having a breed of horses from the strain of Alexander's horse Bucephalus.

85 *Falco cherrug* and *Falco biarmicus* are both large falcons.

86 Probably Shewá, northern Badakhshan.

87 Yule wryly observes: "Yet scarcely any country in the world has suffered so terribly and repeatedly from invasion."

88 An ell is a textile measure based on hand breadths; it was typically 45in.

89 Pashai is almost certainly Peshawar, an ancient centre of learning and an important part of the historic kingdom of Gandhara.

90 Keshimur is Kashmir.

91 Marsden explains that the Brahmins of Kashmir supplied southern India with many of the images of the deities in their temples.

92 The River Jhelum in the Kashmir valley is a tributary of the Chenab, which later joins the Indus.

93 Although predominantly Hindu at this time, the Kashmiris identified by Polo had less than strict observance of any religious restrictions on eating meat.

94 Marco was told also that the wolves killed many wild sheep. Hence quantities of horns and bones were found, which were made into heaps by the wayside to guide travellers when snow was on the ground.

95 Pamier is the region of the Pamir Mountains, which straddle Tajikistan and Afghanistan–Pakistan. The description suggests a high-altitude plain surrounded by the mountains.

96 Cascar is Kashgar or Kashi, a historically important Silk Road trading city located in the Tarim basin at the eastern edge of the Taklamakan Desert (in modern-day China's Xinjiang Uyghur Autonomous Region).

97 According to Yule, Marco tells a story because he was never at Samarkand; if he had been, there would be something descriptive. Instead, his father and uncle may have visited on their first journey.

98 Both Yule and Marsden note that this story is of a kind that earns Marco disrepute. Chagatai was Kublai's uncle rather than his brother. There is no evidence that Chagatai embraced Christianity (though Mangku, Chagatai's nephew, was said to have been baptized). Caidu (Caidou/Kaidu) was neither Chagatai's son nor Kublai's nephew. (For consistency, Chagatai is used here, but Yule spells it Sigatay and Marsden has Zagatai.)

99 Yule suggests this is allegorical, likening it to Protestants taking the fine stone of Catholicism to build their Church on and fearing that one day it will collapse.

100 Also spelled Yarkan/Yarken/Yerken/ Yarkand/Karkan/Carchan.

101 The disorder of the legs is elephantiasis. The tumours are goitres, commonly caused by iodine deficiency.

102 Cotan is Khotan/Khoten/Kotan.

103 Marsden spells this Peyn and notes the confusion over where it is, or was. Yule believes that Pien or Pem was the same as the Pima visited by the Chinese monk Hsüan-tsang (Xuanzang) during his trip

to India and back (629–645), and possibly buried under shifting sands. Yule states that it may be Kiria/Keriya, a later name that incorporates the Tibetan word for sand.

104 Jasper is actually a form of chalcedony.

105 Kashgar or Kashi. See note 96.

106 Marsden prefers Turkistan to Great Turkey.

107 Marsden (again) has Turkistan.

108 Both Lop and Charchan seem to have been lost to desert sands.

109 Yule has a lengthy note about the peculiar experiences of travellers crossing deserts and examines various natural phenomena that would explain the sounds reported.

110 Marsden renders Tangut as Tanguth.

111 The idolatry referred to here is Tibetan Buddhism. The language is Tibetan.

112 This custom is essentially Chinese; it may be here because Tangut was the travellers' first encounter with Chinese peculiarities.

113 Burning is only one method of disposing of their dead, all of which were influenced by the deceased's birth sign.

114 Yule notes that similar practices are found in many other cultures around the world.

115 Yule notes that Camul, or Kamul/Komul (modern-day Hami), does not fall into Marco's line of travel toward Cathay. Polo's notice of it, and of the next province, forms a digression like that he has already made to Samarkand. Again, Marco's father and uncle may have visited on their first journey.

116 The custom Polo speaks of here is also ascribed to eastern Tibet; and elsewhere to others with Mongolian blood.

117 Yule notes the difficulty of identifying the location of Chingintalas (spelled Chinchitalas in Marsden), suggesting it may be in the vicinity of the Tannu-Ola Mountains, in modern-day southern Siberia near the border with Mongolia.

118 The Altai Mountains (of which the Tannu-Ola Mountains are a branch) are probably the location where asbestos (the "salamander" referred to) was found.

119 Yule states that there is part of a *sudarium* ("sweat cloth", but in this Christian context it normally refers to the Veil of Veronica) made of asbestos in the Vatican, but that it came from a pagan tomb on the Appian Way rather than from the Great Khan.

120 Sukchur and Sukchu are both rendered as Succuir by Marsden. It is almost certainly Jiuquan/Suzhou in Jiangsu, China.

121 Marsden has Kampion, but both he and Yule agree that this is Kanchou, once called Ganzhou and today known as Zhangye.

122 The inroads made by Islam later played a major part in exterminating Christianity.

123 A reference to colossal representations of the Buddha, and in particular those in a recumbent pose.

124 References to Tibetan Buddhist monks.

125 Marsden notes that Polo's observations seem to be at variance with modern information that the form of polygamy that exists in parts of Tibet is fraternal polyandry.

126 Yule adds, in a note, "on business of theirs that is not worth mentioning". Marsden observes that three centuries later the Portuguese Jesuit missionary Benedict Goez was also detained for a year in a similar manner before receiving permission to advance further.

127 Etzina is also spelled Ezina/Yetsina/Itsinai.

128 The *kiang* (*Equus kiang*), native to the Tibetan plateau.

129 Caracoron is properly spelled Karákorum (signifying "black camp").

130 By the early ninth century the Tartars appear to have been living around the northern bend of the Yellow River.

131 Chorcha is the Manchu country whose people were at that time called Yuché by the Chinese (and by the Mongols Churché).

132 As Yule states, the idea that there was a Christian potentate, bearing the title Prester, or Presbyter, John, who ruled over vast tracts of the Far East was universal in Europe from the middle of the twelfth

century. The king may be the same one whom the Chinese know as the ruler of the Western Liao dynasty, ruling (with the title of *Gurkhan*) from Kara Khitai until his kingdom was destroyed in 1218. (*Gurkhan* may have become confounded with Johannes. As for his professed faith, it is known only that the last ruler's daughter was a Christian.)

133 Some sources have 1155 as the year of Temujin's birth. Chinese sources put it at 1162; 1187 is not an important year in his history – according to Persian sources he was inaugurated under the name Genghis Khan in 1202 (1206 according to the Chinese).

134 Yule believes that there is a real story at the root of this: that in about 1202, when *un-khan* and Genghis were still acting in alliance, a double union was proposed between *un-khan*'s daughter and Genghis's son and between Genghis's daughter and *un-khan*'s grandson. The union fell through and it contributed to the opening of a breach between the two chiefs. Marsden relates another source, in which the claim is made that before he became Genghis, Temujin was married to *un-khan*'s daughter and was driven to leave his father-in-law's court by the intrigues of his rivals.

135 Marsden explains that the plain (Tanduc/Tenduk/Tenduch/Tangut/Tanguth) is not to be confused with the Tangut in Tibet referred to previously. Rather, the reference may be to the land of the Tangusi, which is around the sources of the Amur near Lake Baikal.

136 Marsden does not mention rival astrologers, Christian and Muslim, in his translation.

137 Yule comments that Prester John was not finally defeated until some time later (in 1203) at a place near modern-day Urga (Ulan Bator), when he was killed by tribesmen in a neighbouring territory.

138 In Marsden, Caaju is named Thaigin. Yule

suggests that this account of Genghis's death arises out of a confusion with the circumstance of Mangku, who died by arrow wound in 1259 at a siege in Sichuan. Yule further states that Genghis survived *un-khan*/Prester John by twenty-four years, dying during an expedition in 1227, aged sixty-five (or seventy-two, according to Chinese and Persian sources respectively, both of which agree the cause was natural).

139 Yule and Marsden both believe Polo is wrong here. The succession of five (not six) *khan*s was as follows: Genghis, Ogodei, Kuyuk, Mangku and Kublai.

140 Levant and Ponent essentially mean "east" and "west".

141 According to Yule, not the Altai Mountains of Siberia but the hills of the Khingan range, and specifically a mountain called Khanoola (Khan Uul, today), near Urga (Ulan Bator).

142 This description of a felt hut or tent (a *yurt*) is common to nearly all the nomadic tribes of Central Asia.

143 "Pharaoh's rats" were the jerboa or desert rodents of Arabia and North Africa – these examples on the steppes may also be jerboa, or perhaps Mongolian gerbils and marmots.

144 No mention is made of Buddhism, then recently introduced among the shamanistic Mongols. The Mongols appear to have called the supreme God Tengri (Heaven).

145 Called *kemurs* or *kemiz* this milk is fermented and can be slightly intoxicating. It is nutritious and keeps for a long time.

146 The bow was the characteristic weapon of the Tartar. Hide was softened by boiling, then shaped and hardened into leather armour (*cuirbouly*).

147 The decimal division of the army was made by Genghis at an early point in his career but it is much older than his time.

148 Frequently made of ewe-milk, this *kurút* is the same as that mixed in Tibet with barley to produce *tsamba*.

149 Yule comments that Marco habitually

suppresses or ignores the brutality of the Tartars, but acknowledges it may have been less in Kublai's time.

150 Idolaters refers to Chinese Buddhism.

151 The Tartars needed no herdsmen to watch over their cattle because the severity of the punishments against theft were a deterrent.

152 Yule explains that the source texts have differences, with one journey of forty days, one journey of sixty days, and one of forty days followed by a second of forty days. Yule has gone with the first. Both Yule and Marsden note that Bargu seems to refer to territory from Lake Baikal to the frozen north, or what we would call Siberia.

153 The image of lakes and marshes swarming with waterfowl is very characteristic of Siberia between Yakutsk and Kolyma. It is likely that Marco is compressing a picture from an eyewitness.

154 What little is said of the *barguerlac* points to a sand grouse of some kind.

155 In the Middle Ages gerfalcons were highly esteemed objects and frequently given as gifts by royals to royals.

156 Marsden spells Erguiul as Erginul and Sinju as Singui. He believes Erguiul/Erginul is the district of Tangut that the Tartars call Kokonor and the Chinese Hohonor, and that Singui is Si-ning (or Selin, modern-day Xining) in western China, only a few days from Hohonor, and the great resting place between Tibet and Beijing.

157 This is the *drong* or wild yak of Tartary (*Bos grunniens*), the bushy-tailed bull of Tibet.

158 The description is good, except the musk deer has canines in only the upper jaw.

159 The pheasant best matching this description is Reeve's pheasant (*Syrmaticus reevesii*), which has long tail feathers, though there are other possibilities, including the blue-eared pheasant (*Crossoptilon auritum*) and the argus pheasant (*Argusianus argus*).

160 Erguiul and Calachan (Kalacha in Marsden) do not appear on any map. Either could be Alashan in modern-day Inner Mongolia; one suggestion (in Yule) is that the former is Alashan and the latter is a summer residence at the foot of the Alashan Mountains. In Alashan today much is made of it being the hometown of camel fabric.

161 The fine wool may well also have been produced from Angora goat mohair.

162 Here Yule has the spelling Tenduc, but this must be the Tanduc (and plain of Tanduc) referred to earlier, which Marsden believes to be the case. (See also note 135.) Yule supposes that the city was actually Kuku-Khotan/Kuku-khoto (Kwei-hwa-cheng) or, possibly, Togto.

163 Argon may derive from a Turkic word for "fair" or "ruddy", though here there is no suggestion that this mixed race is Christian.

164 (Mongul in Marsden rather than Mungul.) Yule cannot conceive why Polo should mention Gog and Magog, except as intimating "here we are beside the Great Wall known as the Rampart of Gog and Magog", and being there he tries to find a reason why those names should have been applied to it. The answer was touched upon previously (see chapter 4, note 13) and the two classes of people whom Marco tries to identify with Gog and Magog substantially represent the Turks and Mongols, or, to use the terms of Rashiduddin, the White and Black Tartars. Yule believes the Ung are the former and the Mungul the latter.

165 Yule believes these cloths are what was known by medieval writers as "Tartary cloth", not because they were made there necessarily but because they were brought from China through the Tartar dominions.

166 Sindachu and Ydifu are difficult to identify. (The two are Sindichin and Idifa in Marsden.) Many places in the area were destroyed during the Ming dynasty.

167 The name Chagan Nor means "White Lake". The palace is thought to have been built in about 1280.

168 These may not all be cranes, but may include the heron or the stork. Yule attempts to identify them as *Grus monachus, Grus leucogeranus, Grus cinerea, Anthropoides virgo* and *Grus antigone*.

169 Chandu is also known as Shandu/Shangtu/Shangdu/Xandu (Coleridge's Xanadu), meaning "upper court" in Chinese, the title of Kublai Khan's summer residence at Kaipingfu.

170 The roof described is of a kind in which the semi-cylinders of bamboo are laid just like Roman tiles. Yule describes bamboo as the "staff of life" used for countless articles and in effect being responsible for maintaining order throughout the empire.

171 The *khan*s usually went to Shangtu/Shangdu in the fourth moon and returned to Cambaluc in the ninth. On the seventh day of the seventh moon there were libations in honour of the ancestors performed by a shaman, who then appointed the propitious day for the return journey to Cambaluc.

172 White horses were presented to the *khan* on New Year's Day (the White Feast). The Horiad probably refers to the Oirad, taken to mean a closely allied non-Mongol tribe who had helped in the victory over *un-khan*/Prester John. That they alone should have this privilege is strange, for the highest position at the *khan*'s court belonged to the Kunkrat tribe out of which the *khan* chose his first wife.

173 The time of year assigned by Polo for this ceremony implies some change has taken place, for many other sources assign this festival to the ninth day of May.

174 Weather-conjuring is often alluded to in the history of the Mongols, performed using a magical stone.

175 It is not clear whether Marco attributes this cannibalism to the Tibetans and Kashmiris, or brings it in as a particular Tartar custom he has forgotten to mention before. Yule examines the evidence for this practice (noting the Tibetan Buddhist use of human skulls and thigh bones for magical cups and musical instruments), much of which relates to events and customs in China.

176 Yule notes that exorcism and magic are prominent in Tibetan Buddhism, influenced strongly as it is by the older shamanic Bon/Bonpo belief system as well as ancient yogic traditions from India, which has a highly developed art of juggling and other extraordinary acts of conjuring. However, he also makes the point that such practices were once found widely in the West, too.

177 Tsongkhapa reformed the Buddhist clergy by prohibiting marriage. Confusion can also arise because there were many lay brothers and sisters in Tibet and Mongolia who did not have to adhere to the vow of celibacy.

178 This bran is *tsamba*.

179 Although the term *sensin* is used, most likely Marco encountered, or heard about, various religious groups regarded as heretical by the Buddhists (from the Taoists to the practitioners of Bon), partly because of their supposed supernatural powers.

BOOK II: PART I

1 The word actually used in the Yule edition is "puissance", rendered here for the modern reader as "power".

2 *Khan* was the title Genghis directed his son and successor Ogodei to assume, and which is explained by the term *khan* of *khan*s, or lord of lords.

3 In fact, as stated previously (see Book I, chapter 51, note 139), Kublai was the fifth not the sixth *khan* (Batu, Genghis's eldest grandson, waived his right in favour of Mangku, his nephew). As emperor of China, Kublai's reign is understood to have commenced in 1280. In Western societies the right of succession would have been in one of the sons of Mangku, but among

the Mongols the dying sovereign generally nominated the family member best qualified, according to age and talent – an appointment subject to the approval of the tribal chiefs in an assembly.

4 Kublai died in 1294. By the Muslim way of reckoning he would have been close to eighty-five. Kublai was the fourth son of Tuli, the youngest of Genghis's four sons by his favourite wife.

5 Not literally true – soon after his accession, in 1261, he led an army against his brother and rival Ariq Böka (Arikbuga/Artigbuga) and defeated him. In his old age he took the field in 1289, though on his approach the rebels disappeared. Kublai and his brother Alaü (Hulagu) began their military careers on Genghis's last expedition (1226–27).

6 Nayan was no "uncle" but a cousin in a junior generation. Kublai was the grandson of Genghis and Nayan was the great-great-grandson of Genghis's brother Uchegin (called in the Chinese annals Pilgutai)

7 Marco, to impress on his readers the great power of the *khan*, is exaggerating on a large scale. Ramusio explained that such was the constant threat of rebellion that garrisons were maintained near every population centre. Marsden believes that this was due, in part, to Kublai wanting to keep his troops from being exposed to Chinese influences in the towns and therefore to provide a semblance at least of their former pastoral life, surrounded with their herds and flocks.

8 A mounted sentry posted to observe the movements of the enemy.

9 A bartizan is an overhanging corner turret on a castle, but used here in the sense of a mobile, battlefield tower.

10 The two-stringed instrument is a *balalaika*. The *naccara*, or *nakkara*, is a kettledrum, perhaps carried here on an elephant.

11 Polo uses this form of words repeatedly to describe a fight.

12 Friar Ricard mentions a Tartar maxim that

if royal contenders kill one another it is improper to spill the blood on the ground and therefore they cause the victim to be smothered or somesuch.

13 Chorcha is Churchin, or Manchuria (subdued in 1233). Cauly or Kauli is Corea (Korea), by which Marco Polo might have meant the northern part, which submitted to the Mongols in 1269, though the ruler of the southern part was a vassal. Barscol or Barskul ("Leopard Lake") seems to have been in the west of Mongolia on the Manchu frontier. Sikintinju is thought by Yule to represent Shangking–Tungking, expressing the two capitals of the Khitan dynasty in this region. (Marsden lists the four as Chorza, Karli, Barskol and Sitingui.)

14 Nayan was said to have been a baptized Christian who had borne the Cross on his banner. This is the only mention by Marco of Jews in China, though much has been written about the settlement of Jews at Kaifungfu (Kaifeng, Henan). Judaism was said to have reached China from Persia during the Han dynasty (206BCE–221CE).

15 Marsden renders Cambaluc as Kanbalu. (This was how the *khan*'s city was known to medieval Europeans, but it is the same place that we now know as Peking/Beijing.)

16 Edited from this edition is Marco Polo's detailed information about the tablets of authority. These were issued in different precious metals and bore engraved symbols. Anyone in possession of such a tablet had significant powers and privileges.

17 We are left in some doubt as to the colour of Kublai's eyes; some of the manuscripts read *vairs* and *voirs*, and others *noirs*. The word has generally been interpreted bluish-grey.

18 The number of wives varies according to the source. Genghis established the practice of four chosen out of four different nomad tribes, and they existed nominally as long as China remained under Mongol domination.

19 Yule believes that Ungrat represents the great

Mongol tribe of Kungurat/Kunkrat (from near the Great Wall), which gave more wives than any other to the princes of the house of Genghis. (Marsden offers the variant spellings Ungut/Ungrac/Origiach/Origiathe. Almost certainly these are the people known today as Uighurs.) See also Book I, note 172.

20 Kublai had an older son who died young. Marco is probably wrong in connecting the name of Chinkin with Genghis. Chinkin died in 1284–85 aged forty-three. Temur, or Teimur, was his third son, but the eldest squinted and the second was rickety in constitution and therefore Temur was named to the throne.

21 The Chinese annals give only ten sons to Kublai, at least by legitimate wives. The annals agree that seven were "kings" of particular territories.

22 Over the gates of Cambaluc there stood lofty tower-like buildings called *lou* by the Chinese. It may be very likely that at the time of Marco Polo the *khan's* war harness was stored in these towers. The dimensions cited in Marsden's edition are much greater, though there is a note that tries to explain the exaggerated dimensions.

23 The stores are now outside the walls of the Forbidden City, corresponding to Polo's palace wall, but within the Imperial City.

24 It seems Polo took the three gateways in the middle gate for three gates and thus speaks of five gates instead of three in the southern wall. (This is the five-arched Meridian Gate still visible today.)

25 Possibly blue-stone, or carbonate of copper, which would turn green through moisture.

26 Genghis captured that city in 1215; in 1264 Kublai adopted it as his chief residence, and in 1267 he founded the new city of Tatu (called by the Mongols Taidu/Daitu/Dadu) a little to the northeast of the old Yenking (Peking/Beijing). Polo explains Cambaluc (*Khan-baligh*) as "the city of the *khan*".

27 The river that ran between the old and the new city must have been the Yu. However, Marsden, while acknowledging in his notes the existence of this "rivulet", may be more reliable in his identification of the river as the Pe-ho, known today as the Hei or Hai He.

28 After the expulsion of the Mongols in 1368 the new native Ming dynasty established their capital at Nanking. But this was found so inconvenient that the third sovereign of the dynasty reoccupied Taidu–Cambaluc. He reduced it in size by cutting off nearly a third of the city at the north end. Polo says that there were twelve gates but old Chinese accounts say eleven (nine remain).

29 The same watchman (using a water-clock) looked out for fires and used a gong to summon the public to help extinguish them.

30 The Chinese lunisolar calendar determines New Year, which usually falls on the second new moon after the winter solstice (21/22 December in the northern hemisphere), which means the date differs each year. In the Gregorian calendar Chinese New Year falls between the third week in January and the middle of February.

31 A bezant (derived from the word Byzantium) is a medieval term for a highly prized gold coin. Venetians used the term to describe the Egyptian gold dinar and the coins of the East.

32 Yule explains that although the number thirteen occurs in many sources, there are good reasons why it could actually be three.

33 This must have been purely a Mongol custom because among the Chinese white was the colour of mourning. Indeed, Marsden notes that when the Chinese Ming replaced the Mongols white was again proscribed for these occasions.

34 The directory of ceremony under the Mongol dynasty explains the *k'o-tow*, or act of prostration described in this passage.

35 There is something unintelligible about this chapter: the 12,000 *keshican* are all elevated to barons, and at the same time the

statement about their changes of raiment seems to be that already made in chapter 14.

36 The boots are described as being of *camut* or *borgal*, which is Russia leather.

37 Yule states that the "cheetah (*Gueparda jubata*) or hunting leopard is very distinct from the true leopard". The cheetah is now classified as *Acinonyx jubatus* and has been used by kings for hunting for millennia.

38 The conception of a tiger seems almost to have dropped out of the European mind during the Middle Ages, hence Polo can only call the tigers "lions".

39 Yule remarks that the Kirghiz people train the *búrgút* (the golden eagle) to fly at wolves and deer, and so on. He cites a British envoy to Kashgar who witnessed a "burgoot" let loose on a huge wild hog – a flabbergasting sight he would not have believed if he had not seen it with his own eyes.

40 The mastiffs were probably Tibetan, but may have come through China. (In the Marsden edition the brothers are Bayan and Mingan, and said to be styled *chivichi*.)

41 Yule disputes the duration of the journey. Peking/Beijing is 100 miles as the crow flies from the nearest point of the coast, which is at least six or seven days' march. The Ocean Sea, as Marsden notes, is the Yellow Sea (Beijing is near the westernmost part, known as Bohai Bay).

42 The oriental practice seems to have assigned one man to each hawk.

43 Yule disagrees that this is a place in east Manchuria, arguing that the return journey from Peking/Beijing would have taken six months. The name Cachar Modun is "land" or "region" and "wood" or "tree". He notes that Jesuit maps have a place called Modun Khotan at just about the correct locality, which is in the region north of the eastern extremity of the Great Wall.

44 It would seem to have been usual to reckon *twelve* suburbs to Peking/Beijing down to modern times.

45 "Public woman" is a euphemism for prostitute.

46 This narrative is peculiar to Ramusio's version. The name of the oppressive minister is printed as Achniach. But Yule argues the letters c and t are so constantly interchanged in the manuscript that he thinks this was a mere clerical error for Achmath.

47 Yule quotes the remarks of a Chinese historian on Kublai's administration, noting that for all his greatness and the success he had with those he appointed, Kublai never placed a Chinese man in his cabinet.

48 The term *bailo* was the designation of the representative of Venice at Constantinople, called *podestà* during the period of Latin rule there. But that term could scarcely have been in use at Cambaluc to designate the powerful minister, and it looks as if Marco had confounded the word in his own mind with some Oriental term of like sound, possibly the Arabic *wáli* (a prince, governor of a province, a chief magistrate).

49 And it is a fact that Marco's presence, and his upright conduct upon this occasion, were not forgotten in the Chinese annals.

50 The *tornesel/tornesol/tornese* was a European silver coin, taking its name from the *denier Tournois*, the *denier* (a coin introduced by Charlemagne) of the city of Tours.

51 In a lengthy note of several thousand words Yule explains in detail the history and workings of paper money in China, which had existed from at least the beginning of the ninth century. He includes the following observation: "Dr Bretschneider makes the following remark: 'Polo states that the Great Kaan causeth the bark of great mulberry-trees, made into something like paper, to pass for money. He seems to be mistaken. Paper in China is not made from mulberry-trees but from the *Broussonetia papyrifera*, which latter tree belongs to the same order of Moraceae. The same fibres are used also

in some parts of China for making cloth, and Marco Polo alludes probably to the same tree when stating (see Book II, Part II, chapter 59) "that in the province of Cuiju (Kwei chau) they manufacture stuff of the bark of certain trees, which form very fine summer clothing"."

52 Yule notes that he can shed no light on the thirty-four provinces into which Polo states the empire is divided, unless they be the provinces and districts described in the second and third parts of Book II. China was then divided into twelve *sheng* or provinces. Yule imagines that the thirty-four provinces refer to the *fu* cities, though according to *Oxenham's Historical Atlas* these numbered thirty-nine.

53 This Mongol word survives in both Persian and Turkish in the senses of both a post-house and a post-horse. It is thought these post-stations were established by Ogodei in 1234 throughout the Mongol empire.

54 The post-system is described almost exactly as in the text by Friar Odoric and the Archbishop of Soltania, in the generation after Polo, and very much in the same way by Magaillans in the seventeenth century.

55 In this Kublai imitated Ashoka, who in his edicts asked for fig trees to be planted along the high roads. There are still remains of the fine avenues of Kublai and his successors in parts of northern China.

56 A kind of yeast is employed, which is often mixed with a flour prepared from fragrant herbs, almonds, pine-seeds, dried fruits, and so on.

57 There was much consumption of coal in northern China, where brick stoves were universal, even in poor houses.

58 The word *tacuin*, or almanac, is from the Arabic *taḵwím*. It is noted in Yule: "Marco does not allude to the fact that almanacs were published by the government. Had Polo not omitted to touch on the issue of almanacs by government he could scarcely

have failed to enter on the subject of printing, on which he has kept a silence so singular and unaccountable."

59 The real cycle of the Mongols, which was also that of the Chinese, runs: Rat, Ox, Tiger, Hare, Dragon, Serpent, Horse, Sheep, Monkey, Cock, Dog, Swine.

60 Ramusio's heading has "Tartars", but it is manifestly of the Cathayans or Chinese that the author speaks throughout this chapter.

61 Filial piety is a fundamental principle of the Chinese polity and the prime virtue in Chinese culture.

62 Calf-length boots.

BOOK II: PART II

1 When Marco leaves the capital, he takes the main road, the "imperial highway", from Peking to Si-ngan fu (Kenjanfu/Xi'an).

2 Pulisanghin is from *Pul-i-Sangín*, which means in Persian simply "The Stone Bridge". We may easily suppose that near Cambaluc the bridge and then the river came to be known to the Persian-speaking foreigners by this name. The river is that which appears in maps as the Hwan Ho/Hun-ho/Yongting Ho/Yongding Ho, joining the Pe-Ho (Hei) at Tientsin (Tianjin on the Hei or Hai He river); and the bridge is that which has been known for ages as the Lu-kou-Kiao (Bridge of Lugou).

3 The city is Zhuozhou. Yule calls the city Chochau and writes that Juju is the name given by Rashiduddin.

4 This bifurcation of the roads is a notable point in Polo's book. For after following the western road through Cathay to the borders of Tibet and the Indo-Chinese regions, Polo will return not to the capital to take a fresh departure, but to this bifurcation outside of Zhuozhou, and thence south to Manzi (Manji in Marsden) – that is, China south of the Yellow River.

5 Yule notes that Marsden translates the commencement of this passage by the words, "At the end of five days' journey *beyond* the ten" – then adds "but this is clearly wrong. The place best positioned, as halfway between Chochau (Zhuozhou) and Taianfu/T'ai-yuan (Taiyuan), would be Cheng-ting fu (Zhengding), and I have little doubt that this is the place intended".

6 Taianfu is modern-day Taiyuan, the capital of the province of Shan-si (Shanxi), and Shan-si is the "kingdom".

7 Pianfu is P'ing-yang fu/Piyingku, now known as Linfen in Shanxi.

8 The name of the castle is doubtful. Yule relates some stories which claim that the Golden King was the *Gurkhan* of Kara Khitai, overthrown by one Kushluk, to whom he had given protection and the hand of his daughter. Kushluk's father had been defeated and slain by Genghis Khan – his name was Taiyang Khan, which translates as Great King John. Thus Taiyang and Kushluk may have been the parties to whom the character of Prester John properly belonged. (See Book I, note 132.)

9 The history of the Tartar conquerors of China is that for one or two generations only were the warlike character and manly habits maintained.

10 Caramoran – from Ḳará-Muren, or "Black River" – is one of the names applied by the Mongols to the Hwang Ho/Huang He, or Yellow River, of the Chinese.

11 Although the abundance of silk is so distinctly mentioned in these chapters, at the time of the Yule edition next to no silk at all was being grown in these districts.

12 A small mention perhaps, but as Marsden points out, the bamboo cane is one of the most useful materials with which nature has furnished the inhabitants of warm climates.

13 *Morus alba* (white mulberry) is grown in northern China for feeding silkworms.

14 Kenjanfu is the city of Si-ngan fu

(modern-day Xi'an), capital of Shen-si (modern-day Shaanxi province). Yule then subjects this route from Pianfu/P'ing-yang fu/Linfen to detailed scrutiny to examine a number of difficulties that arise, but which cannot really concern us here. He believes that the explanation, in part, lies in Polo having confused recollections of his journey westward with those of his return.

15 Kenjanfu is now called Xi'an and was known historically by widely different names, including: Fenghao/Chang'an/ Daxing/Fengyuan/Anxi/Jingzhao/Xijing.

16 Mangalai, Kublai's third son, who governed the provinces of Shen-si (Shaanxi) and Sze-ch'wan (Sichuan), with the title of *wang* or king, died in 1280, which limits the date of Polo's journey to the west. It seems unlikely that Marco should have remained ten years ignorant of his death, yet he seems to speak of him as still governing.

17 Cuncun region must be part of the district of Shen-si (Shaanxi) called Han-chung (Hanzhong/Nanzheng), the axis of which is the river Han, enclosed by mountainous and woody country to the north and south.

18 Yule admits he cannot shed light on the position of Acbalec Manzi, other than to note that Klaproth identified Acbalec with Pe-ma-ching, or "White-horse-town", which once stood on the extensive plain.

19 Sindafu is Ch'eng-tu fu (Chengdu), the capital of Sichuan. Yule suspects Marco's story of the three kings arose from a misunderstanding about the period of the Three Kingdoms (ca.220–263CE).

20 The river Kian-suy is probably the Min, which is a contributary of the Yangtze.

21 Sindu here is applied to the city, suggesting Sindu-fu for the reading at the beginning of the chapter.

22 Tibet was spelled Tebet in Yule's original.

23 Mongu Kaan in Yule's original has been changed here to Mangku Khan, which is therefore consistent throughout this edition.

24 According to Yule, Tibet was always a part of the empire of the Mongol *khans* at its height, but it is not clear how. Kublai may have extended his authority over it by diplomacy and the politic handling of the spiritual potentates who had for several generations been the real rulers of Tibet. Chinese history attributes the organization of civil administration in Tibet to Kublai.

25 Marco exaggerates a little about the bamboo, but before gunpowder became familiar no explosive sounds of this kind were known to people. Richthofen reports that nowhere in China does the bamboo attain such a size as in this region.

26 Marsden believes these oxen to be the yaks (*Bos grunniens*) referred to previously.

27 This alleged practice is ascribed to a variety of people in different parts of the world. Polo has told nearly the same story already of the people of Camul/Kamul.

28 Salt is extracted by condensation from saline springs of great depth.

29 The spiced wine of Kien-ch'ang.

30 Marsden asserts that cloves, cassia or cinnamon do not grow beyond the tropics. However, Yule states on the authority of Baron Richthofen that cassia is produced the length of the valley of Kien-ch'ang, though in no other part of Sichuan nor in northern Yunnan. This valley (thought to be the Anning river valley) is the Caindu referred to by Polo; its name probably derives from an ethnic group in this area called the Kantu, who spoke Tibeto-Burmese.

31 Marsden suggests this may be the N'mai tributary of the Irrawaddy.

32 Yachi/Yachi-fu is modern-day Kunming, which means the province of Carajan (Kárájang of the Mongols) is Yunnan.

33 The existence of Nestorian Christians in this remote country is notable. In 1855 Muslims began a revolt against imperial authority, which for a time resulted in their independence in western Yunnan

under a Sultan Suleiman.

34 This is the first time Polo mentions cowrie, which he calls porcellani. Correctly, this should read "twenty-four *piccoli* each", for this was about the equivalent of a *grosso*.

35 Shambles is an old English word for meat market.

36 Carajan city is Tali-fu (Dali), which was the capital of the ancient Shan kingdom the Chinese called Nan-Chao/Nanzhao. Dali was the capital of Sultan Suleiman until captured in 1873, when a massacre of Muslims took place. (Polo says the king was a son of the *khan* called Cogachin, after telling us in the last chapter that the king at Yachi was also a son of the *khan*, called Essentimur. It is probably an error of dictation calling the latter a son of the *khan*, for elsewhere this prince is correctly described as the *khan's* grandson.)

37 A gyn is a lifting device used on a sailboat.

38 Marco's serpents here are crocodiles. He may have seen only a mutilated specimen. The term *serpent* is applied by many old writers to crocodiles and the like.

39 The demarcation between the two provinces is the Mekong River. *Zăr-dandán* is Persian for "gold teeth". Vochan seems to be around Dehong in western Yunnan, close to Bhamo in Burma.

40 Ramusio says both men and women do it.

41 All diseases in these regions are ascribed to the supernatural.

42 This date is no doubt corrupt. See note 45 for chapter 52.

43 Mien is the name by which the kingdom of Burma or Ava was and is known to the Chinese. Although Polo did more or less confound Bengal with Pegu, the king of Burma may well have had the title "king of Bengal" – Anaurahata, one of the most powerful Burmese kings, extended his conquests to the frontiers of India.

44 Three or four men carried by a war-elephant sounds more reasonable.

45 The Chinese annals fix the date to 1277.

46 A lengthy note in Yule points out the difficulties with this timetable, which suggest some confusion in Polo's mind between the real capital of Mien/Burma/Ava (Pagan, at this time) and the point reached. Polo represents the country traversed as wild and uninhabited, whereas in a journey to Pagan the most populous and fertile part of Burma would be passed through.

47 According to the Yule edition, this chapter offers little evidence that Marco himself visited the "city of Mien", and his account of the conquest is derived from gossip.

48 The Yule edition makes it clear that if Marco had visited Bengal he would have been aware that it was part of India, whilst in fact he seems to regard it as an Indo-Chinese region, like Zardandan, Mien and Caugigu.

49 Perhaps wild buffalo.

50 Marsden spells this province as Kangigu, and speculates it may lie on the route from eastern Bengal to northern Burma. The Yule edition asserts that Laos or some part of that region is meant to be described, with the general direction of the course taken being through the regions east of Burma.

51 The spelling of this province varies. Most editions (including Marsden) have Amu, with some believing the name represents Annam. The Yule edition argues for a location in southeast Yunnan.

52 All the other texts except Ramusio's read fifteen. Ramusio's reading of twenty-five was adopted by Yule.

53 This region on the frontier of Kweichau (Guizhou) has native tribes the Chinese called Kolo-man or Kihlau-man (*man* is "barbarian"). The Kolo-man/Coloman referred to are probably the people the Chinese today call the Miao or Mong.

54 Cuiju is probably Kweichau (Guizhou). Paper money reveals this as a province of China proper.

55 Several Chinese plants yield grass-cloths.

56 Tigers of course are meant.

57 Yule remarks that this trade is an important part of commerce in Kweichau (Guizhou).

58 Marco having got back to Sindafu/Ch'eng-tu fu/Chengdu in Sichuan, Yule reviews the difficulties of the journey. Yule does not believe Polo visited Bengal, though the descriptions probably came from people who had been there. Instead, Yule argues that Polo mistook where he was (Pegu) for Bengal, which was easily done when the kings of Pegu claimed to be kings of Bengal. It seems certain he had been to the upper Irrawaddy, upper Mekong, Laos and southern Yunnan. Yule theorizes that Polo returned from Yunnan to Sichuan through some part of Guizhou, perhaps only its western extremity, but that he spoke of Caugigu, and probably of Anin, as he did of Bangala, from reports only.

59 Here the traveller gets back to the road bifurcation near Juju (that is, Chochau/Zhuozhou), and then travels southward.

BOOK II: PART III

1 Cacanfu is Ho-kien fu (Hejian in Hebei province), southeast of Chochau/Zhuozhou.

2 Changlu is southeast of Ho-kien fu/Hejian (and may be Cangzhou). Polo here introduces a remark about cremation, which, with idolatry and the use of paper money, constitutes a wearisome formula repeated all through the Chinese provinces – and therefore replaced here with "[and so forth]". It is, in fact, his definition of the Chinese people, for whom he lacks a name.

3 According to the Yule edition, Chinangli and Tadinfu seem to have been confused. The position and name of Chinangli point to T'si-nan fu in Shan-tung (Jinan in Shandong). Tadinfu seems to be Yen-chau (Yanzhou). The nobler city of the two was T'si-nan fu/Jinan.

4　The date for this rebellion should be 1262.

5　The Yule edition agrees with both Murray and Pauthier in identifying Sinjumatu with T'si-ning chau (Jining). Polo, according to the route supposed, first comes upon the artificial part of the Grand Canal here.

6　Yule is certain Piju is Pei-chau (Pizhou). Marsden spells it Pingui.

7　Yule claims that Siju (Cingui in Marsden) can be scarcely other than Su-t'sien/Si-chau as Murray and Pauthier have said. (This city appears to be Suqian or Suyu.)

8　The Yule edition makes clear that this is a southern branch of the Yellow River, whose course has altered greatly over the centuries. Presumably at this time (before its 1853 redirection) the river was running southward near Hongze Lake and toward the Yangtze, though it flowed into the Yellow Sea further north than where the Yangtze flows into the East China Sea.

9　Coiganju is Hwaingan chau (Huai'an or Huaiyin). Caiju does not seem to be traceable, having probably been carried away by the changes in the river; but it would seem to have been at the mouth of the canal on the north side of the then flow of the Yellow River.

Manzi (or Mangi) is a name used for Southern China. Or more properly for the territory which constituted the dominion of the Song dynasty at the time when the Mongols conquered Cathay or Northern China from the Qin.

10　"Facfur" is *Faghfúr* or *Baghbúr*, which was a title applied by old Persian and Arabic writers to the emperor of China (an old Persian translation of the Chinese title "Son of Heaven").

11　The history of the conquest shows many instances of extraordinary courage and self-devotion on the part of Chinese officers.

12　Bayan (signifying "great" or "noble") was Kublai's most famous lieutenant. When the emperor died, Bayan took decisive measures for preserving order, and maintained Kublai's disposition of the succession.

13　A note in the Yule edition explains the historical background. The Song emperor had died in 1274. A son, aged four, was put on the throne with his grandmother as regent. When the Mongols arrived the empress sent the great seal of the empire to Bayan and he entered Huaiyin without resistance in 1276. The emperor, his mother and the remaining Song princes and princesses were sent to the Mongol capital. The eldest of the two boys who had escaped was proclaimed emperor but was speedily driven from the province, and in 1278 he died on a desert island off the Canton coast.

14　Paukin is probably Baoying and Cayu is probably Gaoyou.

15　Yule believes Tiju is likely to be Tai-chau (Taizhou), lying to the east of the canal, but apparently connected with it by a navigable channel. Tinju is probably Tung-chau (Tongzhou, later renamed Nantong), near the northern shore of the estuary of the Yang-tzu (Yangtze).

16　Yanju is Yangchau (Yangzhou).

17　*Sing* is used in the sense of governor-general. Yule doubts that Polo was ever governor-general.

18　Nanghin is Nanjing (Nan-ching/Nanking, meaning "southern capital"), one of the four great ancient capitals of China (with Beijing, Luoyang and Chang'an/Xi'an).

19　Saianfu is Siang-yang (Xiangyang). (This is confusing because the city is well to the west of the journey narrative at this point.)

20　A lengthy note in the Yule edition identifies chronological difficulties here. The siege was over by 1273, but according to the narrative the Polos could not have reached Kublai's court until the end of 1274. However, Chinese and Persian histories also record the use of Western engineering know-how (notably the counterpoised lever), solicited by Kublai, to bring prolonged city sieges to an end. No sources agree on who the individual engineers were.

21 Sinju is difficult to identify. The Yule edition names it as Chen-chau or I-ching-hien; Sinju could be Yizheng or Shierxu, near Yangzhou.

22 The Yangtze.

23 One ton equalled about twenty-four *cantar*s.

24 Caiju is probably Guazhou, near Yangzhou.

25 Polo's account of the formation of the Grand Canal is exceedingly accurate.

26 Chinghianfu is modern-day Zhenjiang (referred to elsewhere as Chin-kiang fu/ Chen-chiang/Chingkiang/Chingk'ou/ Jingjiang/Jingkou).

27 Chinginju (Chang-chau/Changchow) is modern-day Changzhou.

28 The Alans of the Caucasus became subjects of the *khan*s of Sarai and were taken into Mongol military service. In 1306 there were Alans fighting in the service of the Byzantine emperors, which renders Marco's story of a corps of Christian Alans in the Bayan's army quite possible.

29 Suju (Su-chau/Soochow) is the celebrated city of Suzhou. It was the capital of the old kingdom of Wu.

30 Ignoring the literal accuracy of Polo's statements as to the bridges, many travellers have noticed the number and elegance of the stone bridges in this part of China.

31 The meanings ascribed by Polo to the names of Suzhou and Kinsay/King-szé/Quinsai/ Hang-chau (Hangzhou) show plainly that he was ignorant of Chinese.

32 These three cannot be identified with confidence, though it seems likely that Vughin is Wujiang.

33 Kinsay is a close representation of *king-szé*, Chinese for "capital", the modern-day city of Hangzhou, which as Lin'an was the capital of the Southern Song dynasty from 1127.

34 There might be some ground for supposing that 100 miles of circuit stood for 100 *li*. The earliest record of the wall, as built under

the Sui, makes its extent little more than thirty-six *li*. But the wall was reconstructed during the Tang dynasty (892) with a circuit of seventy *li*. Moreover, in 1159, after the city became the Song capital it was further extended, thus the circuit of the city may have been not far short of 100 *li*.

35 There is little trace of such an ordinance. Certain trades run in families, though there is no compulsion.

36 The celebrated Sihu (Xī Hú) or "West Lake".

37 The number of bridges appears to be greatly exaggerated.

38 The estuary of the river has undergone great changes since Polo's day.

39 "King" really means a provincial viceroy.

40 In the Yule edition this chapter was included by Yule "after some consideration". He had collected together a number of additional particulars concerning Hangzhou, which are only found in Ramusio. Because they add little to what is in chapter 76, these particulars have been edited and reduced in length for this edition.

41 Pauthier's text seems to be alone in saying that Marco was sent by the Great Khan.

42 A lengthy note in the Yule edition makes it clear that although we know that the traveller's route proceeds from Hangzhou (Kinsay) in Zhejiang southward to Quanzhou (Zayton) in Fujian (Fo-Kien), via Fuzhou (Fuju), we cannot be certain which places are represented by the names in the text. For example, some say Tanpiju is Shao-hing fu/Shaoxing, while others claim it is Fuyan, along the river.

43 As part of a much longer note in the Yule edition, Cordier observes that if it is assumed that Tanpiju is Shao-hing fu/ Shaoxing, the remaining places as far as the Fujian frontier run thus: three days to "Vuju", two days to "Ghiuju", four days to "Chanshan", three days to "Cuju". Zhuji, Jinhua, Changshan and Quzhou are some of the candidate cities for these places,

but their actual identities are not known. (Confusingly, Vuju is mentioned twice, in chapter 75 and chapter 79.)

44 Fuju is the city of Fuzhou, capital of Fujian.

45 Possibly Safflower, *Carthamus tinctorius*.

46 The Yule edition has a lengthy note recording cannibalistic practices in China, which if true appear to have been ritualized forms of vengeance to punish enemies, criminals, and so on. See also Book I, page 116, and the accompanying note 175.

47 Aboriginal tribespeople in the mountains.

48 *Galanga* or Galangal is an aromatic root.

49 The fierce lions are tigers. These are numerous in this province, and tradition points to the diversion of many roads, owing to their being infested by tigers. Tiger cubs are often offered for sale in Amoy.

50 A note in the Yule edition observes that the timings are interesting because they show that Polo reckoned his day at thirty miles.

51 The city is Fuzhou, capital of Fujian. The name here applied to Fo-kien (Fukien or Fujian province) by Polo is variously written as Choncha/Chonka/Concha/Chouka.

52 The Min, the river of Fuzhou, "varies much in width and depth. Near its mouth, and at some other parts, it is not less than a mile in width, elsewhere deep and rapid."

53 The *Laurus* (or *Cinnamomum*) *camphora* grows abundantly in Fujian.

54 Zayton is Quanzhou.

55 The note in the Yule edition reads: "When Marco says Zayton is one of the two greatest commercial ports in the world, I know not if he has another haven in his eye or is only using an idiom of the age. ... From Zayton sailed Kublai's ill-fated expedition against Japan. From Zayton Marco Polo seems to have sailed on his return to the West. At Zayton Ibn Batuta first landed in China, and from it he sailed on his return. When the Portuguese, in the sixteenth century, recovered China to European knowledge, Zayton was no longer the great haven of foreign trade, but the old name was not extinct among the mariners of western Asia.

56 These tattooists were probably employed mainly by mariners frequenting the port.

57 The meager statement in the French texts shows merely that Polo had heard of the Fujian dialect. The addition from Ramusio shows further that he was aware of the unity of the written character throughout China, but gives no indication of any knowledge of its peculiar principles, nor of the extent of difference in the spoken dialects.

The note in the Yule edition continues at some length on this topic.

EPILOGUE

58 Book II ends abruptly, though before Book III (Japan, the Archipelago, Southern India and the Coasts and Islands of the Indian Sea) begins, there is this declaration: "we have still to tell you all about the people of India and the notable things of that country, which are well worth the describing, for they are marvellous indeed. What we shall tell is all true, and without any lies."

In the Yule edition this final piece is presented as the concluding Chapter 34 in Book IV, with this note: "This conclusion is not found in any copy except in the Crusca Italian, and, with a little modification, in another at Florence, belonging to the Pucci family. It is just possible that it was the embellishment of a transcriber or translator; but in any case it is very old, and serves as an epilogue."

FURTHER READING

The original product of Marco Polo's collaboration with Rustichello has been lost. More than 100 early Polo manuscripts exist, but there is no authoritative version of Marco Polo's account. However, scholars accord more significance to some sources, such as the 1559 work by Giambattista Ramusio, than others.

There are about nine significant English-language editions of Polo's text, and two of the most widely respected have been the basis for this edition. The Marsden edition first appeared in 1818 (it uses Ramusio, among other sources); it was revised by T. Wright in 1854, prior to the publication of the 1908 version of Marsden's translation. The 1903 translation by Henry Yule won him the prestigious award of a Gold Medal by the Royal Geographical Society, and it remains a highly respected work, not least for its extensive annotations, some of which were added by Henri Cordier.

PRIMARY SOURCES

The Book of Ser Marco Polo the Venetian Concerning the Kingdoms and Marvels of the East. Translated and edited, with notes, by Sir Henry Yule, R.E., C.B., K.C.S.I., Corr. Inst. France. 3rd edition. Revised throughout in the light of recent discoveries by Henri Cordier (of Paris). Volume I. John Murray: London, 1921.

The Book of Ser Marco Polo the Venetian Concerning the Kingdoms and Marvels of the East. Translated and edited, with notes, by Sir Henry Yule, R.E., C.B., K.C.S.I., Corr. Inst. France. 3rd edition. Revised throughout in the light of recent discoveries by Henri Cordier (of Paris). Volume II. John Murray: London, 1921.

The Travels of Marco Polo. Translated by William Marsden in 1818 and revised by T. Wright in 1854, with an Introduction by John Masefield. J.M. Dent & Sons Ltd: London, 1908.

BOOKS OF RELATED INTEREST

Bergreen, Laurence. *Marco Polo: From Venice to Xanadu*. Quercus: London, 2009.

Blunden, Caroline and Elvin, Mark. *Cultural Atlas of China*. Facts on File: New York, 1983.

Chinnery, John. *Treasures of China*. Duncan Baird Publishers: London, 2008.

Foltz, Richard. *Religions of the Silk Road*. St Martin's Press: New York, 1999.

Hopkins, Peter. *Foreign Devils on the Silk Road*. John Murray: London, 1980.

Liu, Xinru. *The Silk Road in World History*. Oxford University Press: Oxford and New York, 2010.

Rossabi, Morris. *Khubilai Khan: His Life and Times*. University of California Press: Berkeley, California, 1988.

Rossabi, Morris. *Voyager from Xanadu: Rabban Sauma and the First Journey from China to the West*. Kodansha International: London, 1992.

Shaughnessy, Edward L. (General Editor). *China*. Duncan Baird Publishers: London, 2005.

Thubron, Colin. *The Silk Road to China*. Hamlyn: London, 1989.

Tucker, Jonathan. *The Silk Road: Art and History*. Philip Wilson: London, 2003.

Whitfield, Susan with Sims-Williams, Ursula (Editors). *Silk Road: Trade, Travel, War and Faith*. The British Library: London, 2004.

Wood, Frances. *The Silk Road: Two Thousand Years in the Heart of Asia*. The British Library: London, 2003.

Wriggins, Sally Hovey. *Xuanzang: A Buddhist Pilgrim on the Silk Road*. Westview Press: Boulder, Colorado, 1996.

INDEX

A

Acbalec Manzi 176
Acbaluc 169
Achmath 148–151
Acre 10, 16, 27, 28, 29
Aguil 209
Alacou Khan 96
Alaü (city) 26
Alaü Khan (brother of Kublai
    Khan) 20, 47–49, 68–69
Alexander the Great 14, 44–45,
    65, 70, 72–73
Altay, Mount 97
Amien *see* Mien
animals
  crocodiles 188–189
  deer, musk 108, 182
  dogs 141, 183, 203–204
  elephants 193–194, 196–197
  horses 56, 73, 101, 113–116,
      189–190
  oxen 58
  sheep 58, 76
  tigers ("lions") 140–141,
      203–204
  yaks 108
Anin 201–202
Arbre Sol (Arbre Sec) 65
architecture/construction,
    descriptions of 98, 112–113,
    129–130, 175, 198, 232–233
Arghun (ruler of Persia) 11, 33,
    34, 35, 184
Argons, the 110
Armenia, Greater 43–44
Armenia, Lesser 42
Arzinga 43

Arziron 43
Arzizi 43
Asedin Soldan 60
assassins (*ashishin*s) 66–68
astrology 84–85, 95–6, 116, 121,
    162–163, 183, 232
  year signs 163

B

Badashan (Badakhshan) 16,
    72–74
Baghdad *see* Baudas
Baian 141
Balc (Balkh) 69–70
bamboo 174, 178–179, 223,
    236
banditry 56, 60, 182
Bangala 199–200
Baoying *see* Paukin
Bargu, Plain of 107
Barka Khan 20
Barsamo, St, monastery of 53
Barscol 124
Bastra (Basra) 46
Batuy Khan 96
Baudas 46–52
Baudas, *calif of*
  vanquished by Alaü 47–49
  relations with Christians
      49–52
Bayan Chincsan ("100-Eyes")
    215–216, 225
Beijing *see* Cambaluc
birds
  *barguerlac*s 107
  cranes 111–112
  eagles 141

falcons 107, 112, 184
partridges 112
pheasants 108–109
boats, design of 63, 223
Bokhara 9, 22
Bolgana (wife of Arghun) 33
Bolgara 20
Bolor 76
Brius, River 186
Buddhism
  Chinese 163–164
  Tibetan 84–85, 89–90, 116–117
bularguchi ("keeper of lost
    property") 142
Bundokdari (*soldan* of
    Babylonia) 30
Burma *see* Mien

C

Caaju 96
Cacanfu 207–208
Cachanfu 174
Cachar Modun 142–144
Caichu 171
Caidu (nephew of Kublai Khan)
    77, 120–121, 125
Caiju 213, 224
Caindu 184–186
Cala Ataperistan 54
Calachan 109
Camadi 58
Cambaluc 129, 131–133,
    144–146
  Green Mount 131
  palace of the Great Khan
      129–131
  as trading centre 145–146

Campichu 89–90

Camul 85–87

Caracoron 91

Carajan (province) 186–190,
192

Carajan (city) 187–190

Caramoran, River 173–174, 213

Casaria (Caesaria) 43

Cascar 77

Casem 71

Casvin 55–56

Cathay 14, 167–213 *passim*

Cathayans, the
customs 164
religion 163–164
resistance to Tartar rule
149–150

Caugigu 201

Cauly 124

Cayu 218

Chagan Nor 111–112

Chagatai 60, 77–78

Chandu, palaces of 112–116,
145

Changan 226

Changlu 208

Changzhou *see* Chinginju

Chanshan 236

Charchan 81

charity 161–162, 216–217

Chenchu 149–150

Chengdu *see* Sindafu

Chinangli 208

Chinghianfu 224–225

Chinginju 225

Chingintalas 87–88

Chinkin (son of Kublai Khan)
128, 149, 150

chinuchi ("keepers of
the mastiff dogs") 141

Chonka 240, 242

Chorcha 91, 124

Christians 95–96
Nestorian and Jacobite 46,
224–225
relations with Muslims
49–52, 77–78

Clemenfu 30

Clement IV, Pope 27

clothing, styles of 74, 100,
135–136, 139

coal 159

Cobinan 64–65

Cogachin (son of Kublai Khan)
187

Cogatai 150

Coiganju 213, 215–216, 217

Coleridge, Samuel Taylor 9

Coloman 202

Columbus, Christopher 15

communication systems
154–156

concubines 126–127

Conia 43

corruption 148–151

Cotan 80

Cuiju 202–205

Cuju 237

Cuncun 175

Curmosa 56

Curzola, battle of 12

customs and rituals
adoption of unwanted babies
216
business 192
childbirth 191
healing 192–193
hospitality, using wives/women
for 85–87, 179–182, 185
murder, ritual 190
raw meat, eating 187
sacrifice 84

see also cannibalism; charity;
death and burial; justice,
systems of; marriage; money;
religion

Cuy Khan 96

D

Dali *see* Carajan (city)

Dalivar 60

Dandolo, Andrea (admiral) 12

Darius III, king of Persia 14,
65, 72

death and burial 63, 84–85,
97–98, 146, 202, 232

Dogana 70

E

Egrigaia 109

Erguiul 108–109

Erzincan *see* Arzinga

Essentimur (king of Carajan)
186, 193

Etzina 90–91

eunuchs 200

F

Facfur (king of Manzi) 215–217

falconry 142

feast days 116–117, 134–139
birthday of Kublai Khan
135–136
New Year (White Feast) 136–
137

food and drink
cereals 70, 159–161, 224
fish 45, 187
kemiz (fermented milk) 100
melons 69
rhubarb 89, 226
rice 158, 187
spices 176, 186, 200, 226, 237

sugar 240
wine 61, 169
Formosa, Plain of 61
Fujian *see* Chonka
Fuju (Fuzhou) 237, 240–241
Fungul 203
Fuzhou *see* Fuju

G
Ganfu 231–232
Gaoyou *see* Cayu
Genghis Khan 93–96, 113
Genoa 12
George (king of Tanduc)
    109–110
Georgiania 44–45
Ghel or Ghelan, Sea of 45
Ghiuju 236
Gobi Desert 16–17
Gog and Magog 110
Golden King 171–173
government (of Kublai Khan)
    148–162
    charity to the poor 161–162
    communication system 154–
    156
    monetary system 151–153
    provision for times of dearth
    156–157, 159–161
    Supreme Court (*Shieng*)
    153–154
    see also highways; taxation
Grand Canal 212, 224
Gregory X, Pope 10, 27, 29–30
Guazhou *see* Caiju
Guielmo da Tripoli, Fra 30
guilds 229
Guizhou *see* Cuiju

H
Hami *see* Camul

Hangzhou *see* Kinsay
Herodotus 14
highways 157–158, 231
Horiads, the 113
Hormuz 61–63
Huai'an/Huaiyin
    see Coiganju
hunting 111, 112, 139–144
    restrictions 144, 169

I
India 10, 60
Istanit 56

J
Jesus Christ 53–55
Jian'ou *see* Kelinfu
Jinan *see* Chinangli
Jining *see* Sinjumatu
Juju 168, 205
justice, systems of 103–106,
    116, 164

K
Karakorum *see* Caracoran
Karaunas (bandits) 60
Karazan 32
Kasan (son of Arghun) 35
Kashgar *see* Cascar
Kashmir *see* Keshimur
Kelinfu (Jian'ou) 237–240
Kenjanfu 174–175
Kermán 57
keshican (Kublai Khan's
    horseguards) 133–134
Keshimur 75, 116
Khogatal 25, 26
Khotan *see* Cotan
Ki-akato 35–36
Kian, River 222–223
Kian-suy, River 177–178

Kinsay 216, 226, 227–236
Kishim *see* Casem
Kisi (Kish) 56
Kogatin 33
Korea *see* Cauly
Kublai Khan 15, 96–97, 119–
    129, 133–145, 198
    accession 120
    age 120
    appearance 126
    birthday 135–136
    character 15, 23–24
    children 128–129
    and Christianity 10, 24–25,
    124–125
    concubines 126–127
    death 11, 36
    and defeat of Nayan 120–125
    and defeat of Liytan Sangon 209
    and hunting 111, 112, 139–
    144, 169
    and Manzi 215–217, 220–222,
    235–236
    palaces 112–116, 129–131
    and the Polos 9–11, 23–26, 31,
    32, 33, 34–35, 167
    seasonal movements 113–116,
    129, 141–142, 144–145
    wives 126
    see also government (of Kublai
    Khan)
Kunming *see* Yachi
Kurdistan 56
Kurds, the 46

L
Laiassus (Ayas) 16, 42
Leonard, St, convent of 45
Linfen *see* Pianfu
Linju 212
Liytan Sangon 209

Lop 81–83
    Desert of 83
Lor 56

M
magi, the 14, 53–55
Manderville, Sir John 13
Mangalai (son of Kublai Khan)
    174–175
    palace of 175
Mangku Khan 86–87, 96, 98
Manzi 215–217, 232–233,
    215–242 *passim*
    dialects 242
    queen of (wife of Facfur) 216,
    217, 227
Mar Sarghis 225
marriage 80, 90, 98–100, 106,
    109, 179–182, 187
Mescript, the 107
Mien (Amien) 197–199
Mien and Bangala, king of
    193–197
Min, River *see* Kian-suy, River
minerals
    asbestos (salamander) 88
    gold 187–188, 191–192, 202
    rubies, balas 73
    silver 111, 191–192
    spodium (byproduct of zinc
    ore) 65
    turquoise 57
    zinc ore (*tutia*) 65
    see also coal; oil; salt
Mingan 141
miracles, descriptions of 49–52,
    77–78
monasteries 117, 224
money 151–153, 182, 185, 187,
    191–192, 202
    see also taxation

Mongotay 209
Mosolins (merchants) 46
Mosul 43, 45–6
Mulehet 66
Muslims 70–71, 151
    relations with Christians
    49–52, 77–78

N
Nanghin (Nanjing) 219
Nantong *see* Tinju
Natagai (Tartar god) 100, 163
Nayan 120–125
Nescradin 195–196
New Year 136–137
Nicolo da Vicenza, Fra 30
Noah's ark 16, 43
Nogodar (king of Karaunas)
    60

O
oil (as fuel) 43–44
Old Man of the Mountain
    (Aloadin) 66–69
Oukaka 22

P
Pamier, plain of 76
Pashai 74
Paukin 218
pearls 184
Pein 80
Persia 53, 55–56, 53–70 *passim*
Peshawar *see* Pashai
Pianfu 169–171
Piju (Pizhou) 213
Polo, Donata (wife of Marco)
    12
Polo, Marco 9, 10–15, 28,
    31–36, 60–61, 74, 151,
    220–222

and Kublai Khan 10–11, 31,
    32, 33, 34–35, 167
    itinerary 16–17
    positions of responsibility 218,
    235
    return to Venice 11–12, 36
Polo, Nicolo and Maffeo
    (Marco's father and uncle)
    9–11, 20–36, 220–222
    first journey to Cathay 9–10,
    20–23
    first return to Venice 10, 27
    itinerary 15–17
    and Kublai Khan 10–11,
    23–26, 31, 32–33, 34–35
    as Kublai Khan's envoys to the
    pope 10, 26–30
    second journey to Cathay 10,
    30–31
    second return to Venice 11, 36
    porcelain 242
Prester John 91, 93–96
    descendents of 109–110
    and the Golden King 171–173
    prostitution 146
Pulisanghin, River 168

Q
Qingdao *see* Changlu
Quanzhou *see* Zayton

R
reincarnation 163–164
religion 89–90, 100, 163,
    192
    see also Buddhism
Reobarles 58
resistance, Cathayan, to Tartar
    rule 149–150
resources, natural *see* animals;
    birds; food and drink;

minerals; textiles; *and individual entries*
Ruomedam Ahomet (king of Hormuz) 61, 63
Rustichello (Rustician) of Pisa 12, 20

S
Saianfu 220–222
Samarkand 77–78
Sapurgan 69
salt 70, 187, 208, 217, 218
Sarai (Saray) 20
Savast 43
*sensin*s (ascetics) 117
Serazy 56
Shangdu *see* Clemenfu
Shaoxing *see* Tanpiju
Sheberghan *see* Sapurgan
shells, cowrie 187, 188, 202
Siju 213
Sikintinju 124
Sindachu 111
Sindafu 176–178, 205
Sinju (in Manzi) 222
Sinju (in Tangut) 108
Sinjumatu 209–212
Soldaia 20
Soncara 56
Sudak *see* Soldaia
Suju (Suzhou) 226
Sukchu 89
Sukchur 88–89
Suolstan 56
Suqian/Suyu *see* Siju

T
Tadinfu 208–209
Taianfu (T'ai-yuan) 169
Taican (Taloqan/Talikan) 70
Taidu 131

Taizhou *see* Tiju
Tanduc 109–111
Tangut 83–85, 83–91 *passim*
Tanpiju 236
Tartars, the 91–106
  ascent 91–93
  customs 97–100
  justice, system of 103–106
  marriage, posthumous 106
  military organization 101–103
  military victories 93–96, 193–197
  religion 100
  succession of rulers 96–97, 120
tattoos 190, 201, 242
Tauris (Tabriz) 52–53
taxation 235–236, 241–242
Temur (grandson of Kublai Khan) 128–129
textiles
  camel hair 109, 110
  nasich/naques (cloth of gold) 110
  silk 45, 56, 110, 146, 169
Tibet 116, 178–184
Tiju 218
Tinju 218
Tonocain (Tunocain) 56, 65–66
trading 146, 153, 241
  restrictions 73, 184
Turcomania 42
turquoise 57
Tyunju 242

U
Ung and Mungul *see* Gog and Magog
Ungrat, the 126–127
Unken 240
un-khan see Prester John

V
Venice 12
Visconti, Theobald, of Piacenza *see* Gregory X, Pope
Vochan 190, 192
Vokhan 76
Vughin 226
Vuju 226, 236

W
Wakhan *see* Vokhan
Wangchu 149–150
White Feast (New Year) 136–137
Wujiang *see* Vughin

X
Xanadu *see* Changdu, palaces of
Xi'an *see* Kenjanfu
Xiangyang *see* Saianfu

Y
Yachi 186, 192
Yanju (Yangzhou) 218–219
Yangtze River *see* Kian, River
Yanzhou *see* Tadinfu
Yarcan (Yarkand) 78–80
Yasdi (Yazd) 56
Ydifu, Mount 111
Yellow River *see* Caramoran, River
Yule, Henry 12, 13
Yunnan *see* Carajan (province)

Z
Zardandan 190–197
Zayton 241–242
Zhangye *see* Campichu
Zhenjiang *see* Chinghianfu
Zhuozhou *see* Juju

ACKNOWLEDGMENTS

The publisher would like to thank The Society of Authors as the Literary Representative of the Estate of John Masefield for permission to reproduce the introduction and itinerary.

PICTURE CREDITS

The publisher would like to thank the following people, museums and photographic libraries for permission to reproduce their material. Every care has been taken to trace copyright holders. However, if we have omitted anyone we apologize and will, if informed, make corrections to any future edition.

Page 1 Portrait medal of Marco Polo, Scala, Florence/Heritage Images/Science Archive, Oxford; **2** Central Tian Shan Mountains, Kazakhstan, Photolibrary.com/Imagebroker/Nikolay Kuznetsov; **8** Marco Polo sailing from Venice, from *Li Livres du Graunt Caam, Travels of Marco Polo*, c.1400, with miniatures by the artist Johannes and his school, Scala, Florence/BPK, Bildagentur für Kunst, Kultur und Geschichte, Berlin/Bodleian Library, Oxford (Bodley 264); **18** Gondola moorings, Venice with San Giorgio Maggiore in the background, Werner Forman Archive, London; **21** Parekklesion cupola, Kariye Camii, former church of the Chora monastery, Istanbul. Byzantine fresco, c.1320, akg-images/Gerard Degeorge; **22** Ceramic detail, Mir-i-Arab *madrasah* façade, Bukhara, Uzbekistan, Photolibrary.com/Robert Harding Travel/Upperhall Ltd; **23** Nicolo and Marco Polo before the Great Khan, from the *Livre des Merveilles du Monde*, c.1410–1412, vellum, Boucicaut Master, (fl.1390–1430) and workshop. Collected record of travels in the Orient, including those of Marco Polo (1254–1324), Odorico de Pordone (c.1286–1331), Guillaume de Boldensele, the Armenian monk Hayton, Ricaldo da Monte di Croce (c.1243–1320) and the fictitious knight Sir John de Mandeville, Bridgeman Art Library/Bibliothèque Nationale, Paris (Ms.fr.2810); **26–27** Mountains in the Acre region © Chris Kutschera; **28** View of Jerusalem, from *Civitates orbis terrarum*. Originally published 1575, British Library, London (215.f.2 volume 2, 54); **35** Safe Conduct Pass (*Paizi*) with Phakpa script, 1299, iron inlaid with silver, Scala, Florence/Art Resource/Image © The Metropolitan Museum of Art, Bequest of Dorothy Graham Bennett (1993.256); **37** Sumela monastery, near Trabzon, Turkey, Corbis/David Samuel Robbins; **40** Khor Virap monastery and Mount Ararat, near Yerevan, Armenia, Corbis/Wolfgang Kaehler; **41** Mongol silver gilt pendant from a horse trapping. Black Sea 13th–14th century, Art Archive/Alfredo Dagli Orti/Hermitage Museum, St Petersburg; **44** King David Melic of Georgia visits the monastery of St Leonard from *Le Livre des Merveilles du Monde*, akg-images/Bibliothèque Nationale, Paris (Ms. fr.2810, f.8 r); **47** Slip-painted pottery bowl, with an archer on horseback, 13th century, found in Aleppo, Syria

Relics of Anxian county, Hunan; **143** *The Encampment* by Black Pen, depicting figures kneading dough, baking bread, attending to their saddles, and grazing horses, Tabriz or Baghdad, Jalayirid period, c.1350–1370, Topkapi Sarayi Müzesi, Istanbul/Hadiye Cangökçe (2153, f.8b); **147** Chinese knots, Photolibrary.com/Fotosearch Value; **148** *Cizhou* figure of a seated lady, Jin–early Yuan Dynasty, China, 13th century, Scala, Florence/Heritage Images/Museum of East Asian Art, Bath; **152** Hand-painted mulberry paper umbrellas, Alamy/Greg Vaughn; **157** Kublai Khan orders and oversees the planting of trees along China's main roads from *Le Livre des Merveilles du Monde,* akg-images/Bibliothèque Nationale, Paris (Ms.fr.2810, f.47 v); **158** Grey glazed cup with brown splashes, Yuan Dynasty, China, 1279–1368, Scala, Florence/Heritage Images/Museum of East Asian Art, Bath; **160** Aerial view of terraced farms of the Naxi people just upstream from Judian on a tributary of the Yangtze River, Yunnan Province, China, Corbis/George Steinmetz; **165** Burning incense sticks, Photolibrary.com/Tips Italia/William Baker; **167** A frozen pond in a mountainous area, Yulong River, Yangshuo County, Guangxi, China, Photolibrary.com/Keith Levit; **170** Silk drapery in the market at Khotan, Xinjiang province, China, Photolibrary.com/Imagebroker; **175** Yellow River, Lajia, Qinghai province, China, Robert Harding/Occidor Ltd; **177** The bridge of Sindufu, from *Li Livres du Graunt Caam,* Art Archive/Bodleian Library, Oxford (Bodley 264, f.246v); **180–181** A Buddhist *stupa* at Shangri-La (Zhongdian) on the Tibetan border, Yunnan, China, Photolibrary.com/Tips Italia/Angelo Cavalli; **183** Yak-grazing in Tibet, Corbis; **185** Pearl fishing and "winning" turquoise in Gaindu province; the yield is delivered to Kublai Khan, from *Le Livre des Merveilles du Monde,* akg-images/Bibliothèque Nationale, Paris (Ms.fr.2810, f.54 r); **188** Siamese crocodile, Getty images/National Geographic/Joel Sartore; **191** Rice harvesting, attributed to Cheng Chi, Yuan Dynasty, 13th–14th century, China, Art Archive/Freer Gallery of Art, Washington D.C.; **194** Shaffron (armour for the head of a horse), 13th–15th century. Iron, gold, silver, copper, leather and textile, 1500. Found Mongolia, possibly from Tibet, Scala, Florence/Art Resource/Image © The Metropolitan Museum of Art. Purchase, Arthur Ochs Sulzberger Gift (2004.402); **199** The temples of Bagan in Burma at sunset, Getty images/National Geographic/Aaron Huey; **200** Sack of chili powder at a market stall, Tai'an, Shandong province, China, Photolibrary.com/Glow Asia/Red Chopsticks; **203** *Cizhou*-type *sancai* tiger pillow, Jin Dynasty, China, 12th century, Scala, Florence/Heritage Images/Museum of East Asian Art, Bath; **204** A rank badge with Tiger, Qing Dynasty (1644–1911), 18th century, silk and metallic thread on silk, Scala, Florence/Art Resource/Image © The Metropolitan Museum of Art. Fletcher Fund (36.65.11); **206** Dragon sculpture, Mount Tai, Shandong, China, Photolibrary.com/Best View Stock/Shiwei; **210–211** Confucius Temple in Qufu, Shandong, China, Photolibrary.com/Best View Stock/Shiwei; **214** Wheat hanging to dry, Long Quan, Yunnan, China, Corbis/Ludovic Maisant; **219** Seven-lobed carved red lacquer platter ("children at play"), Yuan Dynasty (1279–1368), 14th century, Scala, Florence/Art Resource/Image © The Metropolitan Museum of Art. Promised Gift of Florence and Herbert Irving (L.1996.47.14). Photo: Lynton Gardiner; **222** Yangtze River, Yunnan province, China, Corbis/Liu Liqun; **227** View of the lagoon city Quinsai (Kinsay), in southern China from *Le Livre des Merveilles du Monde,* akg-images/Bibliothèque Nationale, Paris (Ms.fr.2810, f.67 r); **228** Sailboat on Erhai Lake, Dali, Yunnan province, China, Corbis/Keren Su; **231** Lodge carved with exquisite patterns, Longmen Ancient Town, Fuyang county, Hangzhou City, Zhejiang province, China, Photolibrary.com/TAO Images Limited **234** Baskets of dry goods, Zhuozhou, China, Photolibrary.com/Blue Jean Images LLC; **238–239** Bamboo plant in the sunlight, Hongkeng, Longyan, Fujian, China, Photolibrary.com/Thomas Roetting.